Across the Pacific

*Asian
Americans
and
Globalization*

IN THE SERIES

Asian American History and Culture

EDITED BY

Sucheng Chan, David Palumbo-Liu, and Michael Omi

Across the Pacific

Asian

Americans

and

Globalization

EDITED BY

Evelyn Hu-DeHart

Asia
Society
New York City

Temple University Press
Philadelphia

Temple University Press, Philadelphia 19122
Copyright © 1999 by The Asia Society
First paperback edition published 2000
Printed in the United States of America

Text design by Nancy Berliner

∞ The paper used in this publication meets the requirements of the American National Standard
for Information Sciences—Permanence of Paper for Printed Library Materials, ANSI Z39.48-1984

Library of Congress Cataloging-in-Publication Data

Across the Pacific: Asian Americans and globalization / edited by Evelyn Hu-DeHart.
    p. cm. — (Asian American history and culture)
  Includes bibliographical references.
  ISBN 1-56639-710-3 (cloth: alk. paper)—ISBN 1-56639-824-X (paper)
  1. Asian Americans—Economic conditions. 2. Asian Americans—Politics and government.
3. United States—Emigration and immigration—History—20th century. 4. Asia—Emigration
and immigration—History—20th century. 5. Pacific Area—Emigration and immigration—
History—20th century. 6. Competition, International. 7. United States—Foreign relations—
Asia. 8. Asia—Foreign relations—United States. I. Hu-DeHart, Evelyn. II. Series.
E184.O6A28 1999   98–53900
305.895073—DC21   CIP

The Asia Society is an internationally prestigious non-profit, non-political, educational organization
dedicated to fostering understanding and communication between Americans and the people of Asia
and the Pacific.

Asia Society
Division of Cultural Programs
725 Park Avenue
New York, NY 10021-5088
<www.asiasoc.org>

Poetry by Ko Un, Korean poet, translated by Ko Won, is reprinted (on p. 191) with permission from
the translator.

"A Philippine History Lesson," by Alfrredo Navarro Salanga, is reprinted (on p. 209) with permission from Luis H. Francia (Brown River, White Ocean, New Brunswick, N.J.: Rutgers University Press,
1993).

"Song for My Father," by Jessica Hagedorn, is reprinted (on p. 210) with permission from Luis H.
Francia (Brown River, White Ocean, New Brunswick, N.J.: Rutgers University Press, 1993).

"You Must Love," by Indran Amirthanayagam, is reprinted (on p. 215) with permission from the
author.

Contents

Foreword

Vishakha N. Desai

When the "Bridges" project was first conceived in 1994, it was with a notion that two striking trends were affecting life in the United States at the close of the twentieth century. These two trends needed to be studied together. It had been generally acknowledged that many countries in the Asia Pacific region were quickly becoming growth models for the world and were playing an increasingly important role in the international economic and political arenas. The second phenomenon related to the explosive growth of the Asian American communities in the United States. Although both of these trends had been widely known and reported, there was not much discussion of the relationship between them. As we assembled our advisory committee and began working with our co-organizers, Leadership Education for Asia Pacifics (LEAP) and the Asian American Federation of New York (AAFNY), it became very clear that the increased economic power of many Asian countries, combined with the more visible presence of Asian Americans, affected the expectations, perceptions, and experiences of Asian Americans at home and abroad. Much of the complexity of this reality, however, found limited exposition in academic circles and was conspicuously absent from public discussion.

Keeping in mind this need for further discussion and new scholarship, the Asia Society launched a major initiative entitled "Bridges with Asia: Asian Americans in the United States," consisting of regional roundtable discussions, research studies and essays, a national conference, and print and electronic publications. From its very inception, taking into account the diverse patterns of immigration and distinct histories of Asian countries with the United States, the project was intended to highlight the experience of the individual ethnic communities as well as to focus on those topics that may transcend national and ethnic boundaries. To illuminate the complexities of the Asian American experience in a transitional context, and the permeability of identity issues in the globalizing arena, the project was designed to be multidisciplinary, bringing together historians, policy experts, artists, and community leaders.

Another unique feature of the project was its national dimension. As we assembled our advisory committee, it became evident that we needed to take into account not only the ethnic and cultural variations within the Asian American communities, but also the distinct regional nature of these communities' American experience. In other words, Asian connections of a particular Asian American community and the relationships among the diverse groups at the domestic level would be quite different in Houston from those in Los Angeles or New York. In order to understand these regional differences, we organized a series of meetings in Chicago, Houston, Los Angeles, Seattle, and Washington, D.C. These meetings were held in addition to our ongoing discussions with the advisory committee in New York. All of the scholars who have written for this publication went to most of these cities to meet with the local Asian American leaders, and with scholars and activists in related fields, to gain insight into the regional differences of the Asian American experience.

One of the most striking features of these gatherings was the enthusiasm and willingness of the local participants to engage in the international dimension of their experience, which they felt had often been lacking in the more typical Asian American discussions. Similarly, the scholars were often surprised to hear the local variations of the hypotheses they had begun to develop. They were also genuinely pleased to participate in a more community-based dialogue that could help expand their more specialized academic pursuits. A number of articles in the volume refer to these regional discussions.

As a leading organization dedicated to fostering better understanding between the United States and the Asian countries, the Asia Society has increasingly played a vital role in creating connections between Asian Americans and Asia and among the various Asian American communities. In addition to developing a stronger focus on programs dealing with Asian American themes and issues at all of its locations, the Asia Society has made a special effort to serve as a catalyst in creating a national forum for Asian American issues. Recognizing the need for a more nuanced understanding of Asian societies and Asian American complexities, the Asia Society has developed a series of initiatives ranging from art exhibitions to national conferences. "Bridges" was an integral part of this overall objective to infuse the institution with the spirit of Asian American issues and to better understand their role in the multifaceted connections that have been, and continue to be, established between the United States and Asia.

Clearly, such an unprecedented undertaking would have been beyond the expertise of the Asia Society staff; nor would we have presumed that we could proceed on our own. The active collaboration among the Asia Society, LEAP, and AAFNY at all levels of the project was crucial to the conference's successful outcome. Both J. D. Hokoyama of LEAP and Cao 0. of AAFNY were invaluable in their advice about the potential reaction of the communities to the proposed program. With their help and input, we were able to organize an impressive list of members for a program advisory committee. It was one of those unusual committees in which people were not simply lending their names, but were committed to participating fully and were active in helping us shape the agenda for the national project. All of them are acknowledged in the report on the national conference, which was published by the Asia Society in 1997.

"Bridges" was an unusually complex project, involving extensive planning meetings, regional discussions, a national conference, published reports, and this important volume. It is doubtful that we could have gone ahead with this ambitious task had it not been for our major supporters and funders. I would especially like to thank the Ford Foundation for providing major support for the research-oriented aspects of the project. Dr. Mahnaz Ispahani was not simply a program officer, reacting to what we applied for and giving us the necessary funds; she was an active member of the advisory committee, giving us valuable feedback at the conceptual and intellectual levels as well as suggesting names of scholars and topics for potential inclusion in the project. We benefited tremendously from her insightful observations and critical comments as she shepherded the project through the Ford Foundation. The Starr Foundation and the Rockefeller Foundation also provided early support for the national conference, and we are deeply grateful for their willingness to become engaged with a project that, at the time of its inception, seemed futuristic. Our special thanks also go to AT&T for providing corporate sponsorship for the project.

A number of people have worked hard to make the "Bridges" project a great success. At the Asia Society, I would like to thank Dr. Marshall Bouton, our executive vice-president, who was an early champion of programs dealing with Asian Americans at our institution. His keen intelligence and his expertise on sociopolitical and economic issues were crucial in our formulation of the project. Sayu Bhojwani and Sunita Sunder Mukhi in their respective positions as program managers worked hard to bring the project to full fruition. All of the writers who were commissioned to write for this volume have been active supporters of our efforts and have participated fully in all aspects of the project, from traveling throughout the country to conduct regional meetings to presenting papers at the national conference. We are grateful for their commitment and patience as we prepared the volume for publication. Most important, our deepest gratitude goes to

Evelyn Hu-DeHart, the academic editor of this volume who has worked tire-lessly to make it conceptually cohesive and organizationally attractive. I also would like to acknowledge our partners at Temple University Press, who saw the value of the publication and made an early commitment to publish it as part of their Asian American series.

When we began this project in the fall of 1995, we had a palpable sense that we were ahead of the curve: most long-active members of the Asian American communities were not quite sure how the international issues would really help the cause of creating a greater presence of Asian Ameri-cans on the national front. The international policy and business experts, on the other hand, were aware of the potential of Asian Americans to provide special connections to the so-called Asian miracle. Much has changed in the ensuing two years. Controversy over campaign financing has brought the connections between domestic Asian American issues and their international context to a new level of concern and interest. On the economic front, the Asian "miracle" is beginning to have more of a "meltdown" feel in the cur-rent economic climate. Professor Hu-DeHart has elaborated on these issues in her introduction.

Arguably, the need to understand the complexities inherent in the ex-perience and aspirations of Asian Americans has never been greater. It is our hope that this volume will open doors to new forms of inquiry and further exploration of the multiple facets of the Asian American experience.

Acknowledgments

I wish to thank Vishakha Desai of the Asia Society for entrusting me with this part of the multifaceted "Bridges with Asia" project that she conceived and curated. After she had commissioned the essays, she invited me to conceptualize and edit the book, and find a publisher. Although technically an Asia Society project, this book enjoys the kind of total intellectual autonomy that is the hallmark of all credible academic scholarly productions.

I wish to thank Michael Omi and David Palumbo-Liu, co-editors of the Asian American History and Culture series at Temple University Press, for the honor of including this book among its titles, and for their close reading and critique of all the essays.

I wish to thank the contributors to this volume, none of whom "chose" to work with me, but all of whom submitted graciously—even if not always expeditiously—to my nudging, prodding, and occasional desperate nagging.

I wish to thank Janet Francendese of Temple University Press and her fine colleagues, especially Janet Greenwood of Berliner, Inc., and Sue Maier, the superb copy editor. Finally, I thank my own staff at the Department of Ethnic Studies: Karen Moreira and the undergraduate student assistants, Chalane Lechuga and Shiuan Huang.

Evelyn Hu-DeHart
Department of Ethnic Studies
University of Colorado at Boulder

The essays in this volume have been contributed by scholars who participated in a groundbreaking conference, *Bridges with Asia: Asian Americans in the United States,* in May 1996. This conference was organized by the Asia Society together with Leadership Education for Asia Pacifics, Inc. (LEAP) and Asian American Federation. The conference and this volume have been generously supported by The Ford Foundation, The Starr Foundation, The Rockefeller Foundation, and AT&T.

The Asia Society

INTRODUCTION

Asian American Formations

in the

Age of Globalization

EVELYN HU-DEHART

TRANS-PACIFIC ARTICULATIONS

Less than one year after his election as governor of the State of Washington in the Pacific Northwest, Chinese American Gary Locke undertook an official journey to China that included a brief stop at tiny Jilong, his ancestral village in Taishan County, Guangdong Province, in south China (Postman 1997c, 1997d, 1997e). This triumphal ceremonial homecoming of the immigrant's son who had made good in America can easily be the emblematic performance for all Asian Americans at the end of the second millennium, for it captured in a brief script all the conflicting thoughts, beliefs, and expectations by Asian Americans of themselves, and of Asian Americans by others, on the crowded world stage.

Key among those family members who accompanied Locke was his savvy 80-year-old father, the immigrant from the village, who long ago adopted the quintessentially American name Jimmy and Anglicized his Chinese surname to remove any obvious trace of ethnic accent. Patriarch Jimmy publicly lamented not having insisted more forcefully that young Gary learn Chinese from his grandmother in Hong Kong, to whom he had been sent when he was ten and from whom he fled after only a short stay. Jimmy knew that his son's lack of fluency in the Chinese language severely weakened the connection to his Chinese culture (Postman 1997a).

Then there is the large Asian American community, represented by those such as Daphne Kwok, executive director of the Organization of Chinese Americans. This community was also justifiably proud of one of its own. To Kwok and other representatives of Asian American organizations, Locke's election elevated him to a symbol of minority success in America. For Asian Americans specifically, he represented a "tremendous role model." Furthermore, Kwok was curious to find out after Locke's mission to China whether, when he returned, he really was "able to do more in China than someone who is not necessarily Chinese American" (Postman 1997a).

Echoing Daphne Kwok but in a different way, Orville Schell, one of America's leading China observers and currently dean of the Graduate School of Journalism at the University of California, Berkeley, pronounced Locke's history-making trip to China part of the recent surge of Asian economic and commercial power around the Pacific Rim, representing "another piece to the whole Pacific Rim puzzle being repossessed by ethnic Asians, particularly by Chinese." To drive home his point about "race and pride" exemplified by Locke and other prominent Asian Americans, Schell named the phenomenon "ethnic nationalism" (Postman 1997a).

China could hardly contain itself, its glee and pride illustrated by the simple headline reclaiming the "dutiful son" on the cover of a national government-published magazine: GARY LOCKE, DESCENDANT OF TAISHAN, TO RETURN. President Jiang Zemin expressed his "personal pride," and local Taishan officials hoped out loud that Locke's ethnic roots would bring an economic boom to the area (Batsell 1997).

Finally, an exuberant Gary Locke, first Asian American elected governor outside Hawaii, registered distinct reactions to these varied comments. First, he simultaneously paid homage and reconnected himself historically to his roots by remarking that "the people of Taishan, the Chinese people, have given their blood, sweat and tears to the prosperity that America now enjoys." He also delighted in displaying his cultural competence about how things are done "over there," explaining to a non–Asian American reporter that his mission "was very successful in helping establish the personal relationships that are so important to conducting business in Asia" (Batsell 1997; Postman 1997b). While in his ancestral village, in what was probably a less-guarded moment, he expressed consternation at the open sewers, with their stench of "garbage and human waste," and thanked his immigrant father for making possible his more comfortable life in Washington State (Postman

1997e). But most resoundingly, he declared in no uncertain terms: "I am proud to be Chinese. But I am thoroughly American" (Postman 1997a).

In short, can Asian Americans such as Gary Locke claim what Schell calls "ethnic nationalism" without jeopardizing their cultural and political citizenship in the United States? Can these two sources of pride, identification, and belonging be compatible, or must they ultimately clash, at least where Asian immigrants and their descendants in America are concerned? If Asian Americans are to assume the role of "bridge builders" across the Pacific, helping to link the United States more closely to Asian countries, what are the opportunities and the risks, the promises and the perils? Is this even a "natural" role for Asian Americans to undertake? Should someone like Governor Locke, just because he happens to be of Chinese descent and heritage, be expected to take a larger-than-usual role in this enterprise, and what cultural capital is he presumed to possess that would make him more successful in this endeavor than non–Asian Americans if he does not even speak Chinese anymore? Would Gary Locke be equally effective if he were to lead a mission to any other Asian country simply because he is Asian American? Are his Chinese cultural roots and competence transferable from one Asian context to another? Would Asian political and economic leaders be more likely to see him as a successful Chinese or Asian American with some natural or primordial affinity to them, or as another powerful American politician with pragmatic interest in the Pacific Rim?

One of Asian America's preeminent role models at the close of the twentieth century, Governor Locke appears to guide his fellow Asian Americans to cast their gaze spatially across the Pacific, thus temporally projecting themselves into the next century, which has already felicitously been dubbed the "Pacific Century." This is our future, he seems to proclaim, because as Asian Americans, we have the cultural attributes and personal connections to lead the way. To be fair, Governor Locke has also reminded Asian Americans not to forget past struggles in America, to dignify their roots, and to validate their history.

When the Asia Society convened a national conference in New York City in May 1996 to discuss the issue of Asian Americans as physical and metaphorical bridge builders to the Pacific Rim and the next century, it was following up on a theme first articulated at the society's 1991 national meeting in Los Angeles. In fact, it was none other than Mike Woo, then a Los Angeles city councilman and Democratic Party activist, who extolled his fellow Asian Americans as "translators" and "go-betweens" for the Asian and American cultures, thus projecting a "hybrid role" for Asian Americans (cited in Ong 1993: 768) in the Pacific Century of the New World Order. This theme has been picked up repeatedly by Asian Americans and others in the 1990s, more recently echoed by another prominent Asian Californian politician—this time, the Republican Matt Fong. In January 1996, Fong pronounced California, with its large Asian American population, poised to become the "capital of the Pacific Rim" (Fong 1996).

Actually, Woo, Fong, and the others have picked up and are renarrating an already well-articulated theme concerning certain Asian populations around the Pacific Rim, including those in the United States, who have been variously dubbed "Sons of the Yellow Emperor," alluding to the Chinese (Pan 1990); "global tribes" and "global diasporas," referring to Chinese, Japanese, and South Asians (Cohen 1997; Kotkin 1992); and, within certain academic circles, "postcolonials" and "transnationals" living in a state of "postmodernity" (Ong and Nonini 1997). These are Asian cultural and ethnic groups that, over the course of the past three centuries or more, have dispersed themselves and settled in many locations around the Pacific Rim, from Asia to North and South America. In many cases, their arrival predated the advent of European colonialism; they then interposed themselves between colonial masters and colonized natives by functioning as traders and entrepreneurs, and occasionally as government contractors and civil servants. Finally, they lived through national liberation movements to witness their "adopted homelands" becoming independent countries and modern nation-states.

Even after independence, however, these highly mobile cosmopolitans have continued in the role of "essential outsiders" (Chirot and Reid 1997). Incompletely integrated into the newly independent states carved out of colonial empires, they have become the "Jews of the East" (Kotkin 1992: 170). Shut out of politics, which has reverted to the control of indigenous groups, they have gravitated toward commerce and finance, building on "primordial" ethnic ties, networks, and webs to gain competitive advantage. Their collective identity and mutual trust allows for an easy flow of personnel, technology, and, most important, capital across regional and national boundaries around the Pacific Rim (Chirot and Reid 1997; Kotkin 1992; Pan 1990; Seagrave 1995; Weidenbaum and Hughes 1996).

In the post–Cold War era, when the world became a more harmonious whole, according to this narrative—and as Southeast Asian countries positioned themselves to enter the new global economy and join Japan, then South Korea, as smaller economic "tigers" or "dragons"—the diasporic groups, especially the "overseas Chinese," seemed best poised to lead the move toward this New World Order. With their deterritorialized social identities—meaning that they identify first with their co-ethnics wherever they are rather than submit to the hegemonizing claim of exclusive citizenship demanded by a single country or nation-state (Cohen 1997: 157)—they are a perfect match for the postmodern global capitalist ideology: both hold an equal disregard for national boundaries, especially where trade, labor, and capital are concerned. As Robin Cohen, the British sociologist of global diasporas, notes: "There is no longer any stability in the points of origin, no finality in the points of destination, and no necessary coincidence between social and national identities" (Cohen 1997: 175). This deployment of "flexible citizenship," to borrow a term coined by the anthropologist Aihwa Ong (1993), does not serve as a liability; rather, it explains these groups' success. "Chronically insecure" because they are "constantly uprooted," they carry permanently a "refugee mentality" and thus expect little of the state or society in which they settle. Instead, they depend largely on family and kin, on "self-reliance," and on a deep reserve of personal connections (*guanxi* in Chinese) (Kotkin 1992: 185).

Most Western observers have focused on the Chinese, the largest and oldest diasporic Asian ethnic group. In the past few years, a spate of books have been published in the United States by academics and journalists attempting to capture the particular ethos of these hard-driven global capitalists. These sensationalized titles reflect a kind of admiration, to be sure, but they are also prone to exaggeration and betray fear; they can also engender loathing. Two examples stand out and illustrate the point: *The Bamboo Network: How Expatriate Chinese Entrepreneurs Are Creating a New Economic Superpower in Asia* (1996), by the business professors Murray Weidenbaum and Samuel Hughes, and *Lords of the Rim: The Invisible Empire of the Overseas Chinese* (1995), by the journalist Sterling Seagrave.

These books have helped popularize a rearticulated and now oft-repeated neo-Confucian notion to explain Asian successes in the newly globalized Pacific Rim economies. The best spokesmen for these culturalist arguments are none other than Asian leaders themselves, notably Singapore's founding premier and current elder statesman, Lee Kuan Yew, and his neighbor Dr. Mahathir Mohamad, the long-time prime minister of Muslim Malaysia. Ironically, these leaders once blamed Confucianism for stifling the entrepreneurial spirit, holding it responsible for Asia's backwardness and failure to modernize (Woo-Cumings 1993: 138). Today, Lee Kuan Yew and company are recycling Confucianism to form the basis of a regional ideology about "Asian values" that have created an "Asian model" or "Asian spirit" of capitalism. Lee, Mahathir, et al. are fond of subjecting the Western "ethos of individualism" to unfavorable comparison with the Asian "communitarian ethos," where family duties and community obligations come first. Asian culture is first and foremost a "culture of discipline": discipline in politics, in the family, and at the workplace (Jayasuriya 1997: 19). Discipline in turn leads to order, and order leads to productivity. In the words of the eloquent Lee Kuan Yew: "The expansion of the right of the individual to behave or misbehave as he pleases has come at the expense of orderly society. In the East the main object is to have a well-ordered society so that everybody can have maximum enjoyment of his freedoms. This freedom can only exist in an ordered state and not in a natural state of contention and anarchy" (Wong 1994).

Hard work, self-sacrifice, delayed gratification, and love of learning are other important components of Asian values. Again, listen to Lee Kuan Yew in his pointed analysis of why the United States is perceived in Asia to be morally weak and economically vulnerable: "If you have a culture that doesn't place much value in learning and scholarship and hard work and thrift and deferment of present enjoyment for future gain, the going will be much slower" (B. Wong 1994). In case Lee Kuan Yew did not make his point clearly enough, one admiring Western observer drives it home this way: "For the first time since the beginnings of the industrial revolution, the superiority of Western standards of organization, production and technological development have been called into question by the success of a distinctly alien form of capitalism" (Kotkin 1992: 117). Asian neo-Confucianists would flatly and unabashedly claim not only that the Asian model of capitalism is superior by virtue of its cultural underpinnings, but also that disciplined Asians enjoy ethnic and cultural superiority over the decadent West as personified by the United States (Pan 1990: 245). Fortunately for the United States, these Asian values have been carried across the Pacific by generations of Asian immigrants.

If Jimmy Locke, the family patriarch and small shopkeeper, represents an example of the original Asian America—an identity that arose during the Civil Rights movement of the 1960s, when young Americans of Asian descent claimed their rights and their place in this society after a long history of social and legal exclusion—his son the governor heralds the new Asian America. This Asian America has been replenished and revitalized by a tremendous wave of new immigration from Asia, because the Civil Rights movement also reopened the doors of the United States to racialized Third World peoples. For the first time in American history, immigrants from Asia have been given full access to naturalized citizenship; furthermore, they and their children are welcomed into an America that has been newly constructed as multicultural and pluralistic. As a result, the U.S. government has formally adopted what was at its inception an oppositional political concept and converted "Asian American" into a public-policy and census category to measure American diversity, along with "African American," "Hispanic," "Native American," and, of course, "white."

From fewer than one million all told in 1965, the number of Asian Americans in the United States has grown to exceed ten million in the waning years of the twentieth century, making Asian Americans the country's fastest-growing racial-ethnic population. This also means that the vast majority of the Asian American population—70 percent or more—are of the immigrant generation; that is, they are not U.S.-born. If that alone is not enough to make this one of the most dramatic postwar demographic stories, the growing complexity and diversity within this category truly makes it noteworthy. No longer just Chinese, Filipino, and Japanese, the group is enhanced by a long list of post-1965 immigrants distinguished by ethnicity and nativity, such as South Asians, Koreans, Vietnamese, Laotians, Cambodians, Thais, Hmong, Pakistanis, Indonesians, Malaysians, Bangladeshis, Sri Lankans, Burmese, Okinawans and "others," to catch all those not numerous enough to merit their own name yet (LEAP/UCLA 1993: 64; this list is presented in order of numerical size according to the 1990 census).

The Japanese are no longer immigrating to the United States in a significant way. The other original immigrant groups—Chinese and Filipinos—however, have continued to come in ever-larger numbers. In the case of the new Chinese immigrants, the designation "Chinese" increasingly signifies merely an ethnic identity rather than nationality or nativity, for these immigrants now come from a variety of places, such as Taiwan, Southeast Asia (Singapore, Thailand, Indonesia, Malaysia), and Hong Kong, not to mention the Caribbean and Latin America. The same is true of many identified as "South Asians," for they may have been multigenerational residents of various African countries before settling in the United States, and "South Asian" is itself a broad category masking sharp distinctions among Hindus, Ismailis and other Muslims, Sikhs, Jains, Parsis, and others (Kotkin 1992: 205).

Families and children now characterize most new Asian immigrants, resulting in a population that—along with Hispanics, the other large new immigrant group—is younger than the rest of American society and enjoys a good gender balance. Generational distinctions within communities that have both old and new immigrants are stark and signify other differences, such as degree of assimilation into mainstream society. And although Asian immigrants were once almost uniformly poor and rural in origin, and were relegated in the United States to the working class or agricultural and small commercial sectors, today's new immigrants are more likely to be middle class and urban in origin and to make cities their choice for settlement. In addition, many are equipped with considerable education and other human capital that is serving them well in post–Civil Rights America, which officially does not condone racial and ethnic discrimination (Liu and Cheng 1994). Furthermore, these highly skilled, talented, and motivated Asian immigrants were perfectly positioned to benefit immediately from affirmative action— originally enacted in the mid-1960s to help African Americans overcome centuries of slavery and racial segregation—because eligibility for the program was extended to all other "minority" groups just as these Asian immigrants were arriving in large numbers. Consequently, many new Asian Americans have managed to attain the American Dream in far less than a generation's time.

Certainly, collectively and as an aggregate, these immigrants have an impressive profile backed up with strong statistics, even when compared with white Americans. According to the March 1996 "Current Population Survey," Asian Americans are younger and better educated than the rest of America: a whopping 41.7 percent have a college degree, compared with only 23.6 percent for the rest of America. Asian Americans also have stronger "family values," as measured by their much lower divorce rate, which is just 3.8 percent, compared with 8.9 percent for other Americans aged fifteen and over (*AsianWeek* 1997b). While they make up only 3 percent of the U.S. population overall, Asian Americans make up 5 percent of college and university students. Even more impressive, at the most selective institutions (e.g., Stanford, the "ivies," the top University of California campuses), this number rises as high as 30 percent or even more. A recent audit of the Small Business Administration (SBA), an affirmative-action program, disclosed that Asian American–owned small businesses accounted for nearly 24 percent of the total contracts awarded in 1996 (Sharpe 1997). It stands to reason that mainstream America, duly impressed by these indications and abetted by an eager media hungry for success stories in the midst of persistently failing long-time U.S. minorities, would anoint Asian Americans the "model minority."

For those Asian Americans who have even a cursory knowledge of the history of Asians in the United States, the "model-minority" construction stands in sharp contrast to the stereotype of the disease-ridden, racially inferior, inherently unassimilable nineteenth-century coolie, a group that was collectively captured as a "yellow peril" that had no place in a dynamic society characterized by robust republican ideals. But today, although many are clearly uncomfortable with unsolicited attention paid to their successes, it would be disingenuous for Asian Americans to dismiss all evidence of their rapid upward mobility in American society as simply renewed racist fabrications. Perhaps the more appropriate question and concern is how best to manage these images and explain Asian American behavior and practices to the rest of American society, mainstream and marginalized communities alike.

One thing is clear: the perception of Asian Americans' success is inextricably linked to the group's largely immigrant nature. Asian Americans are touted for their discipline and hard work, devotion to family, communitarian ethos, and reverence for learning—the same Asian values that Lew Kuan Yew has been so effectively propounding as essential "Asianness." Furthermore, this success came at a time when the Asian economic tigers were "driving the engine of world growth into the 21st century" (Bello 1998) and China had opened up to foreign investment; a time when foreign investment was flowing into Asia unfettered, and exports were flowing out unrestricted, creating impressive growth rates. These two narratives, which accompanied, respectively, the arrival of new Asian immigrants in America and the extension of globalization to the Asia Pacific region, converged to produce the articulation of a new narrative: Asian Americans as transnationals and bridge builders on the Pacific Rim. As a grand, new narrative, it also posited an articulation between Asia and America, with Asian Americans as the primary instrument of this linkage and connection.

Transnationalism can be defined generally as the "process by which immigrants forge and sustain multi-stranded social relations that link together their societies of origin and settlement . . . [and] whose social fields . . . cross geographic, cultural and political borders." Furthermore, these particular immigrants make decisions, develop identities, and experience life in a "network of relationships that connect them simultaneously to two or more nation-states" (Basch, Schiller, and Blanc 1994: 4–22). Given modern technology and communications systems, most immigrants today are probably transnational to some degree in that they do not pick up all roots and sever all ties—physical, emotional, economic, social, cultural—to one place before forming new ones in another; nor do they immediately transfer their allegiance from one to the other. Modern transnational migration is inextricably linked to the forces of global capitalism, as capital and labor move, and are moved, constantly across borders.

Certainly, it is within this context that so many Asians have migrated to the United States and continue with many transnational practices. The term "bridge-building transnationals," however, refers mainly to middle-class and upper-class immigrants who establish ties, and sometimes citizenship, in two or more places out of desire and necessity. These privileged immigrants, some of whom are already practiced diasporics such as the Chinese, "have the resources to negotiate and exploit the varied conditions of commerce and family residence" in different countries (Ong 1993: 753). The most amusing characterization of Asian transnationals are the aptly named "astronauts," in reference to the inordinate amount of time and energy these people spend in "orbit," vaulting across the Pacific to monitor their transpacific investments (S.C. Wong 1995; Ong 1993). More common are well-educated, professional, and technically trained Asian Americans—who may be U.S.-born but are more likely immigrants with Asian-language skills—who work for U.S. companies in Asian countries, or, conversely, who work for Asian companies in the United States. Many others follow the flow of mobile capital as part of the Pacific "brain flow" (Asia Society 1997: 28, 68). Another kind of transnational Asian American is represented by Jessica Elnitiarta, the daughter of the ethnic Chinese global capitalist and Indonesian national Ted Sioeng, who like many Thai and Indonesian Chinese uses a "native" name. She immigrated to the United States and has established residence in that important Pacific Rim node Los Angeles, where she can better take care of her father's manifold investments, which include a Chinese-language newspaper in the new "Chinatown" of Monterey Park (Risen 1997).

Transnational or otherwise, model minority or not, middle-class, upwardly mobile Asian Americans do desire respect and acceptance from mainstream American society. In a recent column, the print journalist Bill Wong frankly suggested that many Asian Americans aspire to capture the attention of, and seek validation from, mainstream or white America "at some point in our lives." Of course, he also hastened to add, Asian Americans and other "non-whites" would also relish seeing a brown-skinned young person, such as the self-described multiracial (but mostly Asian) Tiger Woods "[whupp] the butts of the white establishment, and [do] it with aplomb, style and elan" (Wong 1997). The prodigious Democratic Party fund-raiser John Huang also cited as motivation the need to increase the influence of Asian Americans "within mainstream American society" (AsianWeek 1997a).

Precisely to gain entree into mainstream American society, a parade of Asian American "advocacy" groups have appeared over the course of the past decade, most with "inside the Beltway" offices in Washington, D.C. These organizations bear names such as National Asian Pacific American Legal Consortium, Organization of Chinese Americans, National Korean American Social and Education Consortium, American Association of Physicians of Indian Origin, Filipino Civil Rights Advocates, and, the most visible of them all, the bipartisan (but mostly Democratic) Congressional Asian Pacific American Caucus Institute, best known by its acronym CAPACI.

These organizations' major goal during the Clinton administration, especially after his reelection, was to place at least one Asian American in the cabinet, building their strategy around an "ascent to the Capitol" (Wu 1996). On the top of a wish list that was actually quite realistic was placing someone such as Chang-lin Tien, at the time the outgoing chancellor at Berkeley, in the cabinet as secretary of energy or education. Among Tien's many achievements was the distinction of having raised more money for the prestigious campus than any of his predecessors, in large part by tapping into his many lucrative Asian connections. Tien has often noted that Asian Americans are "best positioned" to break down "cultural barriers" standing in the way of U.S.–Asian political and business relations. "Versed in both the American mainstream culture and in an Asian 'home country' tradition,

Asian Americans are uniquely poised to promote understanding," he has said (Asia Society 1997: 17–18).

Indeed, the Asian American advocacy groups veritably demanded a presidential appointment at the highest level of the federal government as their well-deserved reward for raising and contributing millions to the president's reelection campaign. Tien's ascendance to the cabinet would be the strongest signal yet that Asian Americans had arrived on the American national political scene, a validation of the calculation that they must seek political clout in order to protect their economic and civil-rights gains in this society and guard against continuing anti-Asian bias, stereotyping, and violence. It would also challenge the glass ceiling that has presented an obstacle to professional, well-educated Asian Americans' reaching their full potential, denying them leadership opportunities in America's institutions and businesses, a point that Tien is also fond of noting (Asia Society 1997: 18).

For successful Asian Americans, it would seem, there is enormous promise in assuming the bridge-building role and in engaging America with Asia. It is as if the frightful old "yellow peril" has been transformed into an overachieving "homo economicus," a version of the model-minority formula (Ong 1993: 764–65) refurbished by "Asian values." But old barriers to Asian American integration into American society remain, and new ones are still being erected. If opportunities arise to boost Asian American centrality in American society and culture, hidden dangers and incalculable risks may also lurk in the wings.

The essays presented in this volume explore the relationships and interactions of Asian Americans in the international context of the Pacific Rim, examining new meanings and practices of Asian Americans in "postality" (San Juan 1998: 157)—that is, the post–Civil Rights, post–Cold War, postmodern, and postcolonial era. Or, in short, in the new era of globalization. They open the discussion but in no way exhaust the topic. They should provide some answers to the field of Asian American studies, which has been both energized and troubled by recent trends toward transnationalism and diasporic studies, and which in other ways has been internationalizing its focus. They should also address some questions for the field of Asian studies, whose practitioners are now wondering out loud how, precisely by internationalizing themselves, Asian Americans, given their biculturalism and transnationality, might help frame new approaches to the study of Asia and its subjects. They also probe into what the commentator and Howard University Law School professor Frank Wu calls the "contradictions of transnationalism" (Wu 1997b), and what Sau-ling C. Wong, professor of Asian American studies at Berkeley, warns of as the "denationalization" of Asian Americans and the increasing "permeability" between Asians and Asian Americans

(S.C. Wong 1995). They interrogate old, and speak to new, Asian American formations in this age of globalization, when the Asia Pacific—David Palumbo-Liu suggests—may have become a "transnational imaginary" (Palumbo-Liu 1999).

Arif Dirlik examines competing orientations facing most Asian Americans today, informed in part by contrasting self-images—that is, whether to look toward the Pacific and hence the "future," or toward their historical legacies in the United States. He sees the new spaces created by globalization and transnational Asian capital at the root of this dilemma between the present and the past, challenging the original ideal that community played in the formation of Asian American consciousness. Changes in the subject matter of Asian American studies, from community-based to diasporic orientations, reflect these changes in Asian American subjectivity. He argues that "the idea of Asian America needs a remapping of the United States, Asia, the Pacific, and the world that is different from the one that produced the original formation of Asian America less than three decades ago." Ultimately, the question is a matter not of ethnic destiny, but of political choice.

In her essay, Lucie Cheng inquires into the impact of the much-touted arrival of the Pacific Century—the rise of the little dragons, the formation of the Pacific Rim economy—on the Chinese in America, their objective condition as well as their changing self-perceptions. She examines the pivotal role that Chinese Americans are playing in the restructuring of U.S.–China relations, not so much in terms of foreign and diplomatic relations as in terms of economic, social, and cultural ones. In this transpacific economy, Chinese Americans are both beneficiaries and victims and can simultaneously contribute and pose challenges to global capitalism.

Le Anh Tu Packard narrates several case studies of Vietnamese Americans engaging with the newly opened economy of their former homeland, then assesses the significance of this engagement to determine whether policies are affected—for example, whether such engagements present the possibility of influencing U.S. economic policy toward Vietnam. Although the relationship between Vietnamese Americans and Vietnam is based primarily on economic exchange, noneconomic considerations of a powerful personal and emotional nature often matter more. Packard also provides interesting comparisons between the perspectives of Vietnamese in Vietnam and their Vietnamese American "cousins."

Paul Watanabe examines Asian American activism in U.S. foreign policy, in part to test the thesis that immigrants and the immigration process are the most important determinant of American foreign policy. In other words, he poses the questions: Are Asian Americans motivated and equipped to become more involved in influencing U.S. foreign policy regarding their homelands? To what extent are they successful? Where are the opportunities, and what are the constraints? He emphasizes that transformations in both the domestic and international contexts may promote or retard Asian American efforts to influence U.S. foreign-policy–making and are crucial in shaping eventual outcomes.

With the passage of California's Proposition 187 in 1995, immigration once again entered the American political scene as a hotly contested issue; the ensuing nativism once again became a troubling phenomenon. Neil Gotanda examines the history of anti-Asian nativism through the series of immigration and naturalization laws, as well as Orientalist constructions of Asians in the United States, framing his analysis within the methods and theories of critical race theory. Throughout, he demonstrates how domestic and foreign policies in the United States mutually act on and influence each other.

Beginning with the premise that Asian Americans—visible as a racial minority yet forever perceived as "foreign"—are vulnerable targets at the intersection of international and domestic tensions, Setsuko Nishi analyzes how U.S.–Asian tensions, when linked to domestic strains, put Asian Americans at risk when there are outbreaks of anti-Asian sentiments and behavior. Nishi's essay studies the interplay between international events and domestic anxieties as they affect American attitudes toward Asian Americans, based on content analysis of a large sample of U.S. newspaper articles from 1989 to 1995.

For Luis Francia, the notion of "home," fundamental to all cultures, begins as a specific site anointed as the matrix of a particular culture. But with global transformations resulting from the movement of people and capital, and the rapid advances in communication, old notions of home and roots have been rendered old-fashioned and meaningless. We close this volume of essays with Francia's critical reading of some well-known Asian American literary works—from the pen of firmly established, canonical writers such as Maxine Hong Kingston and Carlos Bulosan to lesser known, emerging writers such as Theresa Hak Kyung Cha and R. Zamora Linmark, and many in-between—where a consistent theme has been the imaginative, often painful, rethinking of what and where home is, both for the original immigrants and for their American offspring.

THE MORNING DELUGE

Since the end of 1996, events have overtaken the United States and Asia in ways that had not been foreseen. When these essays were originally conceived, and the first drafts were completed in fall 1996, both Asian America and the

Pacific Rim were riding high; since then, both have crashed. First, several Asian American individuals were accused of illegal campaign fund-raising activities, influence-peddling, and complicity with Communist China to infiltrate and corrupt the American presidency. Then, almost a year later, severe currency devaluations, rapid withdrawal of foreign investment, and overproduction in once-vibrant Asian economies led to near-meltdowns and impending misery for untold millions of common people around the Pacific Rim.

All hopes of seeing an Asian American in Clinton's cabinet were dashed, especially when the leading candidate, Berkeley's Chancellor Tien, was tied by his own fund-raising for the university to Mochtar and James Riady—Asian donors to the Democratic Party whose money was deemed illegal (Rosenfeld 1996). The advocacy groups, which until recently felt flush with arriviste fever in the nation's capital, scrambled angrily and frantically to defend themselves against the unfortunate fallout affecting all Asian Americans—which often scapegoated them in a grossly unfair way—from the well-publicized misdeeds of a few individuals identified as Asian Americans.

How did it happen that Asian Americans were fund-raising at such a frantic pace for President Clinton's reelection? The campaign-finance scandal revealed that the White House had targeted the prosperous, increasingly middle-class Asian American community for money and votes. By taking a softer position on immigration issues, the Democrats expected to swing considerable Asian American support in their direction, and away from these voters' previous propensity to support Republicans (Rogers 1997; Kranish 1997). The Democrats had set their sights even higher when it came to prying money loose from Asian Americans, targeting them for $7 million in campaign donations (Weiner and Sanger 1996).

The plan misfired, however, when ordinary Asian Americans did not step up to the donation plate in anywhere near the numbers projected (Squitieri 1997). In a survey conducted in June 1997 of the Chinese in Los Angeles, a predominantly immigrant community (87 percent), 84 percent said they had never given to political parties, and 60 percent of those indicated that they were unlikely to do so (Kang 1997). This posed a big dilemma to those designated to raise the $7 million, led by John Huang of the Democratic National Committee (DNC) and aided by Asian Americans such as Maria Hsia, a long-time Democratic Party activist in southern California (Sterngold 1997). The money gap also created space and opportunity for self-appointed fund-raising freelancers, such as Johnny Chung and Charlie Trie, to step up their efforts and thereby gain favor with the president and party in power (Johnston 1998).

While their personal histories were different in significant ways, these individuals shared a background of having immigrated from Taiwan in the

1970s and 1980s, and each in his or her own way exemplified the practices and subjectivities of transnational Asians in the United States. As the Berkeley professor and Asian American activist Ling-chi Wang pointedly noted at the outbreak of the campaign-finance scandal, the individuals involved were virtually unknown among established Asian American groups working for Asian American empowerment, especially at the grassroots and community levels, until trouble broke (Wang 1996). John Huang—undersecretary of commerce before moving to the DNC—was, however, acquainted with the Beltway Asian American advocacy groups, especially CAPACI, which represented appointed Asian Americans in the federal government. Moreover, he was a member of the exclusive, if not exactly secretive, Committee of 100, formed by some of the most prominent Chinese Americans after the Tiananmen Square massacre to act as a watchdog group on how the U.S. media and the U.S. government deal with China and U.S.–China relations (Asia Society 1997: 63–64).

Mostly on their own and without coordinating all their efforts, these largely Chinese American fund-raisers tapped into "overseas," or transpacific, connections, calling on *guanxi* (personal relationships) to raise the millions of dollars from mostly ethnic Chinese capitalists in places such as Indonesia, Thailand, and Macao (Cooper 1996; Gerth and Labaton 1996; Lowry 1997; Sanger 1997; Sun and Pomfret 1997). As for the now-infamous Riady family of Indonesia who employed John Huang before he catapulted into the upper echelons of the Clinton administration and the DNC, President Clinton had maintained a long-time association with them dating back to his earlier political career in Little Rock—a significant source of *guanxi* (Adams 1995, 1996). Smaller amounts were raised from Asian immigrants in the United States, including from nuns who presumably had taken a vow of poverty (Rempel 1998).

While influence-peddling and selling access to high government officials and political leaders are part of the American political game (Polsby 1997; Van Natta and Fritsch 1997)—as Roger Tamraz, another immigrant entrepreneur, so gamely testified before the Senate hearings on the fund-raising scandal (Rosenbaum 1997)—the Asian American fund-raisers for the Democrats unfortunately accomplished their task in ways that were often clumsy and unsophisticated. Untutored as they were in necessary skills to finesse the intricate web of U.S. campaign-finance laws and regulations, they were charged with illegal solicitation methods and with soliciting from illegal sources. Ultimately bit players in the big drama of America's corrupt system of moneyed politics, these foreign-tinged, transnational Asian American fund-raisers garnered more than their share of blame and media attention—much to the chagrin of a larger community of Asian Americans eager, ironically, to shed their image of "foreignness" by becoming more active in mainstream American politics.

Not long after the campaign-finance scandal broke, with Asian American fund-raisers and Asian money at its center, the Asian miracle began to unravel fast over in Asia itself. Whatever the immediate reasons for the collapse—too much foreign borrowing, too little reinvestment of profits into the domestic consumer market—pundits and analysts now soberly acknowledge that Asia's "fast-track capitalism" had been a ticking time bomb (Bello 1998; Borosage 1997; Richburg and Mufson 1998). Bruce Cumings, the noted scholar of modern Asia who coined the amusing term "Rimspeak" for all the hype that had surrounded the rise of Asia's economic power, warned even before the collapse that the Pacific Rim was a "capitalist archipelago," with Asia functioning primarily as the "workshop of the world," using cheap and efficient labor to manufacture exports for regions with vast consumer buying power, notably the United States. In this archipelago, some nodes on the rim—Singapore, Hong Kong, and Los Angeles, for example—formed the capitalist elite of "transnational power . . . intertwined in various networks and educated in top U.S. and British universities." At the bottom was the majority of the population in Asia, who "are either out or participate only as unskilled or semi-skilled laborers" (Cumings 1993: 33–34).

Another perceptive analyst of the Asian miracle, Bruce Koppel, distinguished between the "buoyant" sector, characterized by "high growth, increasingly modern consumption patterns, and significant dependence on critical resources (labor and savings)," and the "*other*" Asia, which he depicted as the "reservoir of human resources for national development but characterized by low economic growth, traditional low productivity problems, and patterns of exclusion which prevent extensive productive crossover into the buoyant sector" (Koppel 1997: 5; emphasis added).

To put it mildly, global capitalism has been uneven (San Juan 1998: 8, 13–14, 198–200, 221–25). In fact, for the vast majority of Asian peoples, it has been exposed as a cruel hoax, as desperate, laid-off female Thai factory workers recently confided to the *New York Times* reporter Seth Mydans, whose article carried the stark headline: THAILAND ECONOMIC CRISIS CRUSHES THE WORKING POOR (Mydans 1997). Calling it an "underside to the boom," Mydans reported that fully 60 percent of the country's 60 million people remain poor, while half of the nation's wealth is in the hands of the richest 10 percent, producing one of the sharpest gaps between rich and poor in the world. One Thai economist frankly admitted that "the role of the poor in the boom has been to create the wealth. . . . Now when the boom turns to slump, some of them will be cast aside, and they have nothing to cushion them at all."

William Greider, a relentless and trenchant critic of globalization, sums it up well: "Any healthy economy, including the globalized marketplace, will sooner or later be undermined if the broad ranks of consumers lack the wherewithal to keep up." These unrealized consumers are none other than the masses of severely exploited workers now littered all over Thailand, Indonesia, China, and Vietnam. Greider denounces the abundant "lurid examples of the random inhumanity in global capitalism" found in sweatshops and factories (Greider 1997). American consumers have been made uncomfortably aware of the worst examples of such global sweatshops in Indonesia and Vietnam, where female and child workers are paid less than a living wage to sew high-end sneakers for Nike (Norlund 1997; Sanders and Raptur 1997). The intense competition inherent in globalization produces an internal logic that forces factory owners to chase ever-cheaper labor all around the Pacific Rim, including in Los Angeles and New York City, with their vast reserves of immigrant labor. Indeed, the pressures of global competition are repeatedly used to justify low wages and inhumane treatment of immigrant American and Third World workers—in short, to justify the existence of sweatshops, defined as factories and assembly plants that do not comply with minimum local standards on wage and working conditions (Bonacich 1994; Smith 1996).

What is truly ironic in all this hand-wringing and soul-searching about what went wrong in Asia is that, suddenly, the once-touted "Asian values" and "personal connections" deemed intrinsic to the success of Asian capitalism and way of doing business are now denounced and re-coded as "crony capitalism" and corruption (Friedman 1997). What would Lee Kuan Yew and his fellow Asian leaders say now? When their message about Asian values resonated around the Pacific, a few lonely voices did warn that discipline, duty, and order could also be cited as a pretext by the region's powerful authoritarian states to repress political opposition and suppress union activism (Jayasuriya 1997).

Just as there is the Other Asia, there is the Other Asian America. For a long time, putting the spotlight on Asian Americans as a model minority has made it easy for even Asian Americans themselves to elide a very significant segment of the new immigrants, those who are refugees from places such as Vietnam, Cambodia, and Laos. Making up 17 percent of the Asian American population, these "traumatized" immigrants often do not arrive with families intact, and they do not come armed with social skills and human capital that can be readily adapted to modern American society. The young Hmong leader KaYing Yang, executive director of the Women's Association of Hmong and Lao in St. Paul, Minnesota, does not see the role of Hmong Americans as linking the United States and Asia to promote business or improve U.S.–Asian foreign relations; rather, she sees their role as refugees who are concerned with connecting their everyday lives in the United States to still-unresolved feelings for and ties to a lost homeland. For them, the term "Asian American" does not make sense, and "Hmong American" is just barely meaningful. Driven from their homeland by war, the Hmong, a people struggling against all odds to find a place in American society, may find themselves forever refugees, she poignantly notes (Asia Society 1997: 26–28).

Joining the Hmong in the ranks of the Other Asian America are the "illegal immigrants"—among them many desperate workers smuggled into the United States to work in low-skill and extremely low-paid service jobs and in sweatshops (Kwong 1997). For much of American society, however, and for many in the Asian American community, these less-attractive aspects of Asian America are inconvenient and best left unacknowledged until they can no longer be ignored.

Truth be told, the underside of globalization is not just an Asian Pacific phenomenon; it has also been acutely felt in the American Pacific. The Fuzhounese workers were forced into American national consciousness when their overloaded and totally unseaworthy vessel, the infelicitously named *Golden Venture*, ran aground on the New Jersey shore in June 1993 (Kwong 1997). The American public was also genuinely shocked when a garment sweatshop in southern California's El Monte, with its captive female labor force smuggled in from Asia, came to light several years ago. In October 1997, U.S. Labor Secretary Alexis Herman acknowledged that garment sweatshops have reappeared in New York City in force (Greenhouse 1997).

The dark side of global capitalism can also be felt on the Mexican side of the U.S.–Mexican border. There, Asian transnational capitalists have established some 2,700 special assembly plants, called *maquiladoras*, to take advantage of Mexico's cheap labor and the duty exemptions amplified by NAFTA (the North American Free Trade Agreement, an important component of globalization that lifts trade barriers among the United States, Canada, and Mexico) to import finished consumer and industrial products into the United States. In December 1997, Mexican workers in the Korean-owned Han Young factory that makes truck chassis for the Hyundai auto plant in San Diego, California, were denied the right to choose their own union. It was such an egregious violation of the labor rights guaranteed by NAFTA that the *New York Times* was prompted to run an editorial denouncing Han Young's actions (Dillon 1997; *New York Times* 1997).

Asian-owned assembly plants have even spread to Central America, where female garment workers are paid even less than those on the U.S.–Mexican border and fired when they dare to protest (Herbert 1995). New exposés are popping up in the unlikeliest places, the latest in the Northern Mariana Islands, an American possession in the Pacific Ocean. The

$500 million garment industry in Saipan, the capital, employs overwhelmingly foreign female contract workers brought in from China and the Philippines, who are paid $3 per hour, less than the U.S. minimum wage (Alvarez 1998; Silverstein 1998).

The smugglers and employers of cheap, docile, often female Asian migrant labor are typically Asians and Asian Americans themselves—these ubiquitous transnational businessmen from Taiwan, Korea, Hong Kong, and the United States. The owners and operators of the *Golden Venture,* as well as of the El Monte and New York City sweatshops and Mexican *maquiladoras,* all fit this bill, as does the naturalized Asian American Willie Tam, the largest off-shore investor and sweatshop operator in Saipan. Overwhelmingly, Asian and Asian American entrepreneurs fulfill the role of subcontractors in a system of global sourcing in the regional division of labor (Bonacich 1994; Gereffi 1993; Smith 1996).

None of these abuses is necessary to global commerce or to anyone's prosperity, Greider argues. They continue because no one steps in to stop them. But voices are being raised from grassroots Asian America. One of them comes from the labor activist Mai Ngai, who argues passionately in her provocatively titled article "Who Is an American Worker? Asian Immigrants, Race, and the National Boundaries of Class" that Asian Americans can build another kind of "bridge" around the Pacific Rim, one that extends labor solidarity to beleaguered workers organizing to improve their lot in the Philippines, in Los Angeles, in Chinatowns, and wherever they may be (Ngai 1997). Or as Lucie Cheng asks at the end of her essay in this volume, "What is the role of Chinese Americans in a globalized movement of resistance?"

In light of the campaign-finance scandal, which broadly and unfairly implicated Asian Americans in general, and the collapse of the Asian economies, Asian Americans also need to ask themselves whether Asian American bridge builders are "cultural brokers," as many who advocate this as their role, including Chancellor Tien and Governor Locke, persuasively argue. Or do they run the risk of being reduced to *compradores* for non-Asian American global capitalists, who merely use Asian Americans, with their cultural capital, as conduits and instruments to penetrate the Asian market or as subcontractors to manage production and labor relations at the floor level? After all, a prominent Asian American attorney who heads her New York law firm's Asia Pacific division, all but admits that Asian American professionals operating in the Pacific Rim are not primarily "door openers and financiers"—that is, people with true political and economic power and clout—but, more likely, "bridges, links, and compromisers" (Asia Society 1997: 68).

In his keynote address to the Asia Society conference in 1996, the journalist and author Sanford Unger warned his audience not to be seduced by the deceptive rhetoric of America's self-declared membership in the Pacific Rim family of nations, because, he asserted, U.S. foreign policy remains adamantly Atlantic-centered (Asia Society 1997: 36). This European orientation continues to foster notions of Asian "foreignness" while perpetuating the idea that authentic and mainstream Americans are white and of European descent. Nevertheless, Unger and others at the conference urged Asian Americans to become more involved in U.S. foreign- and domestic-policy discussions across the broad spectrum of mainstream issues, not only as they concern Asian or Asian American affairs. Only when seen as actively involved in a broad range of issues can Asian Americans gain access to the mainstream and avert interethnic conflicts that have marked past episodes of American nativism, Unger argued (Asia Society 1997: 37).

In U.S. foreign affairs, Asian Americans have virtually no visibility. Where is the Asian American Kissinger? Brzezinski? Albright? one might ask. All three secretaries of state were themselves immigrants from Europe, yet not only did they rise to the highest and most sensitive unelected position in the executive branch of the federal government, but their loyalties to the United States were never questioned, even when they negotiated with their former homelands. Julia Chang Bloch and William Itoh have been the only two Asian American U.S. ambassadors, and both were assigned to Asian countries (Nepal and Thailand). No Asian American has served at the level of assistant secretary or above, and as of 1996, only five of the 671 highest-level career foreign-service officers have been Asian American (Marshall 1997). Only one Asian American has reached the level of deputy director in the State Department, and this was none other than the intriguing Francis Fukuyama, who became a luminary in elite foreign-affairs circles (Alterman 1997) and was particularly celebrated in the neoconservative circles associated with the magazines *National Interest* and *Commentary* when his widely discussed essay "The End of History" was published in 1989. In the essay, he argued that the passing of the Soviet Union signaled not only the end of the Cold War but the end of history itself, by which he meant the end of the need for further class struggle, leading inevitably to the permanent triumph of liberal democracy and capitalism around the world (Fukuyama 1989). With this thesis, Fukuyama, an Asian American foreign-policy expert, certainly transcended parochial issues of his own community and engaged in "mainstream" discussions.

Yet Fukuyama's intensely debated essay did not seem even to graze the surface of Asian American interest. He is hardly known and rarely mentioned among Asian Americans of any kind, at any forum and in any format, and his neoconservative thesis is rarely if ever discussed or, more important, critiqued. It is as if the idea of class conflict carries no relevance to the Asian

American condition, or to Asia itself. Even Fukuyama's fame in foreign-policy circles is left mostly unacknowledged by Asian American publications, which are usually eager to chronicle and document any kind of Asian American success or notoriety.

On the more practical foreign-policy level, organized Asian American groups—with the exception of the freelancing Harry Wu—have been curiously missing in action. The minute that fingers began pointing at China during the campaign-finance scandal, renewing a new round of vicious China-bashing (*Boston Globe* 1997; *Economist* 1997; Safire 1997; Sanger 1997), the Committee of 100, which was organized to monitor and protest just such developments, became thunderously silent, gun-shy all of a sudden. By contrast, former President Jimmy Carter and former Secretary of State Henry Kissinger both spoke out vociferously against China-bashing (Carter 1997; Kissinger 1997).

In domestic affairs, Asian Americans are definitely more engaged and faring better, although not without some usual bumps and potholes in the road. Just as we began this introduction with an emblematic Asian American for the twenty-first century, Governor Gary Locke of Washington State, so we offer another emblematic Asian American to close it: Bill Lann Lee, a career civil-rights lawyer and director of the Western regional office of the NAACP Legal Defense and Education Fund in Los Angeles. Nominated in mid-1997 by President Clinton to fill the vacant position of chief of the Civil Rights division of the U.S. Department of Justice, Lee waited patiently for six months for Senate confirmation, which never came. Republican senators led by Judiciary Committee Chair Orrin Hatch blocked Lee's nomination because of his vigorous defense of affirmative action, the law of the land, while at the NAACP Legal Defense and Education Fund.

The political right crafted a crude caricature of Lee's distinguished civil-rights career by labeling him the "quota king" (Clegg 1997), paraphrasing the same line that had derailed Lani Guinier, a previous nominee for the same position. The *Wall Street Journal* went so far as to call Lee's defense of affirmative action for African Americans and other minorities "the most anti-Asian law operating in America" because "California's racial preferences in education" unfairly denied better qualified Asian Americans slots given to less qualified "blacks and Hispanics" (*Wall Street Journal* 1997). After these brutal attacks, however, Hatch readily admitted that he could find no fault with Lee's qualifications.

Bill Lann Lee's family and educational background is uncannily similar to Governor Locke's. Lee, too, had an immigrant father from China who, like Jimmy Locke, raised his family on the income from a small business, in his case a hand-laundry shop in Harlem. With discipline and hard work,

Lee graduated from the highly selective, public Bronx High School of Science, attended Yale University on a scholarship, then went to Columbia Law School (Chan 1997). In Lee's own words: "My parents came to this country in search of the American Dream. They became citizens by dint of hard work, respect for the law, and an unshakeable belief in our country's most cherished ideals" (Wu 1997a).

Asian American advocacy groups, still smarting from their inability to gain an Asian American appointment to the cabinet, vowed not to let this fight go down in defeat. They galvanized to pressure President Clinton to support the nomination and not to cave in, as he had with other nominations that ran into political trouble, including Guinier's. The entire civil-rights establishment, led by prominent African American leaders such as Jesse Jackson, gave Lee its strongest endorsement, thereby reinforcing Asian American lobbying efforts on his behalf. Asian American Republicans also rallied to Lee's side (Mok 1997). Finally, in the waning days of 1997, President Clinton appointed Lee "acting" assistant attorney general, by-passing the Senate confirmation process, which refused to budge under Senator Hatch's control (Wu 1997a).

Assistant Attorney General Bill Lann Lee has his work cut out for him. He is likely to supervise the dismantling of certain civil-rights laws and practices, such as affirmative action, if the Republican majority in Congress has its way in the next year or two. But Lee is committed to civil rights because his own personal experience, growing up in New York City during the 1950s where landlords turned his family away and his father suffered ugly taunts and ethnic slurs (Chan 1997), taught him firsthand about racial discrimination. His work as a civil-rights lawyer further honed his sensitivity to institutionalized racism. "America has traveled and is still traveling this long, hard road to redeem this commitment to equal justice. It is a path haunted by the ghosts of slavery, Civil War, Jim Crow, and internment. A path littered with desecrated churches and synagogues, persistent intolerance, and bigotry" (Wu 1997a).

As the nation's highest civil-rights officer, Lee will be aggressively pursuing the work of the Civil Rights division—voting rights; housing, employment, education, and gender discrimination; and hate crimes, to name some major agenda items that should be relevant to the well-being of many Asian Americans. As the first Asian American in this post, he will also automatically assume a highly visible leadership role in race relations. In this respect, he will confront what he probably already knows: that unlike his generation of 1960s Asian Americans, the new Asian Americans, with their immigrant backgrounds, have very shallow knowledge and low appreciation of the Civil Rights movement. When surveyed, the vast majority do not think that race is a problem. Despite a holiday named in honor of Dr. King, many new immigrants do not readily connect with him and his legacy (*AsianWeek* 1998; Guillermo 1998). African American–Asian and Latino–Asian conflicts will probably continue to flare before they subside, as competition for jobs, immigration issues, and the end of affirmative action divide and conquer.

So if Gary Locke can be presented as the outward-oriented Asian American role model, casting his own political fortunes and that of his Pacific Northwest state with the future of the Pacific Rim, Bill Lann Lee is Asian America's inward-directed role model, gathering strength from the roots of the original Asian American movement as he tackles America's unfinished business with race and civil rights.

■ NOTE

Acknowledgment: I wish to thank Professor Ling-chi Wang for sharing over the Internet many of the sources on Asian Americans and the campaign-finance scandal and investigation cited in this essay. I am also grateful to my colleague at Boulder, Professor Lane Hirabayashi, for his careful reading of this essay.

■ REFERENCES

Adams, James Ring
  1995 "What's Up in Jakarta?" *American Spectator* (September), 28–32.
  1996 "John Huang's Bamboo Network." *American Spectator* (December), 24–27, 87–88.
Alterman, Eric
  1997 "Reading Foreign Policy." *The Nation* (October 27), 11–16.
Alvarez, Lizette
  1998 "Congressional Fact Finding in Saipan." *New York Times,* January 20, A14.
Asia Society
  1997 "Bridges with Asia: Asian Americans in the United States. A National Conference, May 2–4, 1996, New York. Summary Report."
AsianWeek
  1997a "John Huang Says Cultural Differences Behind Charges." December 11, 8.
  1997b "Asian Americans Younger, Better Educated than Most Americans." December 18, 8.
  1998 "Perceptions of Race." Editorial, January 22, 4.
Basch, Linda, Nina Glick Schiller, and Cristina Szanton Blanc
  1994 *Nations Unbound. Transnational Projects, Postcolonial Predicaments, and Deterritorialized Nation-States.* Langhorne, Pa.: Gordon & Breach.

Batsell, Jake
  1997 "Locke Returns Home, Calls Trip to Asia 'Very Successful.'" *Seattle Times*, October 13.
Bello, Walden
  1998 "The End of the Asian Miracle." *The Nation*, January 12/19, 16–21.
Bonacich, Edna
  1994 "Asians in the Los Angeles Garment Industry." In *The New Asian Immigration in Los Angeles and Global Restructuring*, ed. Paul Ong, Edna Bonacich, and Lucie Cheng. Philadelphia: Temple University Press.
Borosage, Robert
  1997 "Fast Track to Nowhere." *The Nation*, September 29, 20–22.
Boston Globe
  1997 "Chinese Designs." Editorial, March 2.
Carter, Jimmy
  1997 "It's Wrong to Demonize China." *New York Times*, August 10.
Chan, Ying
  1997 "First Asian for Civil Rights Post; Clinton Taps Son of Bronx." *New York Daily News*, June 12.
Chirot, Daniel, and Anthony Reid, ed.
  1997 *Essential Outsiders. Chinese and Jews in the Modern Transformation of Southeast Asia and Central Europe*. Seattle: University of Washington Press.
Clegg, Roger
  1997 "The Quota King." *Weekly Standard*, November 3, 15–16.
Cohen, Robin
  1997 *Global Diasporas: An Introduction*. Seattle: University of Washington Press.
Cooper, Richard
  1996 "How DNC Got Caught in a Donor Dilemma." *Los Angeles Times*, December 23.
Cumings, Bruce
  1993 "Rimspeak; or, The Discourse of the 'Pacific Rim.'" In *What Is in a Rim? Critical Perspectives on the Pacific Region Idea*, ed. Arif Dirlik. Boulder, Colo.: Westview Press.
Dillon, Sam
  1997 "Union Vote in Mexico Illustrates Abuses." *New York Times*, October 13, A8.
The Economist (U.S. Edition)
  1997 "America's Dose of Sinophobia." March 29, 35.
Fong, Matt
  1996 "From Gold Mountain to the Golden Door." *AsianWeek*, January 19, 7.
Friedman, Thomas
  1997 "Berlin Wall, Part 2: Asia's New Route to Democracy." *New York Times*, December 22, A21.
Fukuyama, Francis
  1989 "The End of History." *National Interest*, no. 16 (Summer), 3–18.

Gereffi, Gary
  1993   "Global Sourcing and Regional Division of Labor in the Pacific Rim." In
         What Is in a Rim?, ed. Dirlik.
Gerth, Jeff, and Stephen Labaton
  1996   "Wealthy Indonesian Businessman Has Strong Ties to Clinton." *New York
         Times*, October 11, A20.
Greenhouse, Steven
  1997   "U.S. Says Many Garment Shops Break the Law." *New York Times*, October
         17, A17.
Greider, William
  1997   "Saving the Global Economy." *The Nation*, December 15, 11–16.
Guillermo, Emil
  1998   "Having a Holiday: APAs and MLK." *AsianWeek*, January 22, 7.
Herbert, Bob
  1995   "In Deep Denial." *New York Times*, October 13, A15.
Jayasuriya, Kanishka
  1997   "Asian Values as Reactionary Modernization." *Nordic Newsletter of Asian
         Studies*, no. 4, 19–27.
Johnston, David
  1998   "Friend of Clinton Surrenders in Campaign Finance Inquiry." *New York
         Times*, February 4, A1.
Kang, K. Connie
  1997   "The Times Poll: Chinese in the Southland: A Changing Picture." *Los Angeles
         Times*, June 29.
Kissinger, Henry
  1997   "The Folly of Bullying Beijing." *Los Angeles Times*, July 6.
Koppel, Bruce
  1997   "Is Asia Emerging or Submerging? Perspectives on the Future of the Asian
         Miracle." *Nordic Newsletter of Asian Studies*, no. 4, 5–10.
Kotkin, Joel
  1992   *Tribes. How Race, Religion, and Identity Determine Success in the New Global
         Economy.* New York: Random House.
Kranish, Michael
  1997   "Clinton Policy Shift Followed Asian-American Fund-Raiser." *Boston Globe*,
         January 16.
Kwong, Peter
  1997   *Forbidden Workers: Illegal Chinese Immigrants and American Labor.* New York:
         New Press.
LEAP Asian Pacific American Public Policy Institute and UCLA Asian American
Studies Center
  1993   "The State of Asia Pacific America: A Public Policy Report. Policy Issues to
         the Year 2020."

Liu, John, and Lucie Cheng
   1994   "Pacific Rim Development and the Duality of Post-1965 Asian Immigration to the United States." *The New Asian Immigration,* ed. Ong, Bonacich, and Cheng.
Lowry, Rich
   1997   "Selling Out? China Syndrome." *National Review,* March 10.
Marshall, Tyler
   1997   "Asian Americans Scarce in the U.S. Corridors of Power." *Los Angeles Times,* October 21, A16.
Mok, Samuel
   1997   "Letter to Editor." *AsianWeek,* December 18.
Mydans, Seth
   1997   "Thailand Economic Crash Crushes the Working Poor." *New York Times,* December 15, A9.
New York Times
   1997   Editorial, December 6.
Ngai, Mae M.
   1997   "Who Is An American Worker? Asian Immigrants, Race, and the National Boundaries of Class." In *Audacious Democracy. Labor, Intellectuals, and the Social Reconstruction of America,* ed. Steven Fraser and Joshua B. Freeman. Boston: Houghton Mifflin.
Norlund, Irene
   1997   "Nike and Labour in Vietnam." *Nordic Newsletter of Asian Studies,* no. 3, 15–18.
Ong, Aihwa
   1993   "On the Edge of Empires: Flexible Citizenship Among Chinese in Diaspora." *Positions* 1, no. 3 (winter): 745–78.
Ong, Aihwa, and Donald Nonini, ed.
   1997   *Ungrounded Empires. The Cultural Politics of Modern Chinese Transnationalism.* New York: Routledge.
Palumbo-Liu, David
   1999   *Asian/American: Historical Crossings of a Racial Frontier.* Stanford: Stanford University Press.
Pan, Lynn
   1990   *Sons of the Yellow Emperor. A History of the Chinese Diaspora.* Boston: Little, Brown.
Polsby, Nelson W.
   1997   "Money Gains Access. So What?" *New York Times,* August 13.
Postman, David
   1997a   "Locke's Asian Trip Is Both Personal and Symbolic." *Seattle Times,* September 28.
   1997b   "Connections Are Critical in China." *Seattle Times,* October 8.
   1997c   "Village Goes All Out for Locke's Entourage." *Seattle Times,* October 10.

1997d "Thousands Fill Town to Greet Locke." *Seattle Times,* October 11.

1997e "Locke's Reunion: Standing Room Only." *Seattle Times,* October 12.

Rempel, William C.

1998 "Buddhist Temple May Be Indicted in Donor Probe." *Los Angeles Times,* January 30.

Richburg, Keith B., and Steven Mufson

1998 "Ignored Warnings. Long Before the Deluge, Storm Clouds Were Gathering over Asia's Economy." *Washington Post National Weekly Edition,* January 12, 6–8.

Risen, James

1997 "FBI Said to Suspect Donor as Agent for China." *Los Angeles Times,* May 12.

Rogers, David

1997 "Battle over Immigration Bill Taught Washington's Ropes to Huang and Hsia." *Wall Street Journal,* May 15, A24.

Rosenbaum, David E.

1997 "Wealthy Oilman Explains Why He Donated $300,000 to Democrats." *New York Times,* September 19.

Rosenfeld, Seth

1996 "Tien Ties to Asia Money May Have Cost Him Job." *San Francisco Chronicle,* December 22, C6.

Safire, William

1997 "Listening to Hearings." Essay, *New York Times,* July 13.

San Juan, E. Jr.

1998 *Beyond Postcolonial Theory.* New York: St. Martin's Press.

Sanders, Bernie, and Marcy Raptur

1997 *The Nation,* Editorial, December 8.

Sanger, David

1997 "The 'Asian Money' Machine Stirs Old Fears in America." *New York Times,* January 4.

Seagrave, Sterling

1995 *Lords of the Rim. The Invisible Empire of the Overseas Chinese.* New York: G.P. Putnam's Sons.

Sharpe, Rochelle

1997 "SBA Program Benefits Asian-Americans." *Wall Street Journal,* September 10.

Silverstein, Ken

1998 "Congress's Beach Boys." *The Nation,* January 12/19, 21–23.

Smith, David A.

1996 "Going South: Global Restructuring and Garment Production in Three East Asian Cases." *Asian Perspective* 20, no. 2 (fall–winter): 211–41.

Squitieri, Tom

1997 "Democrats Knew Huang Might Be in Trouble." *USA Today,* February 18.

Sterngold, James

1997 "Political Tangle of Taiwan Immigrant." *New York Times,* June 9, A13.

Sun, Lena, and John Pomfret
    1997   "Some Sought Access to Clinton, Others' Motives Remain Murky." *Washington Post,* January 27, A1.
Van Natta, Don, Jr., and Jane Fritsch
    1997   "$250,000 Buys Donors Best Access to Congress." *New York Times,* January 27, A1.
Wall Street Journal
    1997   "Bill Lee, Anti-Asian: An Editorial." December 17.
Wang, Ling-chi
    1996   "Foreign Money Is No Friend of Ours." *AsianWeek,* November 8, 7.
Weidenbaum, Murray, and Samuel Hughes
    1996   *The Bamboo Network: How Expatriate Chinese Entrepreneurs Are Creating a New Economic Superpower.* New York: Free Press.
Weiner, Tim, and David E. Sanger
    1996   "Democrats Hoped to Raise $7 Million from Asians in U.S." *New York Times,* December 28, A1.
Wong, Bill
    1994   *AsianWeek,* Commentary, July 1, 9.
    1997   "An American Tiger: Winning Attention, Respect, and Something More." *AsianWeek,* April 18, 6.
Wong, Sau-Ling C.
    1995   "Denationalization Reconsidered: Asian American Cultural Criticism at a Theoretical Crossroads." *Amerasia Journal* 21, no. 1 and 2: 1–27.
Woo-Cumings, Meredith
    1993   "Market Dependency in U.S.–East Asian Relations." In *What Is in a Rim?,* ed. Dirlik.
Wu, Frank
    1996   "The Best and the Brightest: APAs Strategize Their Ascent to the Capitol." *AsianWeek,* November 22, 11.
    1997a   "Clinton's 'Honorable Decision.'" *AsianWeek,* December 18, 11–12.
    1997b   "The Cusp of a New Era." *AsianWeek,* December 25, 19.

2

ASIANS
ON
THE RIM

Transnational Capital and Local Community

in the Making of

Contemporary Asian America

ARIF DIRLIK

An issue of *AsianWeek* in January 1996 contained two items that cogently illustrate the problem I would like to discuss below. One was an invited editorial by Matt Fong (1996), California's state treasurer and "one of the nation's highest elected Asian American officials." Entitled "From Gold Mountain to the Golden Door," Fong's editorial outlined his vision of making California into "the capital of the Pacific Rim." He wrote:

> California's strategic location, coupled with its huge and diverse economic base and available capital, make it an ideal gateway to the Pacific Rim to facilitate trade and capital flows between the Pacific and the rest of the world. California has the opportunity to lead the charge toward dramatically ex-

This chapter is a revised version of an essay published in 1996 in *Amerasia* 22 (3): 1–24.

panded global trade by developing its role as a financial services center to increase the sophistication, speed, volume, reliability, and cost-effectiveness of international commerce. Business, labor, government, and the academic community must aggressively work together to seize this opportunity and chart a new course for California.... As the global economy changes, we must provide a vision and take advantage of opportunities that will make California a better, more prosperous place in which to work, live and do business. California's Golden Door to the Future is the Gateway to the Pacific Rim.

The other was a news item about the appointment to a post with the California Department of Education of Henry Der, who had served as the executive director of Chinese for Affirmative Action in San Francisco since 1974. Superintendent of Education Delaine Eastin, who was able to appoint Der in spite of opposition from the office of Governor Pete Wilson, described Der as a "progressive ... dedicated to the community and to minorities ... who's not afraid to speak for the community." Der himself stated that while his new job made it inappropriate for him to serve as a spokesperson for the Asian American community, "I'm so much rooted in this community that I'm not going to that new job to forget that I am an Asian American." His concerns, however, transcended his Asian Americanness: "I firmly believe we must do everything possible to close the gap between the haves and the have-nots in American society.... I feel very, very strongly that education is one strategy"[1] (Yip 1996).

For *AsianWeek*, Fong and Der are equally illustrations of Asian American success, two of "50 Asian Americans who'll make a difference in the new year" (*AsianWeek* 1996: 13–18). But the success story also conceals deep contradictions that bear directly on our understanding of Asian America and its meaning in the contemporary world. I am not concerned about the political affiliations of Fong and Der, or their trajectories as individuals.[2] My concern, rather, is with their contrasting orientations, which are informed by quite different self-images as Asian Americans: the one looking out to the Pacific, and the future, through the "Golden Door" of California; the other looking to communities rooted in California and their historical legacies, centered on but not restricted to Asian Americans. The difference is spatial, but not in an inert geographical (east–west) sense or even in the sense of spaces as defined by national boundaries. The spaces in this case derive their meaning from associations that are quite contemporary in their implications and from the contradictions that they present: the global, and globalizing, spaces of transnational capital versus the local spaces of communities. Given the significant part that the ideal of community has played in the formation of an

Asian American consciousness, the spatial contradiction appears also as a temporal contradiction between a contemporary Asian American consciousness and the originary assumptions of Asian America.

The contrast between the two orientations, I suggest, is paradigmatic of fundamental contradictions that are essential to grasping contemporary Asian America as a social and ideological formation. The contradiction between the global and the local as structuring moments in contemporary society is not exclusive to Asian America, which is also a reminder that the Asian American experience is but one instance of what is increasingly a common phenomenon not just in the United States but worldwide. The problem of Asian America as I conceptualize it is not a cultural or regional problem; rather, it is a problem in global postmodernity.[3] What is specific to Asian America is its relationship to new centers of global economic power in the Pacific and, to a lesser extent, South Asia that have been responsible for bringing the Pacific to the forefront of global consciousness, in the process challenging Eurocentric conceptions of modernity that were themselves empowered by the apparently unchallengeable supremacy of Euro-American capitalism. What this challenge implies remains to be seen, but in an immediate sense, the emergence of Pacific Asian economies as key players in the global economy has had a transformative effect on the Asian American self-image, as well as on the perceptions of Asian Americans in the society at large. While the most visible effect may be an elevation in the status of Asian Americans vis-à-vis other minority groups, the transformation has not put an end to earlier problems in the conceptualization of Asian America, which persist in reconfigured forms. This has introduced new burdens on being Asian American and has complicated the very notion of Asian America to a point at which it may break apart under the force of its contradictions. Especially important, I suggest, is the increasing ambiguity in the conceptualization of Asian America of Asian populations as members of grounded communities versus as diasporic "Rimpeople."

Although earlier conceptualizations of Asian America seem irrelevant under current circumstances and have come under criticism for being outdated, those conceptualizations may be more relevant than ever, if for reasons different from the ones that inspired them in the first place. We need to rethink earlier conceptualizations because they no longer seem capable of containing the changes within Asian America and in Asian America's relationship to its local and global environments. On the other hand, "forgetting" the past is hardly a way to rethink it, because rethinking requires that we remember differently. Especially important in my view is the community ideal in Asian American consciousness, which has been all but swept away by the enthusiasm over Asian Americans as Rimpeople.

THE PACIFIC AND ASIAN AMERICAN ETHNICITY IN HISTORICAL PERSPECTIVE

A spatial contradiction has shaped the history of Asian America from the arrival of significant numbers of Asians on Pacific shores in the mid-nineteenth century. For the larger part of this history, this contradiction was expressed in the language of a racist Orientalism. I have argued elsewhere that immigration from Asia from the beginning represented a Pacific component in U.S. national history that was suppressed literally by repression and eventual exclusion, and ideologically by the ideology of a Western-moving frontier (Dirlik 1993). By the mid-nineteenth century, the Pacific had already appeared as an extension of an expanding Western frontier, which would not allow for any alternatives to the idea of "civilization" that propelled it, let alone a counter-frontier emanating from across the Pacific. It was across the Pacific that a "Western civilization" destined to rule the world met once again its ancient nemesis, the "Orient" (Gibson 1993).[4]

Gary Okihiro has argued at length the ways in which the Orientalist legacy shaped American views of those who obstructed this frontier, including views of Amerindians but especially of the immigrants from Asia (Okihiro 1994). The very term "Asian" was an invention of this Orientalism. The people who immigrated from across the Pacific did not think of themselves in continental or, until the late nineteenth century, even in national terms. Their primary identifications were with their origins in local societies. Asians were rendered into a racial and cultural formation in their construal as "Asians," "Orientals," or "mongolians" by the hegemonic discourse.[5] This discourse also rendered Asians into permanent foreigners, culturally and even genetically incapable of becoming "real" Americans, an attitude that would serve as a justification for their exclusion from 1882 through World War II. This exclusion did not extinguish memories of ties to their native origins, or even their involvement in politics in their nations of origin, but it did turn affirmation of such ties into a further liability. Even where consciousness of origins was weak, as with generations born in the United States, the very "Asianness" of Americans of Asian descent was deemed to preclude their becoming "real" Americans—as in the social-scientific "dual-personality" thesis, which assumed an Asian coding in the personalities of this group of Americans, regardless of their cultural orientations. The most tragic manifestation of this racist Orientalism was the incarceration in concentration camps of Americans of Japanese descent.

These Orientalist assumptions were to prevail against overwhelming evidence that Asians themselves did not have a sense of unity as Asians, and even against the explicit recognition that different groups of Asians could be used against one another in order to perpetuate their exploitation and oppression, a tactic employed by white capital against Asian laborers. Although groups were able occasionally to unify in struggles against their oppression, there is little evidence that Asians of different nationalities had a sense of kinship for one another on account of being "Asian." On the contrary, to the extent that they identified with their national origins in Asia, conflicts within Asia pitted different groups of Asians against one another, resulting in "disidentification," whereby members of one group distanced themselves "from another group so as not to be mistaken and suffer the blame for the presumed misdeeds of that group" (Espiritu 1992: 20).[6]

Grounded very much on U.S. soil, Americans of Asian descent were excluded from a U.S. national history for more than a century. It was the radical struggles of the 1960s that eventually rephrased the terms of the discourse on Asian America and that produced "Asian Americanness" as a concept and vision. Once it had been coined, the term "Asian American" would acquire enormous power in shaping the discourse on the past, present, and future of Asian America. Yet the term's origins seem to have been fortuitous. According to the distinguished Japanese American historian Yuji Ichioka, who was to become one of the pioneers in Asian American studies, he coined the term in a meeting in Berkeley in 1968 out of analogy with other terms of ethnic identification, especially "African American," which was at the source of much of the ethnic vocabulary of the time.[7] The term would be crucial in uncovering and reconstructing the "buried past"—to borrow the title of one of Ichioka's works—of Asian America. It would also have far-reaching political and intellectual consequences in mobilizing an "Asian American movement," as well as serious institutional consequences in creating official definitions of Asian America.

The term "Asian American" nevertheless bore the imprint of its historical legacy. The "Asian" component was derivative of the hegemonic discourse on Asians rather than the actual experiences and self-images of the Asian peoples that it covered, and by implication it at least shared a commonality with the Orientalist reification of Asia in erasing the significant differences among these peoples. But this is where the similarity ended. Where the Orientalism of the hegemonic discourse had drawn nourishment from a culturalist denial of history to Asia and, by extension, to Asians in the United States, the discourse spawned by the reconceptualization of "Asian" as "Asian American" was informed by a radical historicism that repudiated the fundamental assumptions of the hegemonic discourse. If it bore traces of an earlier hegemonic discourse, the new discourse was informed in its "rearticulation" of the problems of Asian America by the radical challenge to existing social relations of the radical thinking of the 1960s (Omi and Winant 1986).[8]

The historicism of the new discourse was expressed at its most fundamental level in "claiming America" (in Maxine Hong Kingston's words) by rooting Asian Americanness in the ground of U.S. history. In his preface to *Roots: An Asian American Reader*, which was the first collection of its kind, Franklin Odo wrote that "this volume was written and edited with the intent of going to the 'roots' of the issues facing Asians in America. It may, therefore, strike the reader as 'radical'—a term which derives from the Latin *radix*, meaning, appropriately enough, roots." Tortured by questions of identity, he continued, "increasing numbers [of Asian Americans] . . . look to their 'roots.' The central section of this volume deals with the history of Asian Americans, from the emigration period to the present. This was another facet of the title's significance—our 'roots' go deep into the history of the United States and they can do much to explain who we are and how we became this way" (Tachiki, Wong, Odo, and Wong 1971: vii–viii).

Asian Americans, in other words, were not transplantations in the United States of racially and culturally marked Asian peoples without history; they were the very products of the history of the United States in the making, a process in which they had been participants from the beginning. What justified the inclusion of these different peoples in one category was also historical experience: "All Asians have much in common: the history of their exploitation. . . . But there are unique qualities to each of the ethnic groups which make united struggles difficult" (Tachiki, Wong, Odo, and Wong 1971: ix).

If a common historical experience of oppression and exploitation justified speaking of an Asian America, this discourse also presupposed that Asian America was not to be taken for granted, as Odo's statement suggests, but that it was something that was to be created in the course of struggles against oppression and exploitation. Asian America, in other words, was not simply a product of legacy; it was a vision of the future. As John Liu would write nearly two decades later in connection with the problems of Asian American studies: "These attempts at delineating a common culture should admonish Asian American studies instructors to focus on what Asian American meant at its inception: *a political choice*. Asian American studies arose from a *commitment* to build a common identity and a common culture. Most of the people who first worked toward building Asian American studies consciously tried to create a culture that challenged the cultural hegemony of the dominant society. Because many of the early people were political activists, they knew Asian Americans could only be successful in their struggles if they developed an alternative way of seeing and living along with their political demands. It was no accident that the counter culture movement developed during the student, civil rights, women's and ethnic movements. The demand for political change was simultaneously a call to transform the ways in which people did and saw things—that is, a call for a different cultural nexus" (Liu 1988: 123–24).

The grounding of Asian America in U.S. history underlined the commonality of the Asian American experience with the experiences of other oppressed groups in American society while it problematized the relationship of Asian Americans to their distant origins in Asia. In the same preface cited earlier, which affirmed the Americanness of Asians, Odo phrased the problem in the form of questions: "What should be a 'proper' stance toward the inculcation or maintenance of a cultural heritage? How closely, if at all, and in what ways should Asian Americans relate to Asia? Responses vary from 'back to Asia' types to a strictly Americanist, localized point of view" (Tachiki, Wong, Odo, and Wong 1971: x–xi).

The "localized point of view" had the greater weight by far in the originary conceptualization of Asian America. Paraphrasing a statement by Eugene Genovese that "all good Marxist writing leads to an explication of class," Okihiro (1988: 175–83) wrote that "all ethnic studies history may, from one point of view, be judged good or poor by the extent to which it contributes to our understanding of community." What was at issue, however, was much more than an "understanding" of community in the usual academic sense; the fundamental issue was the political one of strengthening communities. Works such as Yuji Ichioka's *Issei: The World of the First Generation Japanese Immigrants, 1885–1924* (1988) carefully delineate in great detail the history of Japanese Americans of the first generation so as to preserve and promote memories of community. The community concerns of the generation of scholars informed by the idea of Asian America, it needs to be emphasized, were not parochial concerns. They saw in the community ideal a concern that was common to all ethnic groups. Community represented for all such groups a basis for resistance to racial and cultural oppression, as well as the source of alternative visions of social organization for the future.

Finally, the idea of community was very much tied in with the perception of ethnic communities as objects of an "internal colonialism," which gave Asian Americans a commonality with colonialized societies worldwide. The Asian American movement, like other ethnic movements of the 1960s, identified externally not with Asia per se, but with other Third World societies that were the objects of colonial oppression. Within the context of the U.S. war on Vietnam, Asian Americans felt a special sense of kinship with the Vietnamese, which distinguished their responses to the war from the responses of others who protested against it. But their responses were couched in terms of Third World solidarity in general, as evidenced in the vocabulary of the Third World employed by political protesters at San Francisco State

University and the University of California, Berkeley, in 1968, which also produced the idea of Asian America[9] (Tachiki, Wong, Odo, and Wong 1971: x).

In her *Asian American Panethnicity*, Yen Le Espiritu (1992: 162) offers a thoughtful account of the successes and limitations of the Asian American movement. Rearticulating the dominant society's exclusionary idea of "Asian," the movement created a new ideological and institutional context for Asian America: "Although the pan-Asian concept may have originated in the minds of non-Asians, it is today more than a reflection of this misperception. Asian Americans did not just adopt the concept but also transformed it to conform to their ideological and political needs. . . . [Y]oung Asian American activists rejected the stereotyped term 'Oriental' and coined their own term, 'Asian American.' Although both terms denote the consolidation of group boundaries, Asian American activists insisted on their term because they wanted to define their own image—one that would connote political activism rather than passivity. . . . Not only did Asian Americans consolidate, but they also politicized, using the very pan-Asian concept imposed from the outside as their political instrument."

Initially consisting mostly of Chinese, Japanese, and (to a lesser extent) Filipino Americans, the movement was making efforts by the mid-1970s to include other groups, such as Koreans, South Asians, and even Pacific Islanders. This spawned another term, "Asian Pacific Americans"[10] (Gee 1976). Movement activity and publications gave Asian Americans visibility on the political scene and spawned institutions that gave its achievements permanence: Asian American studies programs on university campuses, and social and political organizations of various kinds around which to unite Asian Americans and ensure their representation in government programs. Asian American scholarship was to reconstruct the history of Asians in the United States, putting an end to long-standing notions of Asians as temporary residents of the United States and demonstrating Asians' participation in, and contributions to, U.S. history. Asian American literature did much to reveal the complexities of the inner lives of Asians in their efforts to make homes for themselves despite oppression and discrimination. And "Asian American" was quickly assimilated into official language in government programs and censuses.

The movement also faced critical problems almost immediately. In spite of conscious efforts to respect diversity, the rearticulation of Asianness in the language of radicalism did not eliminate the contradiction between the homogenizing implications of an Asian American pan-ethnicity and nationally defined ethnic self-perceptions. Filipino Americans were uncomfortable from the beginning with their inclusion under categories of "yellow" or "Asian," and their discomfort was exacerbated by Japanese American and Chinese American domination of the movement[11] (Espiritu 1992: 104). Within the

Chinese American and Japanese American groups themselves, there was a disjuncture between the perceptions and aspirations of the young radical intellectuals who defined the movement and the ethnic and political identifications of the peoples for whom they spoke. The disjuncture implicit in the term "Asian American" also brought forward generational and class differences.

Other problems were products of the success of the movement. As with other radical movements at the time, the movement in its unfolding brought out significant gender differences, with women demanding that their multiple-layered oppression not be dissolved into categories of ethnic, racial, and class oppression. The institutionalization of the movement, which also required some assimilation to existing structures of power, quickly distanced activists further from the communities for which they spoke. By the early 1980s, Asian American scholars had become acutely aware of the ways in which academic demands distanced them from the radical, community-oriented scholarship that had given rise to Asian American studies programs in the first place. Espiritu has argued cogently that those involved in community programs faced this problem in even more critical ways: success in dealing with government programs required professionalization, which not only distanced community activists from the communities for which they worked, but also exacerbated class divisions between an emergent professional–managerial group and the communities at large (Espiritu 1992: chap. 4). Rather than being defined by the originary radical vision of the movement, the discourse on Asian America was shaped increasingly by the dialectics of state policy and the professional–managerial commitments of an Asian American elite, which, incidentally, further undermined pan-ethnic unity, as the more established groups of Chinese Americans and Japanese Americans continued to dominate this new elite.

Still, it is important to underline that these contradictions were informed by the new ideological and structural context that had been established by the Asian American movement, which continues to this day to serve as a frame of reference for understanding Asian America. The movement embedded the problems of Asian America in U.S. soil. In doing so, it also endowed pan-ethnic identification with normative status, so that although ethnic "disidentification" is ever present as an option (and is perhaps also found in everyday practice), it no longer seems "natural." Instead, it calls for explanation and justification against this new frame of reference. The new ideological and institutional framework, of course, also facilitates pan-ethnic unity when needs and interests require it. Having started as political fiction, in other words, pan-ethnicity has come to be a source of political legitimacy.

These contradictions may not be significantly different from those of other minority groups in the United States whose struggles likewise led to new unities but also to new divisions and conflicts. Asian America, however, was to experience another radical transformation that would lead to a break with the situation created by the struggles of the 1960s and that called into question the possibility of thinking of the problems of Asian America in the language of those struggles. I am referring to the already widely recognized demographic transformation of Asian America, itself bound up with radical changes in the United States' relationship to Asia, as expressed in the new language of the Pacific. What may be less widely recognized is that this new transformation, the future of which is highly unpredictable, may be in the process of constructing new ethnicities that are no longer containable within the national framework that earlier bounded thinking about ethnicity. It may give new meaning to older divisions as well.

The idea of Asian America faced a critical challenge from the outside almost as soon as it came into existence: the challenge of the new immigration from Asia, made possible by the immigration law of 1965, which was to result in a dramatic increase in the number of Asian immigrants. On the surface, the new immigration boosted the power of Asian America by rapidly inflating the numbers of Asians in the United States: from a total of around 1,357,000 in 1970, the number of Asian American Pacific Islanders in the United States would increase to around 3,700,000 in 1980 and to approximately 7,274,000 in 1990. Because of certain preferences in the immigration law, the new immigrants also included a high percentage of educated professionals, who were less likely than their predecessors to keep silent in the face of discrimination and more likely to add their voices to calls for Asian American empowerment.[12]

Equally important, however, was the fact that the new immigration almost immediately made irrelevant the fundamental assumption that had guided the struggle for Asian America: the rootedness of Asian Americans in U.S. history. In 1970, Asians born and educated in the United States made up about two-thirds of the population of Asian America. By 1980, the percentage had been reversed, with the foreign-born constituting 73 percent of the population, up dramatically for all groups except Japanese Americans. The immigration also transformed the relative numerical strength of the various national ethnic groups, moving Chinese and Filipinos way ahead of Japanese Americans, as well as adding immense numbers to groups that were formerly numerically marginal, such as Koreans, South and Southeast Asians, and Pacific Islanders. For this new population, "roots" was more likely to mean roots somewhere in Asia or the Pacific than in the United States or in U.S. history.

The new immigration to the United States coincided with crucial transformations within the Pacific. The United States was to play a crucial part in the new Pacific formation, and, from a U.S.-based perspective, what has been most striking is the flow across the Pacific of Asian peoples. Indeed, with its economic and cultural implications, the new immigration appears to be if not a reversal of the nineteenth-century frontier, then at least a revival of the eastern flow of Asian peoples that was aborted by the ideology of a Western-moving frontier. Nevertheless, it is important to remember that now, as then, the flow of Asian peoples to the United States is part of a larger process of movement of peoples that is both a product and a constituent of a Pacific formation. The major difference between the present and the past is the economic and political emergence of Pacific Asian societies, which has resulted in a restructuring not only of the Pacific but also of global economic, political, social, and cultural relations in general. This has endowed these movements of Asian peoples with a new meaning. The new Asian immigration to the United States partakes of this altered meaning and represents an unprecedented challenge to the very idea of an Asian America.

There is no space here to elaborate on the multiple dimensions of a contemporary Pacific formation, and there is little need to do so, since my concern is with the consequences of the new Pacific formation for people's movement rather than for this formation's inner workings per se. Suffice it to say that past legacy and present circumstances have interacted in complex ways to shape new patterns of immigration—and to blur the differences between the present and the past, especially in the United States. For nearly two centuries, during which a Pacific formation coincided with the U.S. national formation, a Eurocentric racism excluded Asians from the United States, which was to become untenable after World War II. By the end of the war, the United States had achieved its goal of making the Pacific (including East Asia) into an American Lake, but policy by then was dictated by considerations of containing the spread of communism in Asia, which called for a reconsideration of domestic policies that were informed by racism (in the same manner that the fight against Nazi racism had called forth a reconsideration of racism at home). Two tragic wars in Asia would help speed the process whereby those people who were already part of the American Lake could become Americans as well. The 1965 immigration law made up for past injustices by allowing foreign relatives of American citizens to become American citizens. The same law allowed the immigration of those who sought to escape under one guise or another, including under circumstances of economic deprivation and political oppression. Filipinos, colonialized by U.S. aspirations to render the Pacific into an American Lake but long denied "Americanness" nevertheless, would benefit from these provisions. So would Chinese, who were being released from controls by a communist regime that was opening up to capitalism and that did not know how to dispose of a "surplus" population. In these and other cases, immigration has followed an earlier push–pull model of movement of peoples from poor to rich countries in search of economic or political survival. The parallels with the past do not end there. The movement of peoples across the Pacific has again become an occasion for business, reviving earlier practices of indentured servitude, most notably in the case of Chinese migration to the United States, but with other groups as well[13] (Kwong 1994a).

The burden of the past may weigh heavily on the poor, but the parallels with the past must not be exaggerated, for the new migrations take place in a Pacific restructured by contemporary economic forces. U.S. domination provided the context for the new Pacific formation, but it is clear in hindsight that the United States could not dictate the outcome of its own policies. The strengthening of the Western Rim economies to contain communism was to end up creating economic powers that have come to challenge U.S. economic domination of the Pacific. The emergence of these powers has also created a Pacific formation that has brought societies of the Rim much closer economically and culturally, that has rendered their relations much more systemic, and that has introduced a multidimensionality to the flows of capital, commodities, and people. Commodity chains, capital flows, and even transfers of people under the aegis of transnational corporations have bound Pacific economies together. Pacific Asian economies are active players in this economic activity. They are no longer merely the exporters of labor; they are also exporters of capital. And they are crucial to the productive activity of U.S. corporations, which have become major exporters of jobs across the Pacific[14] (Foner and Rosenberg 1993).

Two important consequences of this systemic integration of the Pacific are relevant to this discussion. The first is the generation of diasporic populations, or, where such populations already existed, their transformation into transnational ethnicities. The term "diaspora" has become increasingly current over the past decade, in connection mainly with Chinese but also with Asian Indian and Filipino populations. In the case of the Chinese and Asian Indians in particular, migration abroad is not a new phenomenon but goes back to the nineteenth century and even earlier. But these groups have acquired a new significance in light of global economic developments, and the localized identities that they acquired in their settlements abroad have been overwhelmed in reassertions of cultural nationalism that stress their "essential" unity across global spaces.[15]

The other consequence is the emergence of a highly vocal and visible transpacific professional–managerial class that is the product of the new Pacific formation. As Paul Ong, Edna Bonacich, and Lucie Cheng put it, "as the Asian countries have emerged from their peripheral status within the world economy, their focus on scientific and technical innovation is luring back many of their professional expatriates from the United States. This phenomenon has three consequences. For the developing Asian countries, the return of highly educated and experienced people helps relieve a significant shortage of professionals in selected fields. For the United States, the departure of these highly trained professionals with experience in the most advanced areas of research presents a potential threat. Finally, for the world system as a whole, the frequent movement back and forth of professionals contributes to the internationalization of the professional–managerial stratum" (Ong, Bonacich, and Cheng 1994: 13).

We need to remember that, in addition to family members, the 1965 immigration law gave preference to the professional–managerial group, whose immigration was to make a major impact on Asian American communities, as well as on perceptions of Asian Americans. Their presence would do much to bolster the idea of Asian Americans as a "model minority." Their "movement back and forth" (which is not equally available to the poorer immigrants) has also contributed to the reshaping of Asian American ethnicity.

Because it has come to include groups that can no longer be contained within national boundaries, Asian America is no longer a location just in the United States but, at the same time, is a location on a metaphorical Rim constituted by diasporas and the movement of individuals. To understand Asian Americans, it is no longer sufficient to comprehend their roots in U.S. history or, for that matter, in their countries of origin. Instead, one must understand a multiplicity of historical trajectories that converge in the locations we call Asian America but that may diverge once again to disrupt the very idea of Asian Americanness. It is multiple location in the same physical space that has introduced a new fundamental contradiction to the idea of Asian America, overdetermining the inherited contradictions of pan-ethnicity and of nationally or more locally defined ethnicities. This multiplicity of location is evident in even a cursory examination of Asian American publications, which, unlike in an earlier day, include within their compass everything from local U.S. news and events to happenings in remote locations in Asia, and even elsewhere, as long as they involve "Asians."[16] It also finds a counterpart in discussions of Asian American identity in the new positive value assigned to the idea of hybridity, which in its "dual-personality" manifestation provided the occasion for rejecting the Americanness of Asians, and which Asians earlier struggled against in claiming their history as Americans.[17] While few would object to the openness implicit in cultural inclusiveness or to a hybridity that allows for individual or group "multiculturalism," the diffuseness of Asian American identity that they simultaneously imply may end up, against earlier efforts to construct such an identity, encouraging the ever-present possibility of ethnic insularity.

It seems clear that the idea of Asian America today requires a different mapping of the United States, Asia, the Pacific, and the world than the one that produced the idea less than three decades ago. The old political and economic units, and the spatial directionalities, that informed the older mapping are no longer sufficient to grasp the forces that are in the process of reshaping nationalities, racial affinities, and ethnicities.[18] Ironically, these same changes have revived some of the earlier problems in reconfigured forms. I have already referred to the significant class differences in the experience of the new transpacific movements. Another important problem arises out of the new immigrants' closer relationships to their societies of origin in Asia. To the extent that the contemporary Asian American populations identify with their societies of origin, they are once again vulnerable, in their relationships to one another, to replicating the divisions and conflicts that beset Asian societies. At the same time, closeness to Asia opens the possibility of distancing themselves from their immediate environments in the United States, especially in their relationships with other minority groups. Finally, a kind of Orientalism in reverse, or a self-Orientalization, has reappeared in discussions of Asian American populations. Okihiro (1994) has argued that the idea of "model minority" is a product of just such an Orientalist stereotyping of Asian Americans: "yellow peril and the model minority are not poles, denoting opposite representations along a single line, but in fact form a circular relationship that moves in either direction. . . . Moving in one direction along the circle, the model minority mitigates the alleged danger of the yellow peril, whereas reversing direction, the model minority, if taken too far, can become the yellow peril."[19] Perhaps the most blatant example of a revived Orientalism is the de-historicized culturalism that traces the economic success of Asian societies, and with them of Asian Americans, to some vaguely defined "Asian" characteristic. In the case of Pacific Asian societies, this has taken the form of erasing crucial historical and structural differences under the rubric of "Confucian" values. The same kind of culturalism is visible, as I noted earlier, in cultural nationalist homogenizations of diasporic populations.[20]

FROM JOHN HUANG TO BEIJING:
THE PITFALLS OF DIASPORA DISCOURSE

The reconceptualization of Asian Americans in terms of diaspora or transnationality responds to a real situation: the reconfiguration of migrant societies and their political and cultural orientations. But diaspora and transnationality as concepts are also discursive. Not only do they have normative implications, but they also articulate—in a very Foucauldian sense—relationships of power within populations so depicted, as well as populations' relationships to their societies of origin and arrival. Diaspora discourse has an undeniable appeal in the critical possibilities it offers against assumptions of national cultural homogeneity, which historically has resulted in the denial of full cultural (and political) citizenship to those who resisted assimilation into the dominant conceptualizations of national culture or were refused entry into it, or whose cultural complexity could not be contained easily within a single conception of national culture. This critical appeal, however, also disguises the possibility that diasporic notions of culture, if employed without due regard to the social and political complexities of so-called diasporic populations, may issue in reifications of their own, opening the way to new forms of cultural domination, manipulation, and commodification.

The problems presented by diaspora discourse can be illustrated through the recent case of John Huang, the Chinese American fund-raiser for the Democratic National Committee. When Huang was charged with corruption on the grounds that he raised funds from foreign sources, the Democratic National Committee proceeded immediately to canvass all contributors with Chinese names to ascertain whether they were foreigners, turning a run-of-the-mill case of political corruption into a racial issue. The committee's action reactivated the long-standing assumption that anyone with a Chinese name might in all probability be foreign, reaffirming implicitly that a Chinese name is a marker of racial foreignness. What followed may not have been entirely novel, but it seemed quite logical nevertheless in terms of contemporary diasporic "networks" (perhaps, more appropriately in this case, "webs"). Huang's connections to the Riady family in Indonesia, which surfaced quickly, not only underlined the probable foreignness of the Chinese contributors, but also suggested further connections between Chinese Americans and other Chinese overseas that seemed to be confirmed by revelations that several other Chinese American fund-raisers, or contributors, had ties to Chinese in South and Southeast Asia. As these overseas Chinese had business connections in the People's Republic of China, a petty corruption case quickly turned into a case of possible conspiracy that extended from Beijing, through Chinese overseas, to Chinese Americans.[21]

This linking of Chinese Americans to diasporic Chinese and the government in Beijing has provoked charges of racism among Asian Americans and their many sympathizers. Racism is there, to be sure. But is this racism simply an extension of the historical racism against Asian Americans, or does it represent something new? And if it is something new, is it possible that at least some Asian Americans have been complicit in producing a new kind of racist discourse? These question are fraught with difficulties—chief among them the issue of shifting responsibility to the victim—but they must be raised nevertheless.

The linking of Huang, Chinese overseas, and the Beijing government, I would like to suggest, has been facilitated by the new discourse on the Chinese diaspora, which, in reifying Chineseness, has created fertile ground for nourishing a new racism. The idea of diaspora is responsible in the first place for abolishing the difference between Chinese Americans and Chinese elsewhere (including in China). In response to a legacy of discrimination against Chinese Americans, which made them hesitant even to acknowledge their ties to China and other Chinese, some Chinese Americans and their sympathizers have been all too anxious to reaffirm such ties, in turn suppressing the cultural differences arising from the different historical trajectories of different Chinese populations scattered around the world. The anti-assimilationist mood (expressed most fervently in liberal "multiculturalism") itself has contributed in no small measure to such cultural reification. The question, moreover, is not merely one of culture. Because the very phenomenon of diaspora has produced a multiplicity of Chinese cultures, the affirmation of "Chineseness" can be sustained only by recourse to a common origin, or descent, that persists in spite of widely different historical trajectories. This results in the—often divisive—elevation of ethnicity and race over all the other factors that have gone into the shaping of Chinese populations and their cultures.

In its failure to specify its own location vis-à-vis the hegemonic, self-serving, and often financially lucrative reification of "Chineseness" in the political economy of transnationalism, critical diaspora discourse itself has fallen prey to the manipulation and commodification made possible by cultural reification and contributes to the foregrounding of ethnicity and race in contemporary political and cultural thinking. There has been a tendency in recent scholarship, the publishing industry, and arts and literature, for instance, to abolish the difference between Asians and Asian Americans. In scholarship, there have been calls recently to integrate Asian American studies into Asian studies—contrary to the earlier refusal of Asian studies specialists to have anything to do with Asian American studies—which partly reflects the increased prominence of transpacific population flows, but also suggests the increasingly lucrative promise of reorienting Asian American studies in that direction. Publishers' catalogues, especially those devoted to "multiculturalism" and ethnic relations, freely blend Asian with Asian American themes, and it is not rare to see these days catalogues in which *Woman Warrior* is placed right next to *The Dream of the Red Chamber.* As another example, a series on "Asian American film" mysteriously included many more films from Asia than from Asian America.

Moreover, and more fundamentally, within the context of flourishing Pacific economies (at least until very recently), some Asian Americans—most notably Chinese Americans—have been assigned the role of "bridges" to Asia, a role that they have readily assumed because of its lucrative promises. I referred earlier to the homogenization of Chinese populations in the recent Confucian revival, which attributes the economic success of Chinese, without regard to time or place, to the persistence of "Confucian values"—a concept that was viewed earlier as an obstacle to capitalism, but has been rendered into the source of everything from economic development to the production of "model minorities."[22] Thus, one promoter of Pacific economies writes: "With their cultural, linguistic, and family ties to China, Chinese-American entrepreneurs like [Henry Y.] Hwang are proving to be America's secret weapon in recapturing a predominant economic role in the world's most populous nation" (Kotkin 1996: 25). It may not be very far from a portrayal of Chinese Americans as American economic moles in China to William Safire's depiction of John Huang as a Chinese political mole in Washington, D.C. Finally, widely different Chinese populations have in recent years been endowed with supposedly identical cultural characteristics that further erase their differences. Networked through *guanxi* and driven by Confucianism, Chinese around the world in this representation have been rendered into a "tribe" (in the same description by Kotkin) in relentless search of wealth and power.[23]

The attitudes that lie at the root of these recent tendencies are not the less productive of racism for being produced by or sympathetic to Chinese and other Asian populations. Chinese populations are no less divided by class, gender, and ethnic differences than other populations. Not least among those differences are differences of place and history. If these differences are erased by the shifting of attention from these categories to a general category of diaspora, it is necessary to raise the question of whom such erasure serves. There is no reason to suppose that the government in Beijing (or, for that matter, in Taiwan) is any more reluctant than the government in Washington or U.S. transnational corporations to use diasporic Chinese for its own purposes. On the other hand, from both a political and an economic perspective, some diasporic Chinese are obviously of greater use than others and, in turn, benefit from the erasure of differences among Chinese, which enables them to speak for all Chinese.[24] The reconceptualization of Chinese populations in terms of diasporas, in other words, serves economic and political class interests. (It is not accidental that the Chinese American John Huang was connected with the Riady family, which made him useful in a number of ways.)

In this context, it is also important to raise the question of the relationship between diaspora and national boundaries, for as the notion of diaspora erases differences among Chinese, it seeks also to question national boundaries. Here, too, there is a question of who stands to benefit the most from the erasure of national boundaries. Whatever its own colonizing tendencies, the nation-state is still capable, when properly controlled from below, of offering protection to those within its boundaries. It is not very surprising, therefore, that those Chinese Americans devoted to social issues and community building (such as Henry Der) should be suspicious of the claims of diasporas and of the questioning of national boundaries.[25]

What I am suggesting is not a return to the nation, with its colonial, homogenizing, and assimilationist ideology, but the qualification of diasporic with place consciousness. To raise the question of places is to raise the issue of difference on a whole range of fronts, including those of class, gender, and ethnicity. It is also to raise the question of history in identity. Identity is no less an identity for being historical (is there any other kind?). Contrary to a hegemonic cultural reification or a whimpering preoccupation with the location of "home," which seem to have acquired popularity as alternative expressions of diasporic consciousness, what is important is to enable people to feel at home where they live.[26] This does not require that people abandon their legacies, only that they recognize the historicity of their cultural identities and that those identities are subject to change in the course of historical encounters.

Diasporas are dispersals from some remembered homeland, from some concrete place, which after the fact is conceived in terms of the nation (at least over the past century), although concrete places of origin retain their visibility even in their incorporation into the language of the nation or of diaspora. The dispersed also land in concrete places in the host society, which is captured in national terms as well, even if the very fact of diaspora, if nothing else, disturbs efforts to define nation and national culture. Ling-chi Wang (1991) tells us that one Chinese metaphor for the diasporic condition is "growing roots where landed" (*luodi shenggen*). While a prejudice for the nation makes it possible to speak of "national soil" and demands assimilation to some "national culture," rootedness as a metaphor points inevitably to concrete places that belie easy assumptions about the homogeneity of national soil or culture. As Kathleen Neil Conzen (1990: 9) wrote about German immigrants to the United States: "as change occurred, it could proceed without the kinds of qualitative shifts implied by the familiar notions of acculturation and assimilation. Culture was more strongly localized—naturalized in the literal botanical sense of the term—than it was ethnicized, and the structures of everyday life, rather than being assimilated to those of some broader element within American society, responded to the transforming pressures of modern life on a parallel trajectory of their own." The statement points to both the concrete place-basedness and the historicity of diasporic identity. James Clifford (1997) uses the metaphor of "routes" to capture the spatio-temporality of cultural identity. I will describe it simply as "historical trajectory through places."[27] Encounters in places traversed involve both forgetting and new acquisitions. The past is not erased, therefore, but rewritten. Similarly, the new acquisitions do not imply disappearance into the new environment but, rather, the proliferation of future possibilities.

What attention to place suggests is the historicity of identity. The "assimilation theory" to which Conzen objects presupposed de-historicized and placeless notions of culture; assimilation implied movement from one to the other. One could not be both Chinese and American, but had to move from being Chinese (whatever that might mean) to being American (whatever that might mean); hence failure to become "fully American" could produce such notions as "dual personality," which precluded being American—as well as suggested that such an identity represented the degeneration of the components out of which it was formed.

Such cultural assumptions in the end could only rest on the principle of descent—in other words, race. Ironically, contemporary critiques of assimilation theory, to the extent that they ignore place and history, end up with similar assumptions. A case in point is the currently fashionable idea of hybridity, which "multiculturalism" evaluates differently from the "mono-culturalism" permitted earlier, but which nevertheless retains similar culturalist assumptions (some notion of Chineseness conjoined to some notion of Americanness to produce a hybrid product). And since culturalism still runs against the evidence of difference, it can be sustained only by the reification of ethnicity and, ultimately, race. Diasporic identity in its reification does not overcome the racial prejudices of earlier assumptions of national cultural homogeneity, but in many ways it follows a similar logic, now at the level not of nations but of off-ground "transnations." The "Children of the Yellow Emperor" may be all the more a racial category for having abandoned its ties to the political category of the nation.[28]

The insistence on places against diasporic reification have consequences that are not only analytical in an abstract sense. It draws attention, in the first place, to another, place-based kind of politics. One of the dangerous consequences of paying undue attention to diasporas is that it distances the so-called diasporic populations from their immediate environments, rendering these populations into foreigners in the context of everyday life. Given the pervasiveness of conflicts in American society that pit different diasporic populations against one another, it is necessary, rather than to retreat behind reified identities that further promote mutual suspicion and racial division, to engage others in political projects to create political alliances where differences can be "bridged" and common social and cultural bonds can be formed to enable different populations to learn to live with one another.[29] A Chinese living in Los Angeles has more of a stake in identifying with his or her African American or Hispanic American neighbors than with some distant cousin in Hong Kong (without implying that the two kinds of relationships need to be understood in zero-sum terms). Following the logic of this argument, I suggest that place-based politics offers the most effective means toward achieving such ends. Place-based politics does not presuppose communities that shut out the world; it refocuses attention on building society from the bottom up.

The other consequence is also political, but within the context of academic politics, for there is a pedagogical dimension to realizing such political goals. It is rather unfortunate that recent ideological formations, backed by the power of foundations, have encouraged the capturing of ethnicities in "diasporic" American or cultural studies. In the case of studies of Asian Americans in particular, the most favored choices these days would seem to be to recognize Asian American studies as a field of its own, to break it down into various national components (Chinese, Japanese, Filipino, etc.), or to absorb it into American or Asian studies. Each choice is informed by political premises and goals. Asian American studies as a field is under attack from the inside for its homogenizing implications, as well as for its domination by some groups over others. Breaking it down, however, does not offer any readily acceptable solution, because it merely replaces continental homogeneity with national homogeneities. Why should there be Chinese American rather than, say, Fuzhounese American studies? And why stop at Fuzhou? On the other hand, absorbing Asian American studies into either Asian or American studies would seem to achieve little more than bringing it as a field under the hegemony of the study of societies of origin or arrival.

If education has anything to do with politics, and it does have everything to do with it, the wiser course to follow in overcoming ethnic divisions would be to reinforce programs in ethnic studies, which initially had the bridging of ethnic divisions and the pursuit of common projects (based in communities) to that end as fundamental goals. Ethnic studies since its inception has been viewed with suspicion by the political and educational establishments; it has suffered from internal divisions, as well. Whether these legacies can be overcome is a big question, embedded as they are in the structures of U.S. society and academic institutions. The irony is that while ethnic studies might help ideologically to overcome ethnic divisions, it is not likely to receive much support unless interethnic political cooperation has sufficient force to render it credible in the first place. The ideology of globalization, of which diasporic ideology is one constituent, further threatens to undermine its promise (and existence). Here, too, place-based politics may have something to offer in countering the ideologies of the age.

THE LOCAL AND THE GLOBAL IN ASIAN AMERICA

By way of conclusion, I would like to return to what I described in the introduction as a contradiction between the present and the past; the originary vision of community that defined the term Asian American when it first emerged in the 1960s, and the contemporary understanding of Asian America to which recalling that vision now appears as "the trope of nostalgic-history" (Ono 1995). The original vision of Asian America may no longer be able to contain the forces reshaping Asian America. But is it, therefore, irrelevant? The question is not an abstract question of ethnicity; it is a deeply political one. So is the answer.

The forces that have restructured Asian America over the past three decades have increased the power of Asian America, but they have also created new strains on an already problematic social formation. The new immigration has created new problems in Asian American relations with other minority groups (the African–Korean American conflict comes readily to mind).[30] It has also created problems among different national ethnic groups within a pan-Asian ethnicity and within individual groups. Karen Leonard has documented conflicts between settled Punjabi groups and new immigrants from South Asia, while Peter Kwong has shown the ways in which Chinatowns have been remapped by conflicts between the older residents from Guangdong and the new immigrants from Fujian.[31] The conflicts include basic economic and class issues, but, ironically, they are expressed in the language of cultural authenticity: "real Americans" versus "real Asians."

Although the discourse on Asian America has stayed clear of the language of authenticity, it has undergone noticeable changes in its efforts to accommodate the restructuring of Asian America. By the 1980s, Asian American scholars aready recognized the problems presented to the idea of Asian America by the new immigration and sought to find ways of incorporating the problems and orientations of the new immigrant population into ways of speaking about Asian America. The new immigrants, and the need to include them in Asian American studies, were very much on the minds of the scholars (some of whom were themselves new immigrants) who contributed to the volume *Reflections on Shattered Windows*, published in 1988. The title is itself indicative of their concerns (and an affirmation of the origins of the movement in the windows shattered at San Francisco State). Nevertheless, the volume's contributors were also wary of the consequences for Asian America of the Pacific connection that was ushered in by the same immigration. The volume was prefaced by a poem by Russell Leong titled, "Disarmed/1968–1987: San Francisco State College," which included the lines:

> *Those Who Understand*
>
> America today
> hesitate
> before crossing
> the Pacific bridge
> tomorrow.
> Forty years ago
> the tinge of our skin
> wrongly imprisoned us
> under the shadow of the rising sun
> across the sea.
> Yet today
> we bargain our lives
> for an inflated currency:
> Human capital.
> Transnational investment.
> Economic migrants.
> What does this mean—
> Where does it end?
> The "dominoes" of a defunct theory
> reincarnated into building blocks
> of the Pacific Century
> As Asians, once again
> form the bridge
> toward a new manifest destiny.
> But bridges have been burnt
> whole villages napalmed before.
>
> *Okihiro (1988: xiv)*

Or, as Michael Omi (1988: 31–36) put it, less poetically but with equal passion, in the same volume: "Asian American studies should contribute to an understanding of, and perhaps help to define, the emergent political, economic, and cultural relations between the U.S. and Asia. With the demise of the 'Atlantic era,' Pacific Rim studies is 'hot.' The crucial task for Asian American studies will be to define an approach that avoids the exploitative developmental outlook endemic to international capital. If Asian American studies does not intervene, Pacific Rim studies will be monopolized by the wolves."

The effort to draw a distinction between the new immigration and the Pacific idea that accompanied it was an important one, and one that has continued to inform the debate on Asian America. The effort seems in hindsight to have been quixotic in its urge to preserve the radical vision of communities rooted in an Asian *American* history, for, in the interesting observation of Kent Ono, "The argument that Asian Americans try to make immigrants subjects of the state as quickly as possible may, in fact, work in reverse. In the process of normalizing immigrants, 'Asian Americans' may in fact be socialized to become more like those they serve, more migrant" (Ono 1995). This is indeed what seems to have happened over the past decade, when Asian Americans have appeared increasingly, in the words of Bonacich, as a "middleman minority." The strong affirmation of identity at the origins of the Asian American movement seems also to have retreated before a situation in which the postmodern presents "the moment for the ethnic to be conjoined with the universal, as everything is now in a correlate condition of fragmentation and revision," or erases "at that very moment the specificity of ethnicity" (Palumbo-Liu 1995).

What is interesting is that the questions currently raised about Asian American ethnicity, expressed now in the language of postmodernism and postcoloniality, still take as their frame of reference the ideological and institutional structures created by the Asian American imaginary of the 1960s. This is no doubt due partially to the persistence of organizational structures (including Asian American studies programs) that were products of the movement. I would like to venture, however, that the continuing concern is due also to the persistence of structures of racial, class, and gender division embedded in the capitalist organization of society, which perpetuate in re-configured forms the problems that gave rise to the Asian American movement in the first place and that necessitate the preservation of that frame of reference.[32]

The reconfiguring of the problems nevertheless calls for a reconfiguring of the answers, and this is what necessitates a new understanding, if not a new vision, of Asian America. In her contribution to the special issue of *Amerasia Journal*, "Thinking Theory in Asian American Studies,"[33] from which I have quoted generously, Sau-ling Wong offers a thoughtful appraisal of the problems of reconsidering Asian America that bears some comment. Wong's argument is similar to the argument I have offered in the necessity of drawing a distinction between what she calls "diasporic" and "domestic" perspectives in the understanding of contemporary Asian America—the one stressing the global dimensions of Asian America, the other focusing on the national context (S.C. Wong 1995: 2). Arguing the ways in which these perspectives confound easy definitions of Asian American identity, and undermine cultural nationalism, Wong nevertheless returns to a reaffirmation of identity as a necessity for meaningful political action. In this case, the meaningful political action implies not just a return to earlier notions of community, but the defense of the very notion of community against the developmentalist ideology of a transnational capitalism that is in the process of engulfing the local with the global (in the specific case of Asian Americans, by an ideology of the Pacific, which has become the most recent location for the legitimization of "developmentalism").[34]

Given the strategic importance that Asian America has been assigned in the Pacific economic formation, it may also have a very significant part to play in the reassertion of local welfare against the globalizing forces of transnational capitalism, which returns this discussion to where it started. As the contrasts between Matt Fong and Henry Der reveal, the question of a Pacific versus a community orientation is no longer simply one of Asian America as expressed in the vision of the 1960s or perpetuated in racially or nationally conceived notions of ethnicity. Those questions are themselves embedded in the confrontations between futures mortgaged to the promises of a utopianized transnational capitalism and the very concrete realities of everyday existence at the level of the local, in which there are few differences between old-timers and newcomers, between Asians and others. Where "bridges" are placed under such circumstances is a matter not of ethnic destiny, but of political choice. I conclude with a long quotation that I hope embodies the many themes, and the complex history, of an idea that is Asian America:

> Kathy Nishimoto Masaoka is standing in front of the twelve-foot-tall "Friendship Knot," a double helix of concrete anchored in the mall next to the New Otani. She is scowling at the bronze plaque that dedicates the sculpture to Morinosuke Kajima, the wartime boss of the Hanaoke slaves, but here described as an "international businessman, whose vision and generosity initiated the revitalization of Little Tokyo."
>
> "This used to be the heart of the community," she explains, pointing toward a courtyard of glitzy tourist shops selling Armani suits and English hunting gear under the shadow of the New Otani. "Three old hotels provided affordable housing for elderly Issei [first-generation immigrants] as well as young Latino families. There were scores of traditional, family-run storefronts and cheap restaurants."
>
> But then, in 1973, Kajima created the East-West Development Corporation to oversee the redevelopment of this area. The residents wanted replacement senior housing and the preservation of existing business. The downtown corporate leaders and the city's Community Redevelopment Agency (C.R.A.), on the other hand, pushed Kajima's plan for a luxury hotel

and shopping center. They saw Little Tokyo as a conduit for Japanese corporate investment, not as a vibrant Japanese-American neighborhood. Kajima eventually selected the New Otani chain, headed by a wealthy Japanese family, to manage the hotel[35] (Davis 1996).

According to Mike Davis, Little Tokyo activists, led by a female Salvadoran immigrant, were in touch with elderly Chinese men who had been victims of Kajima operations during World War II, to establish solidarity against Kajima, welcomed otherwise through the "Golden Doors" of the Pacific. That, too, may be transpacific pan-ethnicity, but one that is defined by a different kind of politics that grounds transnationalism in the welfare of local communities.

■ NOTES

Acknowledgment: I would like to thank the Asia Society, especially Vishakha Desai, vice-president in charge of cultural programs, for permission to publish this essay first in *Amerasia*. The views expressed in the essay are strictly my own and are implicitly or explicitly at odds with those of the Asia Society, which initially sponsored the "Bridges" project. I hope the differences are productive in consequence; institutions such as the Asia Society can make important contributions to the resolution of the problems that I have discussed.

1. Governor Wilson's office objected to Der because of his view on "affirmative action, 'English-only' legislation, Proposition 187, and Wilson himself," which obviously differed from those of the governor.

2. It is worth noting here that, although many of the changes I discuss later—especially the revitalized orientation toward Asia and the Pacific—are associated with the post-1965 immigrant population and its immediate ties to countries of origin, this is not the case with Matt Fong, who, according to *Asian-Week*, is a fourth-generation Chinese American. The question, in other words, is not one of being more or less American as conceived in generational or other terms.

3. For further discussion of this problem, see my "The Global in the Local" (Dirlik 1996) and the other essays in the collection *Global/Local: Cultural Production and the Transnational Imaginary*. My interpretation here obviously places structural relationships ahead of culturalist arguments that promote an "Asian" exceptionalism, which are popular especially among non-Asians writing about Asian Americans and the contemporary Pacific.

4. For a recent (and still unabashedly triumphalist) discussion, see Arrell Morgan Gibson (1993), completed with the assistance of John S. Whitehead.

5. I owe the term "racial formation" to Michael Omi and Howard Winant (1986). In the Gibson article cited just above, I explain at some length why, given the

legacy of Orientalism, culture is also an important element in considerations of Asian America.

6. Espiritu derived the idea from David M. Hayano (1981).

7. Ichioka told this story at the conference "Asia–Pacific Identities: Culture and Identity Formation in the Age of Global Capital," held at Duke University, April 13–15, 1995. Other terms of identity available at the time included "yellow" and even "Oriental."

8. Omi and Winant have usefully defined "rearticulation" as "the process of re-definition of political interests and identities, through a process of recombination of familiar ideas and values in hitherto unrecognized ways" (Omi and Winant 1986: 148, n. 8).

9. For differences in Asian American responses to the war in Vietnam, see Espiritu (1992: 44). For the student movement to 1968, see the special issue of *Amerasia Journal* 15, no. 1 (1989).

10. I should note that this inclusiveness has not always been welcomed by those so included. Native Hawaiians, for example, who identify with indigenous rather than ethnic causes, see Asian Americans in Hawaii as participants in the expropria-tion of Hawaiian lands and as part of the structure of foreign domination. From this perspective, the idea of Asian Pacific America is another instance of the imperialis-tic erasure of Hawaiian indigenism. For an example, see the essays in Haunani-Kay Trask (1993). Other Pacific Islanders also often identify more closely with indigenism, and their relationship to Asians is shaped by local experiences with Asian populations that are direct rather than intermediated by what happens in the U.S. (e.g., Asian In-dians in Fiji, or Japanese and more recently Taiwanese investors in the South Pacific).

11. By 1976, an examination of the movement by a Filipino writer had already challenged its pan-ethnic assumptions. See Lemuel F. Ignacio (1976).

12. See, for example, Leland T. Saito and John Horton (1994: 243).

13. In other cases, as with Filipinas and women from Southeast Asia, indentured servitude would seem to be more gender-specific.

14. In his testimony before an incredulous congressional committee in 1877, Henry George argued against Chinese immigration while at the same time defend-ing "free trade" on the grounds that, although the importing of the products of cheap labor benefited the United States, the importing of labor itself did not. George nevertheless backed away from a suggestion that employers should "employ where they can the cheapest." More than a century later, the latter has become common practice in the Pacific economy, which is what I mean by the exporting of jobs. Although there may not be much difference between the exporting of capital and the importing of labor, as some of the congressmen suggested to George in 1877, labor immigration still meets with immediate opposition, while the free mobility of capital usually goes unnoticed. See Foner and Rosenberg (1993: 25–29).

15. For further discussion, see Arif Dirlik, "Critical Reflections on 'Chinese Cap-italism' as Paradigm," *Identities* 3, no. 3 (1997): 303–330. Cultural nationalism is com-plicated, and contradicted, by simultaneous claims to an "Asian" legacy as an explanation of success that seeks to dislodge a Eurocentric conceptualization of

capitalism. For a discussion of the complexities of diasporic identities, see Ling-chi Wang (1991).

16. This blurring of boundaries between Asia and Asian America may be typical of a more widespread phenomenon that pertains to ethnic studies in general. Young Mexican Americans, according to one source, "reject the 'Chicano' label, and even more vociferously, 'Hispanic' and 'Latino.' 'We're Mexicans,' they say" (Castillo 1995). A 1995 Bantam Doubleday Dell catalogue for "ethnic studies" is divided into sections that include "Asian studies" (the "core curriculum" of which includes Chinese novels such as *The Dream of the Red Chamber* and *Wild Swan*), "Middle Eastern studies," "Native American studies," and "Hispanic/Latino/Chicano studies." With the exception of Native American studies, all the sections draw freely on literature from the "areas" from which the ethnic groups presumably hail. In the case of Asian Americans, there have been calls in scholarly circles to bring Asian American studies closer to Asian studies. Asian American studies are much in demand these days, mostly in response to student protests. Very often, however, the impression given by these demands is that Asian American studies should be studies of Rimpeople rather than of Asian Americans within the context of ethnic relations within the United States. I have stressed the importance of the Pacific dimension of Asian America, but as an element that disturbs national histories on both sides of the ocean. There is something quite dangerous politically in overemphasizing the Asianness of Asian Americans, because it renders them "foreign," even if that "foreignness" may be more acceptable at present than it was in the nineteenth century and even if it may have become marketable under the rubric of "multiculturalism" (at least of a transitional corporate "multiculturalism"). It also distances ethnic groups in the United States from one another by identifying them with their various areas of origin rather than the locations that they share and that provide the point of departure for any kind of common political action. A good case can be made that the blurring of area boundaries plays into the hands of existing hegemonic constructions of globalism and "multiculturalism" rather than challenges them, which also reflects the needs of an Asian American elite in complicity with existing structures of power. Against this construction, the call for the original goals of "ethnic studies" seems radical indeed. For an example by a Korean American student activist who stresses the need for "ethnic studies" rather than "area studies," see Ronald Kim (1996).

17. For an example, see the influential essay by Lisa Lowe, "Heterogeneity, Hybridity, Multiplicity" (1991: 24–44). For an early discussion of "hybridity" that stresses its disabling consequences for young Asian Americas, see Chapter XVII, "Cultural Hybridism, in William Carlson Smith (1970).

18. Although different groups may experience this remapping differently, it is clear that the phenomenon itself is not exclusive to any one group. It is a product of what I have referred to as global postmodernity. A seminal work that addresses the question, this time in relation to the African diaspora, is Paul Gilroy (1993).

19. For an earlier critique that emphasized the conservative implications of the model-minority idea, see Keith Osajima (1988: 165–74).

20. For a more detailed discussion, see Dirlik (1995).

21. A great deal of material is available on the John Huang case, although there are no studies as yet. For a blatant example of the unscrupulous linking of Huang with the Riadys and the PRC, see William Safire (1997).

22. It is noteworthy that, with the so-called meltdown of Asian economies in late 1997, "Asian values," among them Confucianism, have once again lost their luster. It turns out once again that Asian values have been responsible for creating a corrupt "crony capitalism" that inevitably led to economic break-down.

23. For critiques of these tendencies in connection with John Huang's case, see Ling-chi Wang (1996) and Nick Cullather (1996).

24. For an important discussion, see Peter Kwong (1997: esp. chap. 5, "Manufacturing Ethnicity").

25. Such suspicion is not limited to Chinese Americans. In a recent conference in Singapore, one paper that foregrounded diasporas and "transnations" was challenged by the well-known sociologist and activist Chua Beng-huat, who declared without qualification that he was Singaporean, not a transnational or diasporic.

26. I am referring here to the title of a conference held in November 1997 at New York University, "Where Is Home?" (previously the title of an exhibition on the Chinese in the United States). The preoccupation has its roots in a particularly narcissistic and manipulative offshoot of cultural studies.

27. See the collection of his essays in Clifford (1997).

28. For a recent, trenchant critique of "hybridity," see Jonathan Friedman (1997: 10–89). My critique here, needless to say, refers not to the intentions of those who employ the concept of hybridity but, rather, to the logic of the metaphor.

29. The divisive effects of diasporic discourse as I approach it here are similar to the divisive effects of the idea of a "model minority."

30. For a critical (and sensitive) discussion of the African American–Korean American conflict, see Nancy Abelman and John Lie (1995). I am grateful to Mette Thunoe for bringing this work to my attention.

31. Karen I. Leonard (1992); Peter Kwong (1994b: 1–5). See also Kwong (1997).

32. For a passionate reaffirmation of the movement's original goals, see Glenn Omatsu (1994: 19–69).

33. This interesting collection contains contributions that range from near-rejection of the idea of Asian America to an affirmation of "Asiacentrism"—or that take on the question, if I may rephrase the subtitle of Sau-ling Wong's essay, of What America Is. I would like to take note of the essay "Asiacentrism and Asian American Studies" (Wong, Menvi, and Wong 1995: 137–47), which argues for an Asiacentrism comparable to Afrocentrism. Although the argument replicates some of the worst excesses of Orientalism in its reductionist argument for a spiritual Asia, it is important because of the case it makes for an alternative development (as well as for its suspicion of "theory" for its inevitably hegemonic premises), which was a goal of the Asian American movement in its radical phase. Interestingly, the idea of Asia proposed in the essay is also radically different from the idea of Asia promoted by the likes of Lee Kuan Yew of Singapore, to whom the defining feature of the Asian spirit is its unquestioning commitment to capitalism.

34. The vocabulary of the local and the global is mine, but I think it is consistent with what Professor Wong is arguing. I hope, at any rate, that my vocabulary does not distort her intentions. Unlike Wong and others, such as Lisa Lowe, I also think that "cultural nationalism" is more a product of contemporary developments than of the original aspirations of the Asian American movement, which, as I have argued, had a much more historicized notion of both nation and culture than seems to prevail at present. The polemics against cultural nationalism should be part of a present-day struggle against the homogenization of identities rather than directed at straw targets of the past. Wong uses the example of Frank Chin and the *Big Aiiieeee!,* which contrasts sharply with the historicist representations in his fiction and, more important, with the 1971 essay that he and Jeffrey Chan co-authored, "Racist Love," published in the volume *Seeing Through Schuck* (Kostelanetz 1972). The shift may well have something to do with the resurgent Orientalism of the present, not least in the works of writers such as Amy Tan, against whom Chin positions himself.

35. Mike Davis (1996). The contradiction between community and transnational capital affects all ethnicities and has become an inescapable issue of contemporary politics. For a recent discussion, see Thomas Friedman (1996).

■ REFERENCES

Ableman, Nancy, and John Lie
  1995   *Blue Dreams: Korean Americans and the Los Angeles Riots.* Cambridge, Mass.: Harvard University Press.
AsianWeek
  1996   January 5, 13–18.
Castillo, Ana
  1995   "Impressions of a Xicana Dreamer." *Bloomsbury Review,* November/ December.
Clifford, James
  1997   *Routes: Travel and Translation in the Late Twentieth Century.* Cambridge, Mass.: Harvard University Press.
Conzen, Kathleen Neils
  1990   "Making Their Own America: Assimilation Theory and the German Peasant Pioneer." German Historical Institute, Washington, D.C., Annual Lecture Series, no. 3. New York: Berg Publishers.
Cullather, Nick
  1996   "The Latest 'Peril' from Asia." *AsianWeek,* November 15, 7.
Davis, Mike
  1996   "Kajima's Throne of Blood." *The Nation,* February 12, 18–20.
Dirlik, Arif
  1993   "Asia–Pacific in Asian American Perspective." In *What Is in a Rim? Critical Perspectives on the Pacific Region Idea,* ed. Arif Dirlik. Boulder, Colo.: Westview Press.

1995   "Confucius in the Borderlands: Global Capitalism and the Reinvention of Confucianism." *Boundary* 2 (fall): 229–73.

1996   "The Global in the Local." In *Global/Local: Cultural Production and the Transnational Imaginary*, ed. Rob Wilson and Wimal Dissayanke. Durham, N.C.: Duke University Press.

1997   "Critical Reflections on 'Chinese Capitalism' as Paradigm." *Identities* 3, no. 30: 303–30.

Espiritu, Yen Le

1992   *Asian American Panethnicity: Bridging Institutions and Identities.* Philadelphia: Temple University Press.

Foner, Philip S., and Daniel Rosenberg, ed.

1993   *Racism, Dissent and Asian Americans from 1850 to the Present: A Documentary History.* Westport, Conn.: Greenwood Press.

Fong, Matt

1996   "From Gold Mountain to the Golden Door." *AsianWeek,* January 19, 7.

Friedman, Jonathan

1997   "Global Crises, the Struggle for Cultural Identity and Intellectual Porkbarrelling: Cosmopolitans Versus Locals, Ethnics and Nationals in an Era of Dehegemonisation." In *Debating Cultural Identity: Multi-Cultural Identities and the Politics of Anti-Racism,* ed. Pnina Werbner and Tariq Madood. London: ZED Books.

Friedman, Thomas

1996   "Balancing NAFTA and Neighborhood." *Rocky Mountain News* (from *The New York Times*), April 13, A44.

Gee, Emma, ed.

1976   *Counterpoint: Perspectives on Asian America.* Los Angeles: UCLA Asian American Studies Center.

Gibson, Arrell Morgan

1993   *Yankees in Paradise: The Pacific Basin Frontier.* Albuquerque: University of New Mexico Press.

Gilroy, Paul

1993   *The Black Atlantic: Modernity and Double Consciousness.* Cambridge, Mass.: Harvard University Press.

Hayano, David M.

1981   "Ethnic Identification and Disidentification: Japanese-American Views of Chinese Americans." *Ethnic Groups* 3, no. 2: 157–71.

Ichioka, Yuji

1988   *Issei: The World of the First Generation Japanese Immigrants, 1885–1924.* New York: Free Press.

Ignacio, Lemuel F.

1976   *Asian Americans and Pacific Islanders (Is There Such an Ethnic Group?).* San Jose, Calif.: Pilipino Development Associates.

Kim, Ronald

1996   "The Myth and Reality of Ethnic Studies." *AsianWeek,* February 16, 7.

Kostelanetz, Richard, ed.
  1972   *Seeing Through Schuck.* New York: Ballantine Books.
Kotkin, Joel
  1996   "The New Yankee Traders." *Inc.* (March), 25.
Kwong, Peter
  1994a "China's Human Traffickers." *The Nation,* October 17, 422–25.
  1994b "The Wages of Fear." *Village Voice,* April 26, 1–5.
  1997   *Forbidden Workers: Illegal Chinese Immigrants and American Labor.* New York:
         New Press.
Leonard, Karen I.
  1992   *Making Ethnic Choices: California's Punjabi Mexican Americans.* Philadelphia:
         Temple University Press.
Lowe, Lisa
  1991   "Heterogeneity, Hybridity, Multiplicity: Marking Asian American Differ-
         ences." *Diaspora* 1, no. 1 (spring): 24–44.
Liu, John M.
  1988   "The Relationship of Migration Research to Asian American Studies: Unity
         and Diversity Within the Curriculum." In *Reflections on Shattered Windows:
         Promises and Prospects for Asian American Studies,* ed. Gary Y. Okihiro, Shirley
         Hune, Arthur A. Hansen, and John M. Liu. Pullman: Washington State Uni-
         versity Press.
Okihiro, Gary Y.
  1988   "The Idea of a Community and a 'Particular Type of History.'" In *Reflec-
         tions on Shattered Windows,* ed. Okihiro et al.
  1994   *Margins and Mainstream: Asians in American History and Culture.* Seattle:
         University of Washington Press.
Omatsu, Glenn
  1994   "The 'Four Prisons' and the Movements of Liberation: Asian American Ac-
         tivism from the 1960s to the 1990s." In *The State of Asian America: Activism and
         Resistance in the 1990s,* ed. Karin Aguilar-San Juan. Boston: South End Press.
Omi, Michael
  1988   "It Just Ain't the Sixties No More: The Contemporary Dilemmas of Asian
         American Studies." In *Reflections on Shattered Windows,* ed. Okihiro et al.
Omi, Michael, and Howard Winant
  1986   *Racial Formation in the United States: From the 1960s to the 1980s.* New York:
         Routledge & Kegan.
Ong, Paul, Edna Bonacich, and Lucie Cheng
  1994   "The Political Economy of Capitalist Restructuring and the New Asian Im-
         migration." In *The New Asian Immigration in Los Angeles and Global Restruc-
         turing,* ed. Paul Ong, Edna Bonacich, and Lucie Cheng. Philadelphia:
         Temple University Press.
Ono, Kent A.
  1995   "Re/Signing 'Asian American': Rhetorical Problematics of Nation." *Amerasia
         Journal* 21, no. 1 and 2: 67–78.

Osajima, Keith
  1988   "Asian Americans as the Model Minority: An Analysis of the Popular Press Image in the 1960s and 1980s." In *Reflections on Shattered Windows*, ed. Okihiro et al.
Palumbo-Liu, David
  1995   "Theory and the Subject of Asian American Studies." *Amerasia Journal*, 21, no. 1 and 2: 55–65.
Safire, William
  1997   "Listening to Hearings." *New York Times*, July 13.
Saito, Leland T., and John Horton
  1994   "The New Chinese Immigration and the Rise of Asian American Politics in Monterey Park, California." In *The New Asian Immigration*, ed. Ong, Bonacich, and Cheng.
Smith, William Carlson
  1970   *Americans in Process: A Study of Our Citizens of Oriental Ancestry.* New York: Arno Press and New York Times. Originally published in 1937.
Tachiki, Amy, Eddie Wong, Franklin Odo, and Buck Wong, ed.
  1971   *Roots: An Asian American Reader.* Los Angeles: UCLA Asian American Center.
Trask, Haunani-Kay
  1993   *From a Native Daughter: Colonialism and Sovereignty in Hawai'i.* Monroe, Maine: Common Courage Press
Wilson, Rob, and Wilmal Dissanayake, ed.
  1996   *Global/Local: Cultural Production and the Transnational Imaginary.* Durham, N.C.: Duke University Press.
Wang, Ling-chi
  1991   "Roots and Changing Identity of the Chinese in the United States." *Daedalus* (spring), 181–206.
  1996   "Foreign Money Is No Friend of Ours." *AsianWeek*, November 8, 7.
Wong, Paul, Meera Menvi, and Takeo Hirota Wong
  1995   "Asiacentrism and Asian American Studies." *Amerasia Journal* 21, no. 1 and 2: 137–47.
Wong, Sau-ling C.
  1995   "Denationalization Reconsidered: Asian American Cultural Criticism as a Theoretical Crossroads." *Amerasia Journal* 21, no. 1 and 2: 1–27.
Yip, Alethea
  1996   "APA [Asian Pacific American] Spokesman." *AsianWeek*, January 19, 9.

3

CHINESE AMERICANS IN THE FORMATION OF THE PACIFIC REGIONAL ECONOMY

LUCIE CHENG

How do the media-touted arrival of the Pacific Century (*Transpacific* 1996), the meteoric rise of the "Four Little Dragons" in Asia (Vogel 1991), the formation of the Pacific Rim (Pacific Basin or Asia Pacific), and other, similar emerging regional phenomena affect the Chinese in America? Do the emerging China Economic Circle (IGCC 1995) and the integration of Taiwan, Hong Kong, and the People's Republic of China into "Greater China" (Harding 1994)—forming a new regional power vis-à-vis other regional developments centered in the United States, such as NAFTA—have something special to offer to Chinese Americans? What roles are Chinese Americans playing, and what roles may they come to play, both in the formation of linkages between the United States and the Asia Pacific region and as a population affected by such linkages? In other words, how do we understand the triangular relationship among Chinese Americans, the United States, and the Asian Pacific Rim regional economy, especially the China Economic Circle?

These questions are being raised by scholars and the media alike. For many scholars, they point to a reexamination of long-held concepts and theories of international migration and development that tend to be unidirectional. Immigrants, even those who are ethnically resilient, are in the long run assimilating, and ties with the "homeland" necessarily weaken through time and generations. Field reports, journalistic accounts, and stories passed through the grapevine seem to indicate otherwise. Ethnic networks created through centuries of diaspora continue to expand. In the case of Chinese Americans, assimilation has neither severed persistent linkages with the old country nor terminated the usefulness of multinational ethnic networks (*Economist* 1988; Weidenbaum and Hughes 1996). In fact, many Chinese Americans are playing a pivotal role in the restructuring of U.S.– China relations, not only in terms of foreign and diplomatic relations, but in economic, social, and cultural arenas as well.

This chapter will focus on three aspects of the triangular relationship among the United States, China, and Chinese Americans. The first has to do with the global commodity chain and the dynamic roles of Chinese Americans as investors, professionals, traders, producers, and consumers as they touch down at different nodes on the chain linking the United States with Asia. The second will focus on the impact of this linkage on the economic and social fabric of the United States and selected countries in Asia. And the third will examine the consequences of this linkage for Chinese Americans in terms of their status and mobility, both positive and negative.

CHINESE AMERICANS AND THE
TRANSPACIFIC COMMODITY CHAIN

Much has already been said about the growing importance of the Asia Pacific region in the global economy and for the economic future of the United States (Jones, Frost, and White 1993). Many have cited figures to show the phenomenal growth of the Asian economy. A recent study by the Australian Department of Foreign Affairs predicts that trade between China and Japan alone will account for 28 percent of world commerce in the year 2015, compared with 13 percent today, and the *Asian Wall Street Journal Weekly* (1996) reported that the Asian economy is likely to continue to grow in the next decade. We have all been reminded that U.S. trade with Asia has long surpassed that with Europe. Even with the recent monetary crisis in Asia, long-term economic forecasts remain optimistic. Compared with the robust economy of Asia, the once hegemonic United States seems clearly in decline. It is against this change of relative position between Asia and the United States that we have to assess the ongoing diversification of Chinese American roles in the transpacific economy.

According to Richard Appelbaum and Gary Gereffi (1994: 43–44), "Global commodity chains (GCCs) have three main dimensions: an input–output structure comprising a set of products and services linked in a sequence of value-added economic activities; a territoriality that identifies the geographical dispersion or concentration of raw materials, production, export, and marketing networks; and a governance structure of power and authority relationships that determines how financial, material, and human resources, as well as economic surplus, are allocated and flow within the chain." It has been argued that the international division of labor today is manifested in the territorial concentration of suppliers and producers in the so-called Third World countries, and the concentration of designers, managers, and investors in developed countries. Young women are especially visible as workers in developing countries that are producing for consumers, who in large part are also women, in more affluent nations. However, the history and recent patterns of Chinese immigration have complicated the race and gender composition of players along the chain, and across the Pacific, in both directions, from raw-material–supply networkers to producers, financiers, traders, retailers, and consumers.

The high population density in the southern coastal provinces of China has always found some relief in overseas migration, resulting in large concentrations of Chinese in parts of Southeast Asia, Australia, North America, and, to a lesser extent, Europe, South America, and Africa (Mei 1984). Since the nineteenth century, Hong Kong has served as the transit point for migration abroad, and would-be migrants, while waiting for opportunities, often took jobs in the colony and became Hong Kong residents (Kwok and So 1995: 16–17). Earlier emigrants were mostly peasants and laborers, with a small number of merchants. Racial hostility and restrictions often circumscribed their choices of economic activities and limited their opportunities for upward mobility. In the case of Chinese Americans, for many decades since their first arrival in the mid-nineteenth century, they had been concentrated in the laboring and small entrepreneurial classes (Cheng and Bonacich 1984). Shunned by most unions, the Chinese American workers typically produced for a limited market. Except for a very few merchants engaged in import-export businesses, most Chinese American entrepreneurs were owner-operators of small mom-and-pop stores, laundries, and restaurants serving the local, sometimes ethnic, economy.

In contrast, post-1965 Chinese immigration to the United States exhibited two parallel movements: the simultaneous development of a professional, managerial class of Chinese Americans and of an unskilled, poorly educated proletariat (Liu and Cheng 1994). The territorial division of labor along the commodity chain is blurred, because both are engaged in production and entrepreneurship on U.S. land for an ethnically diverse local market as well as for a world market that spans all continents.

Two decades ago, industries such as apparel, shoes, and household appliances—termed buyer-driven commodity chains—were typically designed and capitalized in the United States and Europe. Production was organized by named Western companies owned by whites but carried out by small firms in Third World countries, including China, Taiwan, and Hong Kong (Cheng and Gereffi 1994). The roles of Chinese Americans were largely confined to garment workers and small retailers in Chinatowns. Chinese, Taiwanese, and Hong Kong designers and professional buyers were unknown in America. As customers, Chinese Americans in the 1960s had very little choice. Clothes and shoes were limited in their sizes, with little variation in color, style, quality, and price. Club 5'3, Petite Section, and other similar departments that are now very common were nonexistent. Many Chinese Americans found it necessary to buy clothes from boys' departments or to make alterations. The latter undoubtedly supported the livelihood of many Asian American women and men as dressmakers and tailors.

Until recently, much of the garment and shoe production in Asia was driven by retailers in the United States (Bonacich et al. 1994). Working as subcontractors of Asian firms under American ownership or management direction, small producers, often units bound by kinship, geographical, and other non-class affinity, turned out commodities to the specifications of American buyers who rarely had Asian American customers in mind. With the increasing affluence of Asians, especially the rising standard of living of the upper middle class; the convenience of air travel; and the relative ease of obtaining a tourist visa, it has become quite common for Asian visitors to do their shopping in major cities of America, especially in the urban centers where Asian Americans are concentrated, such as San Francisco, Los Angeles, and New York, and in cities frequented by Asian visitors, notably Las Vegas. One has only to walk around major shopping areas in these cities to realize the change in the past decade. Asian mannequins began to appear in store displays, and Asian-language signs emerged in quick succession. Japanese-language signs appeared first, reflecting the early lead that the Japanese economy achieved, followed by Chinese and now Korean signs, informing potential customers from these countries that there were salesclerks inside who could serve their needs.

In terms of household appliances, the Chinese—and, for that matter, Asian—market was hardly noticed by American entrepreneurs. For example, rice cookers, those almost indispensable appliances in Chinese households today, were not easily available in America. And when they were available, the price seemed exorbitant to most Chinese American families. In the 1960s, one of the most treasured gifts an Asian American could receive from visiting relatives and friends was a Sanyo or Tatung electric rice cooker. American businesses were oblivious to the needs of their Asian American customers.

As a more affluent Chinese American population surfaced, this group's increased buying power began to attract American entrepreneurs. And as the occupational structure changed to include more Asians in businesses, Chinese entrepreneurs in both ethnic enclaves and mainstream markets also increased. The development of a professional class among Chinese Americans further expanded their international roles. The careers of Chinese American lawyers, accountants, and engineers were facilitated, if not propelled, by affirmative action and informal pressures, but their presumed knowledge of a rapidly growing Greater China was also a significant factor. Do these Chinese American entrepreneurs and professionals really have a competitive advantage over other Americans?

COMPETITIVE ADVANTAGES: LANGUAGE, CULTURE, AND SOCIAL NETWORKS

Since the open-door policy of 1978, large numbers of outsiders have knocked on the Chinese door, but few have been successful. Among those who succeeded, overseas Chinese figured prominently (Simons and Zielenziger 1994). Language facility, local connections, and knowledge are important for anyone doing business abroad, but in a country where legal uncertainty reigns, these become prerequisites to successful operation. An understanding of *fengshui* (geomancy), *guanxi* (personal connections), *guoqing* (national context), and other cultural, social, and political practices is crucial to doing business in China due to the fact that "rule of law is weak and its administration often chaotic" (Weidenbaum and Hughes 1996). It is assumed that overseas Chinese, including those in America, have a competitive advantage because they possess a bilingual and bicultural background and, perhaps more important, a network that spans both sides of the Pacific. In its May 1995 report on increasing American effectiveness in China's trade and investment environment, the National Committee on U.S.–China Relations argued for using Americans of Chinese origin, including those from Hong Kong and Taiwan, as part of the expatriate personnel in American ventures in China. The committee felt that Chinese Americans could be very helpful in building bridges. Although many Chinese Americans have special skills and backgrounds to offer, this general assumption has several problems. It also presents a number of challenges.

1. A New Myth of Chinese Americans

Not every Chinese has the required facilities to take advantage of the growing Pacific economy. Only those Chinese Americans who have the necessary language skills, the cultural understanding, and the social networks can reap great benefits. The emphasis on presumed abilities has an ironic racist twist that fits the notion of the "unassimilable Chinee." It seems that Chinese Americans have somehow maintained their language, culture, and ethnic networks through generations when, in fact, only a small percentage of native-born Chinese Americans have retained the language of their ancestors (Lopez 1996). This structural requirement reinforces the cleavage within the Chinese American population, since it is mostly the foreign-born who are likely to have these qualifications. The native-born Chinese Americans who refused to learn Chinese and who rejected Chinese culture in an earlier configuration of race and economy in the United States—when biculturalism and bilingualism were stigma rather than virtues—are finding themselves left out of the new opportunities. For decades, connections of Chinese Americans with their ancestral lands have been inhibited by formal and informal practices. Ironically, some non–ethnic Chinese Americans who do not have this burden of denial have been preparing themselves aggressively for the anticipated Pacific Century.

While America's need for individuals who are comfortable with the language and culture of China is rapidly growing, interest in working in China is also growing. There are now job-recruiting firms in Asia that try to identify potential employers for Americans, as well as head-hunting firms trying to locate employees who can meet the requirements (*AsianWeek* 1994).

Given the difficulty of the Chinese language and China's rich cultural heritage, as well as the post-1965 relaxation of Asian immigration, a program to encourage language and cultural retention of young immigrants seems an effective and efficient way for the United States to obtain much-needed bilingual and bicultural personnel to facilitate its dealings with China. Such personnel are less likely to misinterpret Chinese practices and therefore are beneficial to relations between the two countries.

It is important to emphasize that the economic growth of China is restructuring the country's relationship with the United States. This new relationship creates opportunities for upward mobility for some Chinese Americans, but not for others. Those who will benefit must be bilingual and bicultural, which means that they are likely to be foreign born and educated, but with U.S. college or postgraduate degrees. This is only a small group. To presume that Chinese Americans have a general competitive advantage in this new environment would be tantamount to creating a new myth.

2. Transnational Networks

Recent writers have credited the unprecedented transformation of Greater China to the financial and managerial resources provided by an extended network of overseas Chinese (Weidenbaum and Hughes 1996). Similar arguments have also been made regarding the "economic miracle" of Taiwan and, in a much earlier time, the Revolution of 1911. Since the beginning of Chinese diaspora, kinship, village, and native-place associations as well as historical, even legendary, connections have bound the overseas Chinese to their homeland and to one another. These ties may be strong or weak, recognized or submerged, but they are nevertheless "social capital" capable of being mobilized for cultural, social, political, and economic purposes. The overseas Chinese networks have been mobilized for individuals' economic advancement and to facilitate economic development in China.

As in traditional times, linkages with the homeland are still maintained through remittances, investments, and donations by the emigrants. The governments in Beijing and Taipei vie for overseas Chinese, whose material and human resources are much needed. Remittances have long been considered a key element in the balance of payments for China and Taiwan (Lin 1988), and overseas Chinese investments in various development projects have been wooed with especially favorable terms (*Huaqiao,* various years). Donations have taken the form of building and maintaining public services such as schools, hospitals, roads, and bridges. Such activities stem from the desire of overseas Chinese to maintain ties with the homeland and to establish a status in the Chinese community both in and out of China.

The ties maintained by overseas Chinese are not just binational. They are multinational and capable of unlimited extension both vertically and horizontally (Wu 1975; Jones, Frost, and White 1993: 100; Chang 1995; Kohut and Cheng 1996). Termed the "bamboo network," these ties have been instrumental in the transformation of "Greater China" by providing entrepreneurship, risk-taking capital investment, and business-management capability (Weidenbaum and Hughes 1996: 4–6). The Pulitzer Prize–winning *San Jose Mercury News* has reported that overseas Chinese account for 75 percent to 90 percent of the roughly $90 billion in foreign investment in China, whose economy grew 13 percent in 1993 (Simons and Zielenziger 1994).

While the success of overseas Chinese in China is often attributed to their familiarity with the language and culture, more emphasis has been placed recently on the power of multinational networks (Hamilton 1996; Chan 1992; Seagrave 1995; Weidenbaum and Hughes 1996). Taiwan and Hong Kong entrepreneurs who had acquired manufacturing and management know-how from working in and with American companies transferred their expertise and financial resources to set up production on the mainland. There are reports of whole villages specializing in manufacturing textiles or shoes that have moved from Taiwan to Fujian, China (Jones, Frost, and White 1993: 128). The vast business network of overseas Chinese has led to a new configuration of the commodity chain within Greater China. Typically, a product would be designed in Hong Kong, which would provide financial capital and entrepreneurial, marketing, and services acumen. That product might contain a computer chip made in Taiwan, which is well known for its technical and manufacturing capability, and, more recently, for its financial capital. Then the product would be assembled in China, where land, resources, and labor are abundant.

The common factor in these diverse activities is the presence of ethnic Chinese entrepreneurs (Weidenbaum and Hughes 1996). The competitive advantage that overseas Chinese possess is so attractive that common advice to Western corporations doing business in China is to find an ethnic Chinese joint-venture partner. Many Chinese Americans are well integrated into this network. An example is Michael Wu, founder of U.S.–Asia Communication Company. Well versed in the languages and cultures of both China and America, he helps Asian firms develop marketing plans in the United States and assists Americans who are doing business in China. "A lot of Asians complain that every time the American business people stop by, they want to strike a deal. But that is not the way Asians like to do business. There should be socializing, friendship, eating together, meeting the family," Wu says (*Los Angeles Times* 1996b). U.S. corporations that have "teamed up with a bamboo network business group include such distinguished names as Chrysler, Coca-Cola, Kentucky Fried Chicken, Lockheed, Motorola, Procter & Gamble, Wal-Mart and many others" (Weidenbaum and Hughes 1996: 175). After a series of setbacks, McDonnell Douglas recently appointed the retired U.S. Army General John Fugh, a Chinese American, to head its China operation (*Wall Street Journal* 1996: 1). Similarly, when California Governor Pete Wilson opened a trade and investment office in Taipei, he chose Chiling Tong, a first-generation Chinese

American woman, to be its director (*AsianWeek* 1995). A much-discussed, controversial exploitation of ethnic ties is the solicitation of foreign contributions for domestic political campaigns. The case of John Huang, President Clinton's former fund-raiser, has brought mixed feelings in Chinese American communities and is likely to have long-range ramifications.

It is not just transnational business that is created by global capitalism but also transnational crime. Ko-lin Chin's *Chinatown Gangs* (1996) describes some of this phenomenon. Major cities around the Pacific have developed investigative forces in cooperation with others to deal with crimes that transcend national boundaries. One example is Los Angeles. The Asian Organized Crime Unit of the Los Angeles County Sheriff's Department recently received an award from the International Association of Asian Crime Investigators for its efforts. Like any diversified multinational business corporation, Asian organized-crime groups are into everything that is profitable. They hijack cars in America for customers in China, Taiwan, or Hong Kong; extort money from Chinese Americans for their kidnapped relatives in Asia; smuggle men and women from China into the United States to serve as slave labor; and traffic drugs and guns across the Pacific (Kwong 1994; *Los Angeles Times* 1996c, 1996d). Chinese Americans are not unlike other groups who mobilize their resources for economic gain in more ways than one.

Like their "straight" counterparts, Chinese Americans who have the connections to engage in multinational crime tend to be foreign born. While the living standards of the highly educated professionals and capitalists on both sides of the Pacific are drawing closer, that of the poor and disadvantaged in China and the United States are still huge. Human smuggling linking New York, Mexico, Bangkok, Fuzhou, Hong Kong, and Taiwan continues unabated because "so many are willing to travel so far for such meager returns" (Kwong 1994). These immigrants pay exorbitant fees to "snakeheads" to come to the United States to be exploited by American employers, who are often Chinese Americans.

3. Transnational Racism and the Reconfiguration of Domestic Race and Class Relations

Post-1965 immigration has changed the gender, nativity, and class composition of the Chinese American population as well as greatly diversified it. These changes do not just segment the population; they create new relationships, not just within the group, but between Chinese Americans and others. I pointed out earlier how the rise of the Pacific economy created opportunities for some but left others behind, highlighting the nativity and class cleavages. Thus, among Chinese Americans we have the exploited and the exploiters; people who live in poverty and people who spend cash to buy mansions; racists and victims of racism; people who are proud when white Americans compliment them on their fluency in English, which has taken them twenty years to achieve, and those who are angered by the same compliment, because English is their native language. Identities, whether one believes them to have essentialist qualities or to be merely constructed myths, once seemed rather clear and certain but are now fuzzy and questionable. And although they once stood firmly with other racial minorities against oppression, Chinese Americans now seem confused, sometimes feeling rejected by friends and embraced by the enemy.

Transnational racism operates to disadvantage Chinese Americans in the global economy. A familiar problem is pigeonholing. With the emphasis on the competitive advantage of Chinese Americans as bilingual and bicultural and as having access to powerful networks, a stereotypical belief is created that Chinese Americans are good at relating only to the Chinese, thus restricting their choice of careers. The Council on Foreign Relations, in an admirable effort to increase minority participation in international affairs, perhaps overemphasized the affinity of the ethnicity of constituencies to that of the foreign-affairs official (Council on Foreign Relations 1995). Chinese Americans cannot afford to be regarded as able to serve only a Chinese-related constituency or deal with Chinese-related problems, shut out from the much bigger and varied opportunities.

Asians are participating in the conspiracy of American racism. Chinese Americans report that their minority status in the United States is treated as a weakness in their dealings with Asian establishments. Chinese in Taiwan, Hong Kong, and mainland China suspect that Chinese Americans will be less effective in the United States because they are not part of mainstream corporate America. They are perceived as lacking the necessary social networks in America that can bring success to a project. Chinese are not immune to racism themselves.

4. Chinese Americans and Transnational Capitalism

The rise of economies dominated by the Chinese in Taiwan, Hong Kong, Singapore, and that giant country China, and the comparative weakening of the United States in the global economy, changed the relationship between the countries on opposite sides of the Pacific. U.S.-based capitalists (including Chinese Americans) sought cheaper and more flexible labor among immigrants (also including Chinese Americans) and abroad (including China).

Similarly, China-based capitalists are setting up production and service companies in the United States. Well known among Chinese Americans, these firms are not very visible to the general American public. Among the biggest are Tatung and Formosa USA from Taiwan and Citi Steel, a PRC investment.

Banking and real estate are two businesses with well-known Chinese transnational participation. Take real estate, for example. Hong Kong–based capitalists invested U.S. $9.9 billion in the United States in the 1980s. Taiwan investment has been even heavier, and mainland Chinese monies have also found their way into American real estate. They are joined by overseas Chinese from Indonesia, Singapore, and other Southeast Asian countries. Instead of hiring high-profile attorneys and consultants, these overseas Chinese typically use family connections or contacts in fast-growing Chinese communities (*Los Angeles Times* 1996a). Investments from the People's Republic of China have become so huge and invisible that they are causing some people alarm (Timmerman 1997). In Los Angeles, there are more than 250 Chinese American–owned real-estate companies, and in New York City, there are more than 150 (Lai 1992). The growth of Chinese American real-estate companies is clearly related to capital flight from Hong Kong and Taiwan and to the "privatization" program of China's economic reform.

Entrepreneurs here and there have started myriad businesses, from subcontracting to import-export, to take advantage of the new economic relationship. Everyone realizes that the ability to understand and interact with representatives of other cultures is of utmost importance for firms. Successful relations can entail adapting products and services to new markets; it can also help in marketing and selling them and in coping with the legal and regulatory environment in which these activities are conducted. Transnational networks created by earlier members of the Chinese diaspora are being mobilized to serve transnational capitalism. Unlike in traditional entrepreneurship, which relied on family and rotating credit unions for capital, venture capital from transnational networks is now called on to provide huge amounts for large investment projects (Park 1993). Chinese venture capital in the United States, for example, has provided start-up monies for Chinese American entrepreneurs for investment return and technology transfer (Park 1992). Nearly all the Taiwanese venture-capital firms that have invested in the U.S. high-tech industry invested in Chinese American–owned firms. Taiwanese venture capitalists, made up largely of scientists and engineers, target Taiwanese start-ups in America since they mainly rely on existing networks such as former colleagues, classmates, and friends (Tseng 1995).

Chinese Americans are integrated into the sunset and sunrise industries as workers and entrepreneurs. The former generally include apparel, shoes, and so on, and the latter, biotech, multimedia, medical equipment, and other high-tech industries. California and New York are leading the pack with the largest concentration of Chinese-owned firms, as described by Ed Park (1993) and Him Mark Lai (1992).

Chinese Americans have played a crucial role in the establishment of Silicon Valley's high-tech complex. Many well-known high-tech firms are owned mainly by Chinese Americans, such as Solectron Corporation, Unisat, Walker Interactive Systems, Integrated Device Technology Inc., ViewSonic, Trident, and so forth (*Transpacific* 1996: 50–77). More important, their transnational network across the Pacific has also contributed to the establishment of spin-off high-tech industrial complexes in Asia.

The Hsin Chu Science-based Industrial Park in Taiwan is a case in point. A survey in 1985 showed that 44 percent of the firms were foreign-owned, and 4 percent were owned by overseas Chinese firms. However, a close look at the foreign-owned firms revealed that most were owned or managed by Chinese Americans (Castells and Hall 1994: 103). The Taiwanese government seemed to have reversed the brain drain by recruiting Chinese American high-tech professionals through an agency in Silicon Valley. In fact, the first director of the Hsin Chu Park was a Chinese American who had worked for Honeywell for twenty-seven years and was its vice-president of research and development in 1981 when he was recruited by the Taiwanese government.

The new influx of Chinese-speaking immigrants fueled many new information, entertainment, and cultural industries. The popularity of karaoke, which originated in Japan but quickly spread to Taiwan, Hong Kong, and mainland China, is perhaps the most dramatic example. Commercial karaoke clubs and karaoke home parties not only serve the growth of a distinct popular culture in Chinese America, they also form, maintain, and expand a variety of networks.

Closer relations among Asian countries, including China, Taiwan, and Hong Kong, may not be so good for Chinese Americans who are likely to be left out. The huge quantity of goods shipped among ASEAN countries, Hong Kong, Taiwan, and mainland China illustrates how manufacturers are shifting their trade focus from the United States to regional markets. Taiwan's Council for Economic Planning and Development cited its own efforts to diversify export markets, the sagging American economy, the booming mainland China economy, and the imminent formation of a unified European market and the North American Free Trade Agreement as factors convincing Taiwan manufacturers to cultivate traders closer to home. "The economic blocs in Europe and North America will lead to protectionism that will reduce the business opportunities for outside traders" (*Free China Journal* 1993). This will lead more Asian countries to want to limit U.S. involvement in the politics, economy, and culture of this area. How Chinese Americans will be affected remains to be seen.

While Chinese Americans serve transnational capitalism, they are also served by it. In pursuit of self-interest, transnational capitalism broke the glass ceiling in corporate America and facilitated the individual mobility of well-educated Chinese Americans. Chinese Americans have begun to emerge in upper management, especially in corporations that have or wish to have extensive market share in Chinese-dominated economies. This is also true for nonprofit organizations, including universities, which is a reflection of the growth of the highly educated Chinese American population as well as of the demand for talented individuals who have the skills and backgrounds to tap the resources of a prospering Asia.

Scholars and the media have observed the loss of highly trained and talented individuals of less-developed countries to more developed ones, a phenomenon that has been dubbed the "brain drain." It is assumed that the flow of highly trained individuals is always just one way, and that benefits from this migration redounds only to the receiving society. I have argued elsewhere that global restructuring has rendered the concept of "brain drain" obsolete: multidirectional "brain flows" have replaced one-way "brain drain" (Cheng and Evans 1988; Ong, Cheng, and Evans 1992; Cheng and Yang 1998). The ever-increasing movement of capital, goods, and people reflect a continuously expanding world capitalist system. The highly educated professionals, being a product of a Western educational system and steeped in the ideology of individual rights and meritocracy, are becoming the first internationalized segment of the working class. They can and will go where opportunities exist. Any nation that tries to stop them is likely to be condemned as violating their "human rights." We have come to put "individual interest" above all else—the interests of community, nation, and, in fact, humanity.

5. Transnationalism as a Mode of Adaptation in the Global Economy

Transnationalism for Chinese Americans is not new. Chinese Americans historically have been transnationals. Pre–twentieth-century Chinese immigrants returned home periodically; their identity was therefore not constructed only from their experience in America. Even in the 1960s, at the height of the Civil Rights movement when Asian American identity was built on the shared experience of exclusion and oppression, there was always an international dimension—the war in Vietnam. *Roots,* the popular Asian American reader published in 1971, understood the Vietnam war as a racist war against Asians.

Transnationalism among Chinese Americans is more visible today because of changes in the global economy and the relative positions of the United States and China within it. Also, a century ago, there was a greater difference between the living standards of the United States and China, and between the Chinese immigrant workers and the U.S. general public. Immigrants earned money here (U.S.) to support families there (China). In the 1960s, well-endowed Chinese Americans emphasized their Americanness while quietly making periodic trips to visit family and friends in Asia. Today, the differences in living standards between the United States and Taiwan, Hong Kong, and Singapore are much smaller, and the professional class of Chinese immigrants, with real material, human, and social capital, is even doing much better than the majority of the U.S. public. Their transnational characteristic seems to benefit both the United States and China and themselves.

Unlike the previously established conception of immigration as one-way assimilation or integration, recent scholars are more open to considering transnational orientation not as a transitory or evolutionary phenomenon. I propose that we see transnationalism as a mode of adaptation to global capitalism. The sustained involvement of individuals in two or even more nations in work, daily living, and social networks is a "normal" way of living when opportunities are globalized and accessible; when national borders are easily crossed; and when citizenship is commoditized. As global capitalism marches on, it creates opportunities for some and disasters for others. Societies that were once relatively more egalitarian are now polarized into the super-rich versus the devastatingly poor. The gap between rich and poor is widening in China and Taiwan, as it is in the United States. How much of a gap can be tolerated by the public is a question being raised on both sides of the Pacific.

Global capitalism is welcomed as well as met with resistance and temperance. The NGOs and nonprofit organizations that focus on eradicating the ills of capitalism, patching up the tears created by it, or supporting the status quo also are forming bridges with Asia. The recent formation of the Green Party in Taiwan, which tries to bring local environmental issues to international attention, and the increasing activities of international organizations such as Amnesty International in that country are examples. Networks of Asian scholars and professionals that previously sought legitimation from Western participation now exclude it. With the end of the Cold War, NGOs in Asia and the West are reassessing their goals. Asian activists emphasize that "the new world order is not just about seeing Asia as a potential market" or "as a homogeneous mass" (Williamson 1995: 26). Like the linkages of business networks within Asia, closer relations of Asian NGOs to one another and the priority they now give to networking at local and regional levels, in contrast to earlier patterns of linking with Western NGOs, are challenging the wisdom and practice of those Chinese Americans who see themselves as bridge builders between "East" and "West."

A similar situation holds true for the labor unions. A Taiwanese company sourcing for an American apparel firm stated bluntly that the one criterion for choosing where to relocate factories in Asia is the lack of union activity. But she may be in for a surprise. Asian workers are increasingly forming linkages across national boundaries. Recent efforts of the Committee of Asian Women Workers to build a pan-Asian network of female union activists to counter the transnational exploitation of women as garment workers, foreign domestics, and sex providers is but one example (*Asian Women Workers Newsletter* 1996). Another example is provided by the Chinese Telecommunication Workers Union in Taiwan, which sought support from the Postal Telegraph and Telephone International (PTTI) against the government's privatization measures (1997). Organizations such as the Asian Regional Exchange for New Alternatives, based in Hong Kong, are picking up steam as increasing globalization affects intra-regional labor issues. Faced with the Asia Pacific Economic Cooperation (APEC) drive to turn the entire region into one giant free-trade zone by the year 2020, trade unions and various labor groups on both sides of the Pacific are cooperating to demand that APEC leaders integrate labor rights into their consultative processes (International Centre 1995). What is the role of Chinese Americans in a globalized movement of resistance?

CONCLUSION

Chinese Americans are beneficiaries and victims of "Greater China," contributors and challengers to global capitalism. Their identities, which have always had both local and transnational qualities, are being shaped by the arrival of the "Pacific Century." Some are wary that their traditionally community-based local identities will become engulfed by a Pacific Rim ideology, while others are embracing the expansion of a diasporic, global identity (Dirlik 1996).

Whatever the circumstances, Chinese Americans are not easily stereotyped, and there are multiple bridges with Asia that they can choose— or choose not—to build.

■ REFERENCES

Appelbaum, Richard, and Gary Gereffi, ed.
1994 "Power and Profits in the Apparel Commodity Chain." In *Global Production: The Apparel Industry in the Pacific Rim*, ed. Edna Bonacich, et al. Philadelphia: Temple University Press, 42–62.

Asian Wall Street Journal Weekly
1996 May 2.

AsianWeek
1994 September 30.
1995 April 29.

Asian Women Workers Newsletter
1996 Hong Kong: Committee of Asian Women Workers.

Bonacich, Edna, et al., ed.
1994 *Global Production: The Apparel Industry in the Pacific Rim*. Philadelphia: Temple University Press.

Castells, Manuel, and Peter Hall
1994 *Technopoles of the World: The Making of Twenty-First Century Industrial Complexes.* London: Routledge.

Chan, Wellington K.K.
1992 "Chinese Business Networking and the Pacific Rim: The Family Firm's Roles Past and Present," *Journal of American–East Asian Relations* 1 (spring): 1–2.

Chang, Maria Hsu
1995 "Greater China and the Chinese Global Tribe." *Asian Survey* 35, no. 10: 955–67.

Cheng, Lucie, and Edna Bonacich, ed.
1984 *Labor Immigration Under Capitalism: Asian Workers in the United States Before World War II.* Berkeley and Los Angeles: University of California Press.

Cheng, Lucie, and Leslie Evans
1988 "Brain Flow: The International Migration of the Highly Skilled—A Theoretical Introduction." Paper presented at the University of California, Los Angeles, International Workshop on the Movement of Highly Educated Labor in the Pacific Rim, Los Angeles, August 29–September 2.

Cheng, Lucie, and Gary Gereffi
1994 "U.S. Retailers and Asian Garment Production." In *Global Production*, ed. Bonacich et al., 63–79.

Cheng, Lucie, and Philip Yang
1998 "Global Interaction, Global Inequality and Migration of the Highly Trained to the U.S." *International Migration Review* 32 (fall): 626–53.

Chin, Ko-lin
1996 *Chinatown Gangs: Extortion, Enterprise, and Ethnicity.* New York: Oxford University Press.

Council on Foreign Relations
1995 Unpublished conference position paper, April 25.

Dirlik, Arif
  1996   "Asians on the Rim: Transnational Capital and Local Community in the
         Making of Contemporary Asian America." *Amerasia Journal* 22, no. 3: 1–24.
The Economist
  1988   December 24, 39–47.
Free China Journal
  1993   April 13.
Hamilton, Gary, ed.
  1996   *Asian Business Networks.* Berlin and New York: Walter de Gruyter.
Harding, Harry
  1994   *The Evolution of Greater China and What It Means for America.* New York:
         National Committee on United States–China Relations, Inc.
Huaqiao tongji yaolan (Statistical Abstracts on Overseas Chinese)
  Various years.   Taipei.
Institute on Global Conflict and Cooperation (IGCC)
  1995   *Newsletter* 11 (spring), 1.
International Centre for Human Rights and Democratic Development
  1995   News Release. Osaka, November 16.
Jones, Eric, Lionel Frost, and Colin White
  1993   *Coming Full Circle: An Economic History of the Pacific Rim.* Boulder, Colo.:
         Westview Press.
Kohut, John, and Allen T. Cheng
  1996   "Return of the Merchant Mandarins." *Asia, Inc.,* vol. 5, no. 3 (March),
         22–31.
Kwok, Reginald, and Alvin So
  1995   *The Hong Kong–Guangdong Link: Partnership in Flux.* Armonk, N.Y.: M.E.
         Sharpe.
Kwong, Peter
  1994   "China's Human Traffickers." *The Nation* (October), 422–25.
Lai, Him Mark
  1992   *Cong Huaqiao dao Huaren* (From Overseas Chinese to People of Chinese
         Descent). Hong Kong: Sanlian.
Lin, Jinzhi
  1988   *Jindai huaqiao touzi guonei qiye gailun* (A Survey of Overseas Chinese
         Investments in Domestic Enterprises). Amoy, China: Xiamen Daxue.
Liu, John, and Lucie Cheng
  1994   "Pacific Rim Development and the Duality of Post–1965 Asian Immigra-
         tion to the United States." In *The New Asian Immigration in Los Angeles and
         Global Restructuring,* ed. Paul Ong, Edna Bonacich, and Lucie Cheng.
         Philadelphia: Temple University Press.
Lopez, David E.
  1996   "Language: Diversity and Assimilation." In *Ethnic Los Angeles,* ed. Roger
         Waldinger and Mehdi Bozorgmehr. New York: Russell Sage Foundation,
         139–63.

Los Angeles Times
   1996a February 11.
   1996b February 20.
   1996c April 10.
   1996d April 12.

Mei, June
   1984 "Socioeconomic Origins of Emigration: Guangdong to California 1850–1882." In *Labor Immigration Under Capitalism,* ed. Cheng and Bonacich.

Ong, Paul, Lucie Cheng, and Leslie Evans
   1992 "Migration of Highly Educated Asians and Global Dynamics." *Asian and Pacific Migration Journal* 1, no. 3–4: 543–67.

Park, Ed
   1993 "Asian Americans in Silicon Valley: Race and Ethnicity in the Postindustrial Economy." Ph.D.diss., University of California at Berkeley.

Seagrave, Sterling
   1995 *Lords of the Rim: The Invisible Empire of the Overseas Chinese.* New York: G.P. Putnam's Sons.

Simons, Lewis M., and Michael Zielenziger
   1994 *San Jose Mercury News.* Special Report, June 26–28.

Timmerman, Kenneth
   1997 "China's 22nd Province." *American Spectator* (October), 39–45.

Transpacific
   1996 "Marching into the Asian Century." No. 64.

Tseng, Yenfen
   1995 "Beyond 'Litle Taipei': The Development of Taiwanese Immigrant Businesses in Los Angeles." *International Migration Review* 29, no. 1 (spring): 33–58.

Vogel, Ezra F.
   1991 *The Four Little Dragons: The Spread of Industrialization in East Asia.* Cambridge, Mass.: Harvard University Press.

Wall Street Journal
   1996 May 22.

Weidenbaum, Murray, and Samuel Hughes
   1996 *The Bamboo Network: How Expatriate Chinese Entrepreneurs Are Creating a New Economic Superpower in Asia.* New York: Free Press.

Williamson, Hugh
   1995 "New Agendas: European NGOs Rethink Their Strategies in Asia," *Far Eastern Economic Review,* June 15, 26.

Wu, David Yen-ho
   1975 "Overseas Chinese Entrepreneurship and Kinship Transformation: An Example from Papua New Guinea." *Journal of Ethnology,* Academia Sinica, 39 (spring): 85–105.

4

ASIAN AMERICAN ECONOMIC ENGAGEMENT

Vietnam Case Study

LE ANH TU PACKARD

I. INTRODUCTION

Vietnamese American economic engagement with Vietnam is at a formative stage. The potential of the Vietnamese diaspora to contribute to the economic development of their ancestral country is often the subject of extravagant speculation by Vietnamese both in Vietnam and abroad. The number of ethnic Vietnamese living outside Vietnam is estimated at 2.6 million;[1] some 1 million are thought to live in the United States. Like the overseas Chinese and Jewish communities—which have made rich contributions to the economic development of China and Israel, respectively—the overseas Vietnamese are portrayed in the popular press as a hardworking, well-educated, high-achieving group, and many wonder whether they can make similar contributions.

In their public statements, Vietnamese government officials are unreservedly optimistic. They are keen to tap this brainpower potential, and they talk up the filter role of the overseas Vietnamese as cultural bridges and conduits to accelerate the transfer of modern technology and management techniques. Noting the contribution of overseas Chinese who started their own "high-tech" firms in Taiwan's Hsin Chu Science-based Industrial Park,[2] they hope that their overseas compatriots will play a similar role and facilitate Vietnam's integration with the world economy.[3]

Vietnamese Americans have their own reasons for wishing to engage with their country of origin. These include the desire to remain connected with the ancestral country and with family members and friends who stayed behind. Among the younger generation, those with ambivalent feelings about American mainstream culture may seek to use this engagement to clarify and consolidate their cultural and ethnic identity. There is also the economic motive, propelled in part by the business cycle in U.S. regional economies.[4] Cyclical downturns in localities with a high concentration of Vietnamese Americans (for example, the recession in California's Orange County in the early 1990s) had an especially strong adverse effect on their ethnic Vietnamese communities. The opening of the Vietnamese economy and the introduction of market-oriented reforms came at a fortuitous moment. Many Vietnamese Americans were hard hit by the economic recession in their regions. Some were hopeful that the sea change in Vietnam would give them the opportunity to capitalize on their comparative advantage— their language and cultural skills—to develop trade and investment projects for themselves, or to use these skills in the service of foreign companies with business interests in Vietnam.

This chapter reviews in broad outline the recent history of Vietnamese American economic engagement. Policy decisions in both countries will influence how Vietnamese Americans relate to their country of origin and will shape the future path of this engagement. Clarification of nomenclature is provided in Part II (Nomenclature, Attitudes, Perceptions). We are better equipped to understand the likely time path and scope of this engagement if we do not lump the overseas Vietnamese into a single undifferentiated category. They vary from one another with respect to class background, time period of departure from Vietnam, and political stance. These differences influence the content of their engagement with Vietnam. Part III (History and Impact of Government Policy) briefly reviews past policy decisions—both Vietnamese and American—that shaped the evolution of this engagement. Part IV (Current Forms of Economic Engagement) surveys the current forms of engagement and presents preliminary findings regarding their impact on the economies and societies of both countries. Part V concludes with a discussion of future prospects for engagement.

II. NOMENCLATURE, ATTITUDES, PERCEPTIONS

How is "economic engagement" defined, and what nomenclature should be used to describe the protagonists? By the term "engagement," I include the broad set of activities undertaken by Vietnamese Americans in relation to Vietnam and residents of Vietnam that have economic consequences. As regards the protagonists, it should become evident to the reader that the ambiguities of nomenclature reflect not only the fluidity of national status but also the fluidity of cultural identity. I refer to citizens of Vietnam as "Vietnamese nationals." *Viet Kieu,* a commonly used Vietnamese term that has come to acquire a pejorative connotation, refers to persons of Vietnamese ancestry who live abroad. "Vietnamese Americans" are defined as U.S. citizens or permanent residents whose ethnic origins are Vietnamese. This *Viet Kieu* subcategory itself covers a broad spectrum. It includes newly arrived adult refugees with varying attitudes toward both their country of origin and their host country. For example, in this subset are those who consider themselves temporary exiles: they feel intensely that Vietnam belongs to them and that they have a role and a right to determine Vietnam's future. What distinguishes the "exiles" from others is their near-total obsession with their home country. Another subset are refugees who seek to build a new future in the host country. Although their interest in Vietnam remains strong, they are reconciled to the belief that Vietnam no longer belongs to them, that the country's future will be determined by those who live in Vietnam, not by those who live outside Vietnam. Yet another subset are refugee children with vivid memories of their country of origin who quickly learn to adjust to the customs and mores of their host country. There are also children of refugees born in the host country with no memories of their country of origin. Other subsets are refugees from Vietnam of Chinese descent (*nguoi goc Hoa*), children of Vietnamese descent adopted by American parents, and children of mixed marriages in which one parent is not of Vietnamese descent.

Readers familiar with Vietnam's recent history will have no trouble recognizing the imprint of that history in this discussion of nomenclature and taxonomy. With respect to the Vietnamese American population, we can identify distinct phases in the process of its assimilation into the American mainstream. We can also make the broad observation that each distinct phase is associated with a particular form of economic engagement with Vietnam. The following case history illustrates this point: the newly arrived refugee in 1978 at first sees his stay in the West as temporary, an unfortunate byproduct of the sudden rapid collapse of the Thieu government in the South. During this early phase, he frantically searches for ways to send money back to distressed relatives who were left behind in Vietnam. However, by 1995, after reuniting with these family members through the Orderly Departure Program (ODP), he considers his future (and the future of his children) more firmly rooted in America. Over time, the amount of money he sends to Vietnam will diminish if many of the recipients have themselves rejoined him through the ODP. As for his children's generation, we would not expect to see as strong a family link to Vietnam, because they will feel the opposite pull of their host country and its culture. This story, in broad outline, typifies the experience of thousands of Vietnamese American households. Aggregated, a probable time path for remittance sent to Vietnam can be hypothesized if family connections are the sole determinant of these transfers. However, they are not. Policy also matters, as I discuss in Part III.

With this example in mind, and taking into account changes in household demographics (aging parents, children growing up and forming their own households, and so on), it is reasonable to suppose that this particular form of engagement has a definable life-cycle, with a peak and eventual trough. From the U.S. macroeconomic perspective, the size of these financial outflows is insignificant. They make hardly a dent in the American balance of payments, let alone other important economic indicators. Not so for Vietnam. Estimated at around U.S. $1 billion a year, remittances by overseas Vietnamese can finance about 20 percent of the value of Vietnam's 1995 merchandise imports. These transfers also place hard currency in private hands, which reinforces the multicurrency economy and provides its citizens with partial shelter from domestic inflation. For individual families, it has given them the means not only to increase their consumption significantly relative to their non-recipient neighbors, but also to invest in business ventures as opportunities expanded during the *doi moi* (renovation) phase of Vietnam's transition to a market-oriented economy.

Eroding Stereotypes

With the opening of the Vietnamese economy, greater personal contact between Vietnamese nationals and Vietnamese Americans helped to dispel many misperceptions each had about the other. Over time, stereotypical images of rich, ostentatious, and arrogant *Viet Kieu* on the one side, and of ignorant, backward, and beggarly "country bumpkins" on the other, have been replaced by more nuanced views. Initially, Vietnamese nationals were confused by the large disparities in purchasing power between developed and developing countries. What they thought were impressively high *Viet Kieu* salaries in reality could not buy very much in the West. A stereotype often found in Vietnamese lore and narratives at the time was the rich *Viet Kieu* relative who provided capital to entrepreneurial households. An example from the Vietnamese theater is a biting satire of Vietnam's early experience with the market economy called *Tro doi* (The Game of Life), which played to full houses in Hanoi during the early 1990s. This play chronicled the rise to riches of husband–wife owners of a restaurant specializing in keg beer and dog-meat delicacies. Seed money for the restaurant came from the couple's *Viet Kieu* aunt in Paris. Many visiting *Viet Kieu* were loath to dispel this myth because it allowed them to enjoy the respect and attention that they could not command in the West (as poor new immigrants).

Ironically, an unintended effect of Vietnam's outward-oriented policies and strong economic performance during the early and mid-1990s was to accelerate the demise of the myth of the rich *Viet Kieu*. The new climate gave increasing numbers of Vietnamese nationals the opportunity to travel abroad for business, study, and even pleasure. They were able to see for themselves, and to report back on, how their *Viet Kieu* friends and relatives actually lived. Over time, the local "bumpkins" became more sophisticated and better versed in technology and international business practices. A proliferation of computer classes sponsored by government offices and private firms gave rise to a rapidly expanding pool of computer-literate young Vietnamese professionals. Bookstores in Vietnamese cities abounded in translations of well-known business and law publications[5] that introduce Vietnamese readers to trends in the global economy and market economics. Thus, as Vietnamese nationals have become better acquainted with the global marketplace and its technology, their awe for their "worldly" *Viet Kieu* cousins has diminished.

What about the *Viet Kieu* perspective? Not surprisingly, there is considerable variation in how members of this group view their country of origin. Those more actively engaged with Vietnam have different perceptions from those who are less engaged. Ideology and political orientation also matter. This diversity of views was apparent in an informal survey of Vietnamese Americans conducted by the author in 1995 and 1996. For news of Vietnam, many said that they relied on first- and secondhand reports by friends and relatives. Other news sources cited were the foreign press and *Viet Kieu* newspapers. Reflecting technological advances, many professionals also reported obtaining their news from electronic mail and the Internet. Asked whether the *doi moi* reforms were on balance good for Vietnam, and whether these reforms made Vietnam a friendlier place for overseas Vietnamese, a few said yes. The rest were almost evenly divided between those who said no and agnostics who said they did not know. Interestingly, even those who were "bullish" on Vietnam were deeply pessimistic about the outlook for *Viet Kieu* economic engagement. They believed that most overseas Vietnamese investments in Vietnam were unsuccessful. Given the absence of reliable data on this subject, their perception strongly suggests that word of mouth within the overseas community continues to be a powerful force. It is also consistent with their reported high level of reliance on friends and relatives for news of Vietnam. Reflecting the tendency of emotional views to cloud the facts, most of the respondents underestimated by a substantial factor the actual value of approved foreign-investment projects in Vietnam.

Their opinion of business opportunities in Vietnam ranged from "not good" to "excellent"; nearly half believed that the opportunities were "fair," and less than one-third believed that they were "very good." Except for a very small minority who rated the opportunities "excellent," the rest believed that they were "not good." Curiously, there was no apparent correlation between their evaluation of business opportunities and their assessment of the annual rate of return they believed was required by foreign investors. Approximately 20 percent of those who gave a "fair" rating thought that a return in the range of 6 percent to 10 percent would be acceptable. In general, their responses followed a normal (bell-shaped) distribution, with most believing that a rate of return in the 21 percent to 35 percent range was acceptable, followed by equal numbers believing that rates of return in the 11 percent to 20 percent and in the 36 percent to 60 percent range were acceptable. These responses are significant regardless of whether the answers are "correct," because they are indicative of the level of knowledge and expectations many Vietnamese Americans have, which color their approach to economic engagement.

III. HISTORY AND IMPACT OF GOVERNMENT POLICY

In an enlightened world, nations with diverse ethnic populations see value in their citizens' bicultural attributes. "Hyphenated" citizens are natural bridges. They can help expand mutually beneficial relations between their host country and their country of origin. Yet this does not often happen for reasons that can be traced to the emotionally scarring historical experiences of nations and individuals. Vietnam is such a case. For more than two decades, the attitude and policy of both governments toward Vietnamese American engagement was colored by the degree of hostility and suspicion each felt toward the other. During the Cold War years, U.S. policy was not concerned with helping Vietnamese Americans connect with their homeland. For the Vietnamese refugee population, the anguish caused by war and loss of homeland did not warm them to Vietnam or to its new rulers. Nevertheless, they were willing to put aside their distaste for the communist government in order to maintain contact with family members. Thus, by default, it was the

Vietnamese government's own attitude and policy toward the *Viet Kieu* that became the single most important factor in determining the tenor and progress of Vietnamese American engagement. This policy was determined by the state of Vietnam's foreign relations. Thus, when the government had cordial relations with the West, it was reflected in its friendlier attitude toward the *Viet Kieu*. When relations with the West soured, that, too, was reflected in the government's more suspicious and unfriendly stance.[6]

U.S. Government Policy

Before 1975, the Vietnamese American population in the United States numbered only in the thousands. Following the collapse of the U.S.-supported regime in southern Vietnam, the exodus of refugees caused this population to balloon to the hundreds of thousands. They left behind mothers, fathers, brothers, sisters, sons, daughters, uncles, aunts. Often with help from government agencies, refugee-resettlement organizations, neighbors, friends, and church groups, the newly arrived refugees found jobs, made use of various educational and job-training opportunities to better their lives, and laid down roots in their newly adopted communities. As soon as they could, they looked for ways to reestablish contact with loved ones in Vietnam.

Whatever their desires, their actual behavior was circumscribed by institutional factors, the laws and regulations in both countries that defined what was permissible regarding the interactions between the *Viet Kieu* and their loved ones in Vietnam. These factors also shaped their perceptions of the options available to them, which limited even further the range of activities in which the refugees actually engaged. Inadequate access to information compounded misperceptions about U.S. law, especially during the 1975–79 period (Packard 1976). For example, before the U.S. trade embargo was lifted, when Vietnam was officially a Category Z country under the Trading with the Enemy Act, many Vietnamese Americans were confused about what activities would be considered legal and what would be considered illegal by U.S. government authorities. Most did not know the actual content of this act, and consequently feared that any contact with persons living in Vietnam would be considered illegal.

An early pioneer of Vietnamese American economic engagement was the Vinamex Corporation, a New York-based company founded by a group of Vietnamese Americans to facilitate fund transfers between residents of the United States and Vietnamese nationals and to distribute Vietnamese publications to North American subscribers. Ngo Thanh Nhan, a principal of Vinamex, recalled the 1977–78 period, when even Vinamex's staff were unsure of the legality of these fund transfers. To avoid the risk of breaking the law, Vinamex in the beginning took care to avoid becoming involved in the actual transfer of funds. Instead, it provided information to refugees to help them use remittance channels set up by *Viet Kieu* associations in France and Canada,[7] which had friendly relations with the Vietnamese government. They explained to the refugees what was permitted by law and what was not.[8] Under the Trading with the Enemy Act, any financial transaction by an American individual or organization must be licensed by the U.S. government (Charney and Spragens 1984: 2). However, relatives were allowed to send money to their families in Vietnam in amounts up to $300 in any three-month period, or $750 on a one-time basis, for the purpose of emigration (Charney and Spragens 1984: 6).

Since the U.S. trade embargo was lifted and relations between the two countries have become normalized, the U.S. government's stance on Vietnamese American economic engagement has become more neutral. It has done away with ceilings that had been imposed on the amount of money American residents could send to Vietnam. However, many, including the government of Vietnam, consider the FBI's anti-espionage campaign to be an unfriendly diplomatic gesture. In March 1996, leading newspapers in North America and Asia[9] reported that the FBI had posted advertisements in Vietnamese-language newspapers in the United States asking readers to denounce suspected spies of the government of Vietnam. Among the *Viet Kieu* there was considerable outrage[10] because of the campaign's polarizing effect on communities that already suffered from a surfeit of political strife. Although the FBI denied any intent to intimidate, many Vietnamese Americans acknowledge that the threat of FBI scrutiny has caused them to feel uneasy about developing business ties with Vietnam.

As diplomatic and trade relations between the two countries continued to progress, however, the U.S. attitude toward engagement became increasingly sympathetic. A September 1997 report from the American Embassy in Hanoi[11] was remarkably informative about the effect of new legal and regulatory changes on the status of overseas Vietnamese returning to Vietnam. To convey both its extraordinarily positive tone and content, an excerpt is reproduced:

> Recognizing that a market economy cannot flourish without a rational, predictable, and secure legal environment, one crucial area prioritized for reform in Vietnam is the law. The country has passed many new laws and law codes in recent years. . . . The new laws have increased transparency and have measurably improved the business environment. Changes to Vietnamese law mak[ing] it easier for overseas Vietnamese to return, live and

work have succeeded in persuading many *"Viet Kieu"* to return to Vietnam and contribute to its growth. Previously, a Vietnamese citizen was allowed to sponsor only immediate family members over the age of 60 for return. This limited the number of returning Vietnamese to only five hundred or so between 1975 and the end of 1996.

The new regulation eliminates age restrictions and allows a Vietnamese citizen to sponsor extended family members. Overseas Vietnamese without family here, but with a "constructive" purpose including investing and transferring western high technology and education, can seek sponsorship by a government organization. Returnees are allowed to retain the citizenship of their adopted country. Approximately an additional five hundred *Viet Kieu* have returned in the first six months of 1997 due to the easing of the restrictions. Overseas Vietnamese are returning mostly from the U.S., Canada, Australia and other Western and Northern European countries. Most opt to live in the large cities such as Hanoi, [Ho Chi Minh City], Hai Phong and Da Nang, where there is a greater scope for lucrative business investment.

Currently the Vietnamese government is considering revising its citizenship laws to benefit overseas Vietnamese. Until now, Vietnam has not recognized dual citizenship status. The absence of Vietnamese citizenship makes it almost impossible for *Viet Kieu* to register or sell their property. As such, the government is reviewing the issue of dual citizenship and has requested the ministry of justice to put forth recommendations based on a series of meetings with representatives of Vietnamese communities in other countries.

Vietnamese Government Policy

Similarly, the Vietnamese government's attitude and policy toward the *Viet Kieu* since 1975 has not been consistent.[12] Its stance has been alternately (and sometimes simultaneously) welcoming and hostile.[13] On the one hand, the president of the Vietnam Union of Science and Technology Associations (VUSTA) in Hanoi declares that his government's policy is "to invite [the *Viet Kieu*] to come home because we desperately need their training and know-how" (DeVoss 1995). At the same time, visiting *Viet Kieu* wonder how welcome they really should feel in light of the notorious Politburo directive[14] calling for strict control of communication channels such as telephone, fax, and e-mail to curb activities that the Vietnamese Communist Party considers hostile. This ambivalence also is displayed in the bewildering procession of resolutions and decrees that govern relations with the *Viet Kieu*.[15] Even the most recent government ruling, Decision 767/TTg signed by former Prime Minister Vo Van Kiet on September 17, 1997, grants special privileges (reduced visa fees and price discounts similar to those enjoyed by Vietnamese nationals), but only to defined categories of overseas Vietnamese such as those "who are activists in the patriotic movement of Vietnamese abroad, and who are intellectuals invited to visit and work in the country by competent agencies." This sends a warning to the overseas Vietnamese community that the history of past allegiances continues to factor into policy decisions in Vietnam.

IV. CURRENT FORMS OF ECONOMIC ENGAGEMENT

There is a "building block" relationship between the different forms of engagement. Participation in one type of activity very often lays the groundwork for becoming involved in other activities. Thus, individuals and families who have one type of engagement with Vietnam are more likely to participate in other types of engagement. Remittance is an example. Sending money to loved ones, by building trust and reinforcing family and friendship ties, creates opportunities for overseas donor families and their relatives in Vietnam jointly to explore and develop business projects.

Remittances

Sending money to loved ones, who are generally but not exclusively family members, has been and continues to be the most common form of economic engagement. The primary reasons for sending money are to assist the family, especially to support aging parents, and to refurbish ancestral gravesites. With respect to family maintenance, funds earmarked for consumption are generally spent on home improvements; home furnishings, including household durable goods (refrigerators, stoves); consumer electronics (television sets, radios and cassette players); and transportation vehicles (bicycles, Honda motorcycles). Not surprisingly, donor families prefer to finance what can be broadly characterized as investment projects so recipient families can eventually achieve economic independence. These include buying a house, paying for schooling, and providing seed money to finance family enterprises. From the perspective of donor families, this form of engagement has both positive and negative aspects. On the positive side, it promotes goodwill, strengthens family bonds, and lays the groundwork for future family cooperation in other spheres, including business ventures. On the negative side, many donor families worry about contributing to excessive dependence and a "beggar" mentality among their relatives in Vietnam.

There is a defined "life-cycle" aspect to this form of engagement. It is driven by demographics and by Vietnam's economic-development trajectory. The hypothesis is as follows: first, remittances earmarked for economic dependents in Vietnam, especially aging parents, will cease when they die. It is also likely to cease, or at least decline considerably, when the donors, usually members of the first generation, themselves die, and their second-generation children feel less committed to sending money to relatives in Vietnam. Second, economic changes in both countries also influence the flow of remittances. Changes in the level of remittances are negatively correlated with the level of economic prosperity in Vietnam and only somewhat positively correlated with the state of the U.S. economy (which determines how much discretionary income donor families have at their disposal to send to Vietnam).

More research is needed to determine how much weight should be placed on the second variable (the state of the U.S. economy), because a significant portion of remittances to Vietnam may be viewed by donor families as essential non-discretionary spending and invariant with respect to changes in family income. Indeed, the state of the Vietnamese economy may matter more. If the Vietnamese economy can maintain into the next decade a high rate of growth, similar to that recorded during the mid-1990s, many donor families will see less need to send money to their increasingly prosperous relatives in Vietnam.

While the flow of remittances will eventually decrease because of these "life-cycle" considerations, it has not yet peaked for two reasons. First, transaction costs (for sending money to Vietnam) are still in the process of declining as donor families rely less on the occasional personal courier and more on established commercial channels such as banks and Vietnamese American companies that specialize in providing services between families in the United States and Vietnam. Second, as the length of their stay in the United States has increased, the donor families' income-earning capacity (and hence their capacity to give) has also increased (Gordon 1989: 30).

Throughout the late 1970s and 1980s, most recipient families suffered severe economic hardship because the Vietnamese economy was itself in a state of crisis (Ronnas and Sjoberg 1990: viii–ix). During this period, many *Viet Kieu* families felt moved to send money and presents to ease their relatives' impoverished circumstances. Fortunately for them, they did not have to take much out of their salaries to make a difference in the living conditions of their relatives. Because of the very low cost of living in Vietnam, even U.S.$20 a month—the equivalent of the average state worker's salary—went a long way. After reliable channels for transferring funds were established, many donor families reported sending U.S.$1,000 to U.S.$4,000 a year to relatives in Vietnam. This allowed the fortunate recipients to live extremely well relative to their neighbors. Today, the cost of living in Vietnam has risen appreciably, so the purchasing power of U.S.$20 is a fraction of what it used to be. At the same time, the income-generating capability of households in Vietnam is much greater than it used to be. By 1989, the *doi moi* reforms and Vietnam's transition to a market economy had begun to open up new economic opportunities. Some recipient families were able to take advantage of these opportunities and became prosperous. In many of these cases, not only did they not need any more financial aid from their overseas relatives, but often they insisted on feting their *Viet Kieu* relations in grand style when they returned to visit.

CASE NUMBER ONE. During the 1980s, a well-to-do physician living in Pennsylvania began to send money on a regular basis to several of his brothers who lived with their children in Ho Chi Minh City and Hanoi. By 1992, Vietnam had discarded Soviet-style central planning and launched comprehensive economic reforms; at this point, his family asked for seed money to take advantage of new economic opportunities that had emerged. The physician readily agreed for several reasons: first, he wanted to help his brothers' families become financially independent so they would not have to rely on his help in the future; second, having visited them in Vietnam, he was confident of their ability to manage their business venture, which was to assemble garments for export; and third, he had substantial means and was personally interested in exploring projects that might yield attractive returns. The garment business did moderately well. The family in Ho Chi Minh City, which enjoyed the happy combination of entrepreneurial skills and strong political connections (one of his nieces was an officer in the Vietnam People's Army), eventually branched into the construction industry and other sectors catering to domestic demand, which during the mid-1990s was rising more rapidly than external demand. They soon shifted their focus to their new business ventures, which they considered more promising than the highly competitive, low-margin garment business. At the time of this writing, the family businesses are thriving, and the Vietnamese families no longer need financial help from their *Viet Kieu* brother. When he visited them in the fall of 1995, they greeted him at the airport in a brand new Toyota car and insisted on taking him to Ho Chi Minh City's most sumptuous restaurants. Although very happy about his family's economic success, the Pennsylvania physician is placing on hold his own plans to invest in Vietnam because he is uncomfortable with local business practices. "I think I have been living in the U.S. too long," he explains. "Here we are careful to do everything within the law, because it's not worth it to get into trouble with the IRS. In Vietnam, people are used to fudging their books and hiding as much from the authorities as possible. I understand why they do it that way, but it makes me nervous, so I think I'll stay out until things change more and I can trust the legal system."

CASE NUMBER TWO. A young California-raised *Viet Kieu* attorney, who is currently living in Hong Kong, regularly flies to Hanoi and Ho Chi Minh City to conduct business for her firm. She is pleased that her employment has given her the opportunity to become more familiar with her Vietnamese counterparts and to gain what she says is a more realistic picture of the situation in Vietnam today. From a professional point of view, she believes that her Vietnam experience will give her an edge in the highly competitive California legal environment. "Things were very tough," she says. "Too many lawyers and not enough work to go around. I had to figure out what I could do to make myself stand out from the crowd. With my Vietnam experience, I have something special to bring to the table." Her priority and filial mission, however, is to realize her parents' deepest wishes regarding their family in Vietnam. Speaking with great feeling, she revealed that her parents' emotional ties to family who remained in Vietnam, as well as their feelings of guilt for leaving their aging parents, were so powerful that they were moved to send, over a fifteen-year period, what eventually added up to more than U.S.$30,000 to various family members. "My parents were always very sad about leaving Vietnam and leaving behind their family in Vietnam," she says. "It is a sadness that touches me deeply because they are my parents, so I can't help but feel strongly their pain. When I arrived in Vietnam, one of the first things I did was to go visit our relatives, which my parents had urged me to do, because they wanted to know if the money they sent was well spent. Well, what I saw made me feel upset. My parents worked very hard all the time; they scrimped and saved so there would be enough money to send to our relatives. They could have been using that money for their own pleasure, but instead they sacrificed and denied themselves a lot of pleasure for the sake of the family in Vietnam. Anyway, I got upset when I saw that some of our relatives in Vietnam were simply living like parasites off my parents' hard work. Instead of using the money constructively, to make something of their lives, they were lazy and lived extravagantly. I didn't have the heart to tell my parents about that. But now that I'm going to Vietnam on a regular basis, I intend to look after my family's interests, protect my parents, make sure that the money they send through me will be put to proper use, like education for the children or seed money for family members who want to set up their own businesses."

These case histories are illustrative and reflect the experience and views of many individuals, but they capture only a small part of the larger story.

Unfortunately, to date, there is not much survey data[16] to provide a fuller picture of how Vietnamese Americans relate to their country of origin. We see a partial glimpse from the initial results of a small sample survey conducted in 1995 by Anne Talsma,[17] a university student who polled forty-four Vietnamese Americans from Michigan and California and a self-selected group from the Internet. The respondents in the Talsma survey do not constitute a representative sample because they are better educated and earn higher incomes than the underlying Vietnamese American population, and because they are predisposed to respond to academic surveys. Nevertheless, their answers are instructive. With respect to remittances, 63.6 percent reported that they send money to Vietnam on a regular basis; 17.9 percent send money less than once a year; 64.3 percent send money several times a year; and 17.9 percent send money at least once a month. All the respondents said their purpose was to support family members in Vietnam. Asked about their usual channels for sending money, 3.6 percent said they used direct mail, 14.3 percent used bank transfer, and an overwhelming majority—71.4 percent—used a personal courier. To analyze the impact over time of policy-induced changes in the legal and financial infrastructure governing remittances sent to Vietnam, as well as anticipated changes in the financial circumstances of both donors and recipients, a representative annual survey will be useful to monitor changes in remittance patterns and channels.

Tourism

The *Viet Kieu* did not return to Vietnam in large numbers as visitors until they were made to feel reasonably welcome. This did not happen until 1989, when the government's open-door policy became noticeable. That year, more than 31,000 *Viet Kieu* returned to visit. The following year, 30 percent more went. Of the more than 40,500 *Viet Kieu* who returned in 1990, nearly 16,000—roughly 40 percent—came from the United States. Some 5,600 came from France, 5,400 from Australia, and 3,600 from Canada (Marr 1993: 350, 357).[18]

After the U.S. normalized relations with Vietnam in 1994, many Vietnamese Americans felt safer returning for a visit. They relied mainly on word of mouth, and the word-of-mouth experience was generally reassuring. Tales by returning travelers, even when peppered with unpleasant vignettes of grasping relatives and corrupt customs officials, whetted their listeners' desire to go back to see for themselves what present-day Vietnam was like, especially after the much-touted *doi moi* reforms. As more Vietnamese Americans made the journey, communist-but-reforming Vietnam became better known and less frightening. Where fear of unknown dangers had previously been the primary impediment to travel, lack of time, money, or interest became the more important obstacles.

Tet, the Vietnamese Lunar New Year, is the peak visiting period for *Viet Kieu* because it is the traditional time for families to reunite. It is the most important holiday on the Vietnamese calendar, a period of such heavy consumer spending that statisticians take into account the "Tet" effect in their analyses of price fluctuations. It is also a very busy travel period even for the domestic population, because it is the time when urban Vietnamese return to their ancestral villages and exchange gifts. For these reasons, it is not surprising that Vietnam specialists estimate that on average, taking into account both gifts and assorted expenditures while in Vietnam, visiting families add about U.S. $4,500 each to the Vietnamese economy. Thus, in 1995 *Viet Kieu* visitors are estimated to have injected about U.S.$800 million into the economy.

There is significant overlap between families who send money home and families who return to visit. Those sending money home are more likely to visit, because both forms of engagement indicate strong emotional links with the home country. In addition, visiting *Viet Kieu* are often asked to bring in money on behalf of others, so the large sums of money brought in by *Viet Kieu* travelers are not solely gifts for family members or for their own personal expenditure. The widespread use of couriers is due to distrust of the state. They do not wish to give the government any opportunity to have access to information about inter-family transfers because they are afraid that the money will be confiscated or taxed. Since 1995, the overseas Vietnamese have been finding it easier to send money more cheaply through official channels. For example, one *Viet Kieu* physician sends money via Chemical Bank, which uses Vietcombank to effect the fund transfer. While some overseas Vietnamese experiment with new channels, old habits and suspicions do not disappear overnight, especially when they are reinforced by arbitrary changes in state regulations. For example, in May 1996 the government imposed a 5 percent tax on every fund transfer of more than 2 million Vietnamese dongs (about U.S.$180). VINA USA, a private company based in Ho Chi Minh City that provides remittance services, reported that its turnover fell by about 50 percent after that policy was introduced. The tax was eventually rescinded after it became apparent that its main impact was to reduce sharply the flow of remittances through official channels.

CASE NUMBER THREE. Mrs. L. is a Chinese Vietnamese hospital worker who came with her husband and three children to Philadelphia in 1981. She has no close family members left in Vietnam, but her husband does. On learning that T., a friend, was planning a trip to Vietnam in 1990, Mrs. L. asked T. to take U.S.$1,500 in cash for her husband's brother. This elderly man was then living in Cho Lon, the twin city of Ho Chi Minh City (Saigon), which is home to Vietnam's ethnic Chinese population. T. returned with letters and gifts from Mrs. L's brother-in-law and his family. After reestablishing contact through T., the two families in Philadelphia and Cho Lon began to correspond on a regular basis, and on special occasions they even talked on the telephone. Mrs. L. says she would like to return to Vietnam to visit one day when she has enough time and enough money, but for her it is not a high priority. Today she has more important concerns, such as finding a good house to buy and making sure that her children are making the most of their educational opportunities. Her brother's family visited Hong Kong, Taiwan, and Vietnam in the summer of 1994 and reported that they had a good time. Mrs. L. reports that during the summer of 1996, more than half of her fifteen ethnic Vietnamese hospital co-workers, many of whom are former ARVN[19] officers, decided to go to Vietnam for a visit. To ensure continuous coverage, the hospital asked that they stagger their vacations, so they were not able to travel to Vietnam in one large group as they had wished. Mrs. L. laughed heartily upon telling this story because, as she explained, these former ARVN officers were staunch anticommunists who hated and distrusted Vietnam's present rulers. They had never given any indication that they were interested in traveling to Vietnam, she said, until some of their friends made the trip and recounted their experiences. Then, when some made the decision to go, everyone suddenly wanted to go see for themselves what *"doi moi"* Vietnam was like.

Philanthropy

Today, *Viet Kieu* from all walks of life are engaged in a broad range of philanthropic activities related to Vietnam. Vietnamese American professionals living in the San Francisco Bay Area have a tradition of organizing successful concerts and other cultural events to raise funds for people-to-people humanitarian-aid projects. Ethnic Vietnamese physicians and other health workers have joined volunteer medical teams who spend their vacation time working without charge in hospitals and clinics in Vietnam. To honor their father's memory, a group of siblings expanded the scholarship fund he had started for indigent high-school students in Hue, their hometown. A growing number of churches and pagodas in Vietnam rely largely on *Viet Kieu* contributions to finance their renovation projects. A Vietnamese American woman whose dramatic autobiography was turned into a major Hollywood movie established a multimillion-dollar foundation to support medical clinics, schools, and orphanages in her home province in Central Vietnam. Visiting *Viet Kieu* professors and social workers contributed to support a foundation set up by intellectuals in Vietnam to promote research and publish books on child psychology. To preserve historical documents written in *Nom,* a writing system based on ideographic script used by the Vietnamese since the tenth century, a group of Vietnamese American computer professionals joined forces to design the first *Nom* Proper Code Table.[20]

These examples illustrate the diversity of Vietnamese American philanthropic activity and its continuing evolution. Reflecting generational changes in Vietnamese American society, the more traditional forms of giving, such as donating to church or pagoda reconstruction or involvement in family projects to assist the ancestral village, coexist with Western forms of philanthropy. In the latter instance, individuals—related to one another not by blood but by shared interests and values—work together in nonprofit organizations to implement common philanthropic objectives. The importance of these philanthropic activities lies in their potential to support the creation and development of civil society in Vietnam.

In the transitional economies of Asia, Eastern Europe, and the former Soviet Union, widespread concern about the breakdown in society's moral values has lent immediacy to the age-old desire to build civil society. The yearning for a "peaceful civic space"—long celebrated in Greek, Norse, and Hindu mythology—becomes urgent in times of social disorder. Even in India in the third century B.C.E., the Emperor Ashoka recognized the need to support what we today would agree is a basic tenet of civil society: the building of community based on mutual social concern and shared social responsibility (Boulding 1988: 8–10). And so it is with Vietnam. Many families interviewed by the author openly worry about the erosion of traditional values. They wonder whether the economic transformation of Vietnam will widen inequalities and produce a selfish, amoral society. Like other traditional Asian families, they fear the effects of Western pop culture, which their adolescent children find so seductively exotic. They worry that it will cause their children to lose interest in their own cultural heritage and abandon traditional values, including respect for their elders.

How can *Viet Kieu* philanthropy alleviate these concerns? By supporting cultural events and helping to make accessible ancient arts and traditions, Vietnamese American philanthropy generally reaffirms traditional Vietnamese values of altruism and the preservation of culture.[21] By example, it encourages private-sector growth of caring social entities and directly assists in the growth and development of nongovernment organizations (NGOs). During periods of social change and upheaval, NGOs play a stabilizing role by contributing to the social safety net. For this reason, measures of human development have begun to use as a variable the number of in-country NGOs to represent the status of civil-society development.

Sharing Professional Skills

Opening to the outside world, Vietnam became an official participant in the United Nations TOKTEN program, which is designed to "reverse the Third World brain drain." Under TOKTEN sponsorship, developing-country professionals working in the industrialized countries could return to their country of origin for a fixed period to share professional skills and "technological know-how." However, poor governance and ineffective implementation caused the program's resources to be vastly underutilized. Bypassing the TOKTEN framework, *Viet Kieu* professionals in significant numbers have made independent contact with interested nationals to share their knowledge. Visiting *Viet Kieu* computer professionals have shared software and technical skills with their national counterparts. *Viet Kieu* business-school professors, accountants, economists, and lawyers have participated in seminars organized by enterprising state agencies[22] to teach state enterprise managers about global marketing and market economics. Through skills sharing, these *Viet Kieu* professionals and their local counterparts have become better acquainted with one another and established good working relationships. For many, it has laid the groundwork for collaboration in other areas, including business ventures.

Scholarly Research and Academic Exchanges

This form of engagement is at an embryonic stage. While many *Viet Kieu* students and scholars have traveled to Vietnam for educational reasons, the numbers thus far are not significant. They will grow as the search for roots among younger Vietnamese American students leads increasing numbers to elect to do their academic fieldwork and student-exchange programs in Vietnam.[23] A growing number of Vietnamese American college graduates have chosen to embark on a course of independent study in Vietnam for a period of time—usually from three to eighteen months. The topics are varied. History, anthropology, literature, the arts, environmental studies, ethnic studies, community health, traditional medicine, and agriculture appear to be popular choices. Summer study programs also have been developed for high-school students.[24]

Working for Foreign NGOs and Foreign Corporations

International organizations tend to have ambivalent views about hiring West-ern-trained *Viet Kieu* professional staff. The latter's ability to cut through language and cultural barriers is considered a strong advantage. At the same time, there is concern that they may have private agendas that could conflict with the objectives of the organization.[25] Regarding *Viet Kieu* staff with responsibility for managing local hires and interacting with local officials, suppliers, and distributors, they may have contradictory fears. They worry about potential friction between *Viet Kieu* and local staff.[26] They also worry that *Viet Kieu* staff, acting as cultural bridges and go-betweens, may withhold vital information to make themselves indispensable.[27]

For their part, *Viet Kieu* staff gripe about the three-tier compensation system, a widely practiced form of wage discrimination. Under this system, expatriate country managers receive living expenses and other hardship-post allowances in addition to their regular salary. *Viet Kieu* employees often are not given the hardship-post allowance. Reflecting low wages in the local labor market, Vietnamese nationals are paid considerably less. According to *Viet Kieu* professionals, this three-tier compensation system creates resentment among local employees, who feel that *Viet Kieu* staff should work longer hours because they are paid more. As a result of these and other problems, many *Viet Kieu* professionals in Ho Chi Minh City report suffering from severe stress, which they attribute to their bicultural characteristics. They complain of not feeling fully trusted by their employers, who, they say, exploit their desire to connect with their homeland to pay them less than Westerners with equivalent skills.

They also feel that the government's attitude toward them is ambigu-ous. For example, they are uncertain about how to interpret the govern-ment's actions in the high-profile arrest of Nguyen Trung Truc, a fellow *Viet Kieu* and former managing director of Peregrine (an investment company that went bankrupt in 1998), on tax-evasion charges.[28] They wonder if it should be read as a hostile move by party hardliners who fear a *Viet Kieu* role in fomenting "peaceful evolution" in Vietnam.[29] Another view holds that Truc did break the law, but in Vietnam's murky business environment, the authorities have "the goods" on many lawbreakers who go unprosecuted. Thus, the decision to prosecute Truc may have been the result of infighting among the ruling elite.

The "Peregrine incident" and similar experiences are indicative of the complex and ambiguous environment in Vietnam during the transition pe-riod of the 1990s. The system of "cronyism" endemic in Vietnam is not vastly different from business practices commonly found elsewhere in Asia.

From this perspective, Vietnamese Americans working in this environment are in a situation similar to that of other Asian Americans working in their countries of origin, whether it is in China, Thailand, Indonesia, Malaysia, the Philippines, or Korea. At the same time, *Viet Kieu* employees of organizations that possess substantial international "clout," such as the World Bank, Citibank, or Proctor & Gamble, enjoy greater protection from arbitrary actions by the authorities. Like other expatriate professionals, they are in the habit of operating in more transparent and predictable business environments, and their business behaviors tend to follow internationally accepted norms. Through extensive contact with indigenous affiliates, they become conduits for transmitting internationally accepted business practices to the local economy, helping to facilitate and cement Vietnam's integration with the world economy.

Participating in Family-Run Businesses

While this form of economic engagement has a rich anecdotal history, it is difficult to capture in statistical detail because business arrangements made between the principals tend to be informal. Trust between the major parties is necessarily very high: rarely are legal documents involved. Most *Viet Kieu* investment is covert because the protagonists deeply distrust the state and fear the loss of their investment. Consequently, they are reluctant to provide any information to any state authority.[30] The desire to avoid taxes is another important factor. For these reasons, officially registered *Viet Kieu* investment is insignificant: it amounts to less than 1 percent of total registered foreign investment. As of May 1997, the government has licensed fifty-seven *Viet Kieu* projects capitalized at U.S.$223 million;[31] twenty-three of these projects, capitalized at U.S.$148.9 million, are in Ho Chi Minh City. However, it is widely believed that this sum represents the tip of the iceberg. If just 25 percent of annual remittances to Vietnam were used to finance business ventures, including micro-enterprises, the *Viet Kieu* would rank among Vietnam's top-ten foreign investors.

The experience of developing economies with Vietnam's profile indicate that prosperity is most quickly achieved in an export-oriented environment that is friendly to small private businesses. Strengthening this sector's viability is essential if the domestic economy is to avoid becoming wholly dominated by state enterprises and foreign corporations and their joint ventures. *Viet Kieu* participation in family-run businesses has the potential to help strengthen the micro-enterprise and export-oriented small-business sector. It is commonly known that many thriving family enterprises in Vietnam received their initial financial boost from overseas family members. These *Viet Kieu* relatives played a critical mentoring role, sharing market smarts and operating as go-betweens to foreign customers. *Viet Kieu* participants in family-run businesses tend to be older than 35 years of age and have close ties with family members in Vietnam, some business experience, and some accumulated savings. Typically, they are motivated by the desire to help family members prosper economically and, in varying degrees, to share in that prosperity. During the 1990–95 period, the most popular investments with *Viet Kieu* participation were family run mini-hotels, cafés, and storefront shops offering services such as photocopying, appliance sales, and equipment repairs. Given the *Viet Kieu* partner's own prior business experience and comparative advantage, these family-run businesses tend to be concentrated in the tourism sector and other areas of business with an external orientation. These are areas in which the *Viet Kieu* investor has 1) comparatively greater knowledge to identify income-generating opportunities, and 2) the skills needed to implement the business plan. In one particular instance, the initiative for a family business project, manufacturing handknit sweaters, came from the family in Vietnam. However, design suggestions and international marketing contacts came from *Viet Kieu* relatives in the United States and Europe.

Business Ventures

As noted earlier, despite legislation giving *Viet Kieu* investors favorable tax treatment, by official tally the overseas Vietnamese account for less than 1 percent of all foreign investment in Vietnam. In contrast, the overseas Chinese account for about 80 percent of all foreign investment in China. What explains the difference? First, the Chinese government's attitude toward the overseas Chinese is genuinely friendlier than the Vietnamese government's toward overseas Vietnamese. Second, the overseas Chinese population dwarfs the overseas Vietnamese population in both numbers and economic clout; thus, the overseas Chinese are in a position to contribute more. Some 55 million ethnic Chinese live outside China; fewer than 3 million ethnic Vietnamese live outside Vietnam. Moreover, the Chinese diaspora began much earlier than the Vietnamese, which means that the overseas Chinese have had more time to build up their vast economic base. The combined annual output of the overseas Chinese is currently estimated at nearly U.S.$600 billion. Overseas Chinese family-run conglomerates, popularly referred to as the "bamboo network," routinely mobilize resources on a scale that allows them to participate as principals in ambitious infrastructure projects.

In contrast, the overseas Vietnamese do not have an equivalent strong tradition in commerce. Although ethnic Vietnamese entrepreneurs have started new businesses in North America, Western Europe (mainly France), Australia, Eastern Europe, and the former Soviet Union, these firms are small in scale compared with ethnic Chinese businesses. Reflecting the backgrounds of their founder-owners, they include nail salons and firms in the engineering, computer-software, waste-management, and financial-services fields. In Vietnam, a low-profile entrepreneurial *Viet Kieu* presence has emerged in many economic sectors: cement, steel, hotel and office construction, food and beverages, light manufacturing, agricultural processing and distribution, financial services, and hospitality services. Many *Viet Kieu* entrepreneurs are descendants of former business magnates who left Vietnam after 1975.

The role of the ethnic Chinese (*Hoa*)—families who have lived in Vietnam for many generations—provides an interesting contrast. Vietnam's conflict with China in the late 1970s led to an exodus from Vietnam of the ethnic Chinese population. Similar to ethnic Chinese in other Southeast Asian countries, ethnic Chinese Vietnamese have a strong entrepreneurial tradition, and support from other ethnic Chinese communities helped them succeed in North America. The largest and most successful restaurants and supermarkets in ethnic Vietnamese communities in the United States, Canada, and Australia are owned by the *Hoa*. Their common ethnicity gave them access to the "bamboo network," which has provided them with the resources to participate in big investment projects in Vietnam. A number of highly successful Chinese Vietnamese businessmen interviewed by the author described their role as a bridge between local ethnic Chinese networks in Cho Lon and the highly capitalized overseas Chinese communities in Hong Kong, Taiwan, Singapore, and Thailand. In contrast to the segment of ethnic Vietnamese who consider themselves temporary exiles (described in Part II), the Chinese Vietnamese do not have a competitive attitude toward the Communist Party and have no ambition to displace it. They do not feel that Vietnam belongs to them. Their business ventures in Vietnam tend to be more successful because their attitude is less emotional and more objective. This enables them to evaluate risk more dispassionately.

V. ECONOMIC ENGAGEMENT: FUTURE PROSPECTS

Although Vietnamese Americans' involvement with Vietnam is at a formative stage, there are three areas in which they have the potential to make significant contributions. They are: 1) in supporting local efforts to revitalize Vietnam's cultural heritage and—through the example of people-to-people humanitarian-aid projects—in promoting the development of a cohesive and caring society; 2) in acting as a bridge to facilitate Vietnam's integration with the global economy; and 3) in helping to give vitality to the micro-enterprise and small-business sector, potentially the Vietnamese economy's greatest source of dynamism. Additional ongoing research is needed to arrive at a more comprehensive assessment of this engagement, whose actual parameters and fluctuations are not fully known. At the time of this writing, there is no systematic collection of data to capture this activity. For example, reliable estimates of trends in remittance flows cannot be obtained from existing survey data because the sample size is incomplete and unrepresentative.

It should be noted as well that the progress of this engagement faces many hurdles. The most formidable is imposed by the authorities. In the past, both host- and home-country governments have shown considerable ambivalence toward this engagement. For understandable reasons, they tend not to trust "hyphenated" citizens with divided loyalties. The authorities in Vietnam are especially wary of opening their doors to *Viet Kieu* whom they consider politically hostile.[32] Yet they also are reluctant to forgo the potentially rich benefits of engagement. Caught between hope and fear, the door swings tentatively open. For their part, a number of *Viet Kieu* are not themselves without ill will and suspicion and would just as soon leave *their* doors closed. Pessimists point to the high-profile Nguyen Trung Truc/Peregrine case as an egregious but not uncommon example of a *Viet Kieu* project gone sour and predict a bleak future for economic engagement.

Are the prospects so hopeless then? Is it solely up to policymakers in the United States and Vietnam to determine the terms and scope of this engagement? What can individuals and private organizations do to make a difference? As we saw in the early history of Vietnamese American engagement, the ties of kinship and homeland were certainly powerful enough to overcome the many obstacles arising from postwar hostility between the two nations. Relations between home and host country have warmed considerably over time. Consequently, the obstacles today are nowhere near as great as they were in previous decades.

Going forward, the question to ask is: What about the ties? Are they evolving? Yes, says Andrew Lam, a Vietnamese American journalist. He notes the generational differences: "Ironically, while my father's generation finds it harder to return home, we children have returned many times, searching for ways to help and influence the future of our homeland."[33] However, Lam may be mistaken in thinking that his father's generation, as a group, has turned its back to its ancestral land. A growing number who have visited Vietnam have expressed interest in spending their retirement years there. Whether this will actually materialize in significant numbers will depend on how hospitable the future environment in Vietnam is for members of that generation.

At the same time, Lam was correct in implying that the most interesting and innovative engagement trajectories probably will be forged by the second generation, the children of the "exiles." Citing friends who claim that the normalization of U.S.–Vietnam relations "will mark a new phase in the Vietnamese diaspora—a reverse exodus," Lam told of one friend who took issue with Thomas Wolfe's oft-quoted assertion that "You can't go home again." "I see my future as going back and forth," Lam's friend averred. A sampling of *Viet Kieu* narratives suggests possible trajectories for this evolution.[34] It also strongly suggests that the forms of engagement favored by the younger generation of *Viet Kieu* should not threaten any state authority. On the contrary, the themes they favor—economic development, social responsibility, respect for their cultural heritage—should reassure policymakers in both countries. What will be especially interesting to monitor are the evolving forms of engagement.

Philanthropy is the area in which *Viet Kieu* contributions have been the most positive and creative. Many of these projects are characterized by enormous warmth, close cooperation, and mutual respect among the participants, *Viet Kieu* and nationals alike. They contribute to the growth of civil society in Vietnam and serve as models to inspire future philanthropic projects. NGOs are founded not just by *Viet Kieu* but also by Vietnamese nationals. One of the best known is the Center to Research Child Psychology, founded by Vietnam's leading intellectual, the late Dr. Nguyen Khac Vien. This NGO has received *Viet Kieu* assistance, but its work is directed by Vietnamese nationals. Cooperation between nationals and *Viet Kieu* in humanitarian-aid programs reinforces people-to-people ties and increases mutual understanding. By helping policymakers visualize what is possible, creative and visionary forms of *Viet Kieu* philanthropy extend the parameters of engagement and lead the way to more welfare-improving forms of engagement.

■ **NOTES**

1. From a preliminary survey reported by Tran Trong Dang Dan, a sociologist at Vietnam's National Center for Social Sciences and Human Studies. His research indicates that as of 1994, there were 2,645,750 ethnic Vietnamese living in eighty countries and territories. About 1 million live in the United States, 400,000 in France, 300,000 in China, 160,000 in Australia, 150,000 in Canada, 120,000 in Thailand, and 100,000 each in Germany, Cambodia, and Russia. These figures underestimate the actual size of the overseas Vietnamese population because of the

well-known problems of underreporting of immigrant populations, particularly when the immigrants do not have legal status. Moreover, some republics of the former Soviet Union that are known to have ethnic Vietnamese residents are not included in the survey. According to Dan, not included in the official statistics are some 300,000 ethnic Vietnamese who reside in Eastern Europe and the former Soviet Union without legal status.

2. Eighty-one of the 195 firms in the park are headed by Western-trained Chinese who conducted their research overseas.

3. Personal interviews with Vietnamese government officials, including Tran Sy Luong, department director of the Committee for Overseas Vietnamese, September 1995.

4. Orange County, California, is an example. It has one of the largest concentrations of Vietnamese Americans in the United States. More than 100,000 Vietnamese Americans live in Westminster, Santa Ana, Stanton, and Garden Grove.

5. Recent titles that have been translated include *Japan as Number One: Lessons for America*, by Ezra F. Vogel; *Japan in Asia*, by Nigel Holloway, ed.; *Joint Ventures: An Accounting, Tax and Administrative Guide*, by Joseph M. Morris; *Le Droll Civil* (Civil Law), by Christian Atias; *L'Economie du Tourisme*, by Robert Lanquar, *L'Economie Mixte*, by Jean-Dominique Lafay and Jacques Lecaillon; *Managing in Turbulent Times*, by Peter Drucker; *Microeconomics*, by Robert S. Pindyck and Daniel L. Rubinfeld; *Preparing for the 21st Century*, by Paul M. Kennedy; *The Economics of Money, Banking and Financial Markets*, by Frederic S. Mishkin; *The Japanese Experience of Economic Reforms*, by Juro Teranishi and Yutaka Kosai; *The Japanese Social Structure: Its Evolution in the Modern Century*, by Todashi Fukutake; *The McGraw-Hill Guide to Starting Your Own Business: A Step-by-Step Blueprint for the First-Time Entrepreneur*, by Stephen C. Harper; *The Next Century*, by David Halberstam; *The Order of Economic Liberalization: Financial Control in the Transition to a Market Economy*, by Ronald McKinnon; *The Political Economy of Japan*, by Yasusuke Murakami and Hugh Patrick, ed.; *The Rise and Fall of the Great Powers*, by Paul M. Kennedy; and *The Stock Market: A Guide for the Private Investor*, by Neil F. Stapley. I am indebted to David Marr for providing this list.

6. Personal interview with Dang Phong, a Vietnamese economic historian, Hanoi, Vietnam, September 13, 1995.

7. Both these countries allow the voluntary transfer of funds to Vietnam.

8. Telephone interview with Ngo Thanh Nhan, March 14, 1996.

9. Lena H. Sun, "FBI Advertises for Tips on Spies From Vietnam," *Washington Post*, March 8, 1996, A3; Carey Goldberg, "FBI Using Newspaper Ads to Seek Vietnam Informers," *New York Times*, March 12, 1996, A1. Similar stories were published in the *Los Angeles Times*, *South China Morning Post*, and other major papers.

10. Commenting on the story, *Dien Dan*, a Paris-based *Viet Kieu* publication, acidly declared that Britain's "mad cow" disease had crossed the Atlantic and struck the FBI.

11. "Status of Overseas Vietnamese Returning to Vietnam," Telegraphic Report from the American Embassy in Hanoi, U.S. and Foreign Commercial Service, September 22, 1997.

12. Vietnam specialists attribute these inconsistencies to the absence of a coherent policy and fears on the part of the state security apparatus that the *Viet Kieu* could undermine the ruling Communist Party's hegemony in Vietnam. In a December 19, 1997, article published in *Quan Doi Nhan Dan*, Vietnam's official military newspaper, Colonel Nguyen Van Thuc, chief of the Security Protection Service under the Fourth Region Military Command, wrote: "There are still elements who carry out underground activity, waiting for support from exiled reactionaries and for assistance from imperialist forces to seek vengeance when the opportunity arrives. They have caused disturbances and violent incidents in the past. They distributed reactionary documents and harmful cultural products in the society and also in party and state agencies and the armed forces. . . . All officials and combatants should have a clear knowledge and resolute standpoint on complicated incidents and the 'peaceful evolution' scheme of the enemy" (FBIS-translated text document number FBIS-EAS-98-023).

13. I am indebted to Dang Phong for his detailed discussion and analysis of the history of Vietnamese laws and regulations governing relations with the *Viet Kieu*. According to Dang Phong, Resolution No. 127-CP was a very progressive and open-minded document. Regarding those who for various reasons were not able to return to their home country, this official statement of government policy clearly articulated the need to assign to them the responsibility for carrying out research to support Vietnam's postwar reconstruction program. Regarding the *Viet Kieu* who study abroad, Resolution 127-CP directed Vietnamese embassies in these countries to provide the assistance and guidance necessary to help them choose appropriate fields to meet the needs of the home country. The embassies were even instructed to look into ways to assist students with economic difficulties. With respect to *Viet Kieu* technicians, Resolution 127-CP declared that the government was prepared to repatriate those who wished to participate in Vietnam's reconstruction; they would be accorded the same status as Vietnamese nationals who were employed as specialists in state enterprises. With respect to elderly *Viet Kieu* who wished to spend their retirement years in Vietnam, the government declared it was ready to open its doors in welcome. With respect to the children of the *Viet Kieu*, Resolution 127-CP admonished the embassies to organize Vietnamese language and history classes for the children to strengthen their ties to their ancestral land.

14. This report, entitled "Decree to Strengthen the Preparation, Management, and Offensive Against the Conspiracy by Enemy Forces Using the Means of Communication to Attack the Party," was posted on the Internet by an anticommunist *Viet Kieu* organization. I am not aware that its authenticity has been verified. However, according to Vietnam specialists, its contents appear to be plausible.

15. The government's ambivalent policy toward the *Viet Kieu* was evident in *Quyet Dinh* (Decision) No. 122-CP, which came into effect a month before Resolution No. 127-CP (discussed in Note 13) was promulgated. At this time of writing, this decree officially remains in force although in practice a number of its exacting provisions have been set aside. No. 122-CP ruled that a visiting *Viet Kieu* must reside in a place designated by the government agency responsible for him or her. *Viet Kieu*

were not allowed to stay at the home of family members, but could visit and have a meal. At present overseas Vietnamese are allowed to stay with family members or friends, but they must register their place of residence with the state security office. Article 5 of the same decree would overwhelm the visiting *Viet Kieu* with red tape, requiring that they register not just once but several times with the local security office, and each time they must redo the legal paperwork. Another inconsistent aspect of the government's stance were the restrictions placed on money remittances and gifts from overseas Vietnamese, which contradicted its stated intent to encourage *Viet Kieu* contributions to Vietnam's economic development. For example, Circular No. 5 NHTT of the State Bank of Vietnam promulgated May 5 1980 and *Quyet Dinh* No. 32-CP effectively prohibited visiting *Viet Kieu* from transferring hard currency to private hands. Decision No. 103 of the Ministry of Domestic Commerce, issued March 9 1983, ruled that the value of merchandise sent to private individuals could not exceed 2000 VND (Vietnamese dong). As it turned out, these elaborate regulations and restrictions did not prevent the private sector from accumulating large amounts of hard currency and in recent times they have not been enforced. During Vietnam's hyperinflation crisis (1985–1988) private households began to hoard gold and U.S. dollars, transforming Vietnam into a dollarized economy. The macroeconomic impact of *Viet Kieu* monetary transfers to friends and relatives in Vietnam is not trivial, since annual inflows are estimated to reach magnitudes equivalent to one quarter of Vietnam's yearly merchandise imports. By channeling significant quantities of hard currency to the private sector, the overseas Vietnamese made it difficult for Vietnam's monetary authorities to control domestic liquidity and enabled the private sector to protect itself—to a certain extent—from inflation and currency devaluation.

16. Most refugee surveys are sponsored by the U.S. federal government, whose primary concern is helping the refugees adjust to the United States (Gordon 1989: 24). Because they focus on adaptation, there are no questions that would seek to explore and understand the relationship between the refugees and their country of origin.

17. E-mail communication from Anne Talsma, April 25, 1996. Forty-one percent of the respondents were from Grand Rapids, Michigan; 34 percent were from California, and 25 percent came from an e-mail solicitation.

18. According to the Overseas Vietnamese Committee, Ho Chi Minh City itself received an estimated 190,000 *Viet Kieu* in 1997. The committee estimates that 70,000 to 80,000 returned for the Year of the Tiger (1998) Tet festival.

19. ARVN is the popular acronym for the U.S.-supported Army of the Republic of Vietnam.

20. Private e-mail communication from Ngo Thanh Nhan, May 29, 1996, a key participant in the project. Vietnam's historical documents dating since the tenth century are written in *Nom*, which only a handful of scholars know how to read. *Nom* documents can be found in Vietnam, China, Japan, Singapore, England, France, Australia, Germany, the United States, and the Vatican. According to Nhan, the only way to save these historical documents is to "read" them into a computer file. An important aspect of this task involves establishing international standards for the

design of *Nom* characters for coding. According to Nhan, this table consists of 1,773 characters and was adopted as the first *Nom* computer standard in Vietnam in December 1993. This standard, combined with existing International Standards Organization (ISO) standards for Chinese, Japanese, and Korean, has allowed Vietnamese scholars to print and process more than 10,000 characters. This group of Vietnamese Americans is continuing to work with Vietnamese scholars in Vien Han Nom and the General Department of Standards, Metrology, and Quality Control to adopt a second standard for more than 3,000 characters.

21. Exoticism is in the eye of the beholder. The same fascination with the new and unfamiliar that makes Western culture so attractive to the younger generation in Vietnam motivates their young Vietnamese American counterparts to visit Vietnam. For them, Western culture is old hat, and they are driven by the desire to explore their more exotic roots.

22. During the early reform years, belt-tightening in the state sector forced state agencies to look to the market to supplement their budgetary allotment. A number of these agencies managed to make extra money by organizing seminars, taught by *Viet Kieu* professionals, which managers of state-owned enterprises paid to attend in order to learn to adapt successfully to the new market-oriented economy.

23. It is not unusual to find queries placed on the Internet by *Viet Kieu* students on summer study programs, such as the following sent to Australia Vietnam Science–Technology Link (AVSL), a popular Vietnam Internet discussion group: "I'm a student from the College of Charleston in the U.S. I am planning to study abroad this summer and I am trying to find more information about the programs that the University of Hanoi and Saigon offer. However, I cannot seem to find any information over the Web. Do you know if the University of Saigon or Hanoi offer such a program? I am a Vietnamese born and raised in the U.S., this experience would greatly benefit me. Thanks" (e-mail communication to AVSL, February 11, 1998).

24. For example, a group of *Viet Kieu* students toured Vietnam from north to south. While the students were in Ho Chi Minh City, the *Saigon Times Daily* (July 29, 1997) reported that they had learned to make handicrafts and soya milk at NGO establishments for street children.

25. There is a prevailing view in international organizations that foreign expatriates are less likely to have private agendas. However, there is no evidence to support this view. Expatriates who marry locals may be just as likely as *Viet Kieu* staff to have their own private agendas.

26. For example, one Western business consultant claims that hiring *Viet Kieu* is a common "mistake" made by foreign investors. Vietnamese workers defy orders from *Viet Kieu* managers, he asserts, because they resent the *Viet Kieu* and consider them traitors to their culture. *Viet Kieu* managers interviewed by the author observe that resentment by local workers is not uncommon, but they believe that it is largely exacerbated by the large wage differential between *Viet Kieu* and local staff due to the three-tier compensation system. They caution against broad generalizations about relationships between *Viet Kieu* and locals. According to them, the quality of

management supervision is the single most important factor governing relations between local workers and *Viet Kieu* managers.

27. These concerns basically revolve around trust, a fairly typical issue in human-resource management.

28. "Vietnam: Warning Foreign Investors 'No One Is Above the Law,'" IPS news article from Hanoi, August 8, 1996, which says: "Flamboyant entrepreneur Nguyen Trung Truc, previously hailed as one of the most successful businessmen in Vietnam, seems set to face tax evasion charges in a case the state media says should serve as a warning to crooked foreign investors." *Nhan Dan*, the official newspaper of the Vietnamese Communist Party, is quoted as saying: "The whole of Peregrine's business in Vietnam amounts to underground economic activity." Commenting on the case, the newspaper *Lao Dong* (Labor) added: "The case of Peregrine is a precious lesson for foreign businessmen inducing them to observe Vietnamese laws." Truc is accused of using Vietnamese front companies to evade taxes. Vietnamese officials allege that Peregrine Vietnam violated laws prohibiting foreign firms from directly distributing goods in Vietnam by establishing "nominee" companies that are in fact controlled by Peregrine itself. In June 1996, Ho Chi Minh City officials raided Peregrine Vietnam's headquarters and thirteen local distribution companies, seizing more than one hundred boxes of documents and computer data on Peregrine's tax, license, and import situation ("High Flyer Is Grounded," *Business Vietnam*, September 1996).

29. In a December 15, 1997, interview in *Quan Doi Nhan Dan*, Defense Minister Lieutenant-General Phan Van Tra said: "Hostile forces still consider Vietnam a major point of attack. They continue the implementation of a strategy of 'peaceful evolution and subversive violence' in order to eliminate socialism in Vietnam. Their short-term strategic targets are to 'transform' and 'change the color' of the Communist Party of Vietnam, and to promote political and economic liberalization with a view to transform[ing] Vietnam."

30. Nazli Kibria (1993: 26–27) has observed this, as well. She writes of the Vietnamese Americans in Philadelphia: "In part, their unwillingness to participate in the organizations [Vietnamese ethnic associations] reflected a deep, historically rooted suspicion of formal government. French colonization followed by the long years of war, and finally a period of Communist rule, had engendered widespread antipathy toward political institutions. As a participant-observer, for example, I was almost invariably initially 'screened' through intense questioning about my background for possible connections to the United States government or any social service agency. It was only in the absence of such connections that the participants of the study were willing to talk openly to me."

31. According to the Ministry of Planning and Investment, the total value of officially approved foreign investment, from January 1988 to June 1997, is U.S.$29 billion.

32. This covers a broad spectrum, from ancien régime diehards who actively seek to end Communist Party rule to more liberal advocates of "multiparty pluralism" and "peaceful evolution."

33. Andrew Lam, "Vietnamese in America Bid Farewell to Exile Identity," Pacific News Service, July 11, 1995.

34. "First Time Home" by J. H. Phan (Internet: phanjh@pacificu.edu) is a good example. Andrew Lam's *Viet Kieu* narratives is accessible from web site http://www.pacificnews.org/lam/index.html, and Anh Do's "Feeling the Pace of One's Birthplace" from web site http://kicon.com/anhdo/vietnam.html.

■ REFERENCES

Boulding, Elise
    1988   *Building a Global Civic Culture. Education for an Interdependent World.* Syracuse, N.Y.: Syracuse University Press.
Charney, Joel, and John Spragens, Jr.
    1984   *Obstacles to Recovery in Vietnam and Kampuchea.* U.S. Embargo of Humanitarian Aid. Boston: Oxfam America.
DeVoss, David
    1995   "Deja Vu for the *Viet Kieu.*" *Asia, Inc.* (January).
Gordon, Linda W.
    1989   "National Surveys of Southeast Asian Refugees: Methods, Findings, Issues." In *Refugees as Immigrants: Cambodians, Laotians, and Vietnamese in America,* ed. David W. Hains. Totowa, N.J.: Rowman and Littlefield Publishers, Inc.
Kibria, Nazli
    1993   *Family Tightrope: The Changing Lives of Vietnamese Americans.* Princeton, N.J.: Princeton University Press.
Marr, David
    1993   "Education, Research, and Information Circulation in Contemporary Vietnam." In *Reinventing Vietnamese Socialism: Doi Moi in Comparative Perspective,* ed. William S. Turley and Mark Selden. Boulder, Colo.: Westview Press.
Packard, Le Anh Tu
    1976   "The Vietnam Evacueed . . . What Now?" In *Counterpoint: Perspectives on Asian America,* ed. Emma Gee. Los Angeles: UCLA Asian American Studies Center.
Ronnas, Per, and Orjan Sjoberg
    1990   *Doi Moi. Economic Reforms and Development Policies in Vietnam.* Papers and Proceedings from an International Symposium in Hanoi, December 12–15, 1989. Stockholm: Swedish International Development Authority.

5

ASIAN AMERICAN ACTIVISM AND U.S. FOREIGN POLICY

PAUL Y. WATANABE

INTRODUCTION

In a recent report on minorities and U.S. foreign policy, Leslie Gelb (1997: vii), president of the Council on Foreign Relations, observed, "Current demographic projections suggest that the U.S. will enter the next century with a plurality of minorities even more so than in the past. These groups within society will affect America's involvement in the world and our foreign policy agenda." According to Gelb, this dynamic represents one of the "new challenges" the United States faces "that will define its foreign policy."

Assuredly, ethnic-group activism in American foreign policy offers challenges, but the discovery of its importance did not await the dawn of the third millennium. Writing nearly twenty-five years ago, Nathan Glazer and Daniel Moynihan (1975: 23–24), for example, asserted that, "the immigration process is the single most important determinant of American foreign policy. This process regulates the ethnic composition of the American electorate.

Foreign policy responds to that ethnic composition. It responds to other things as well, but probably first of all to the primal facts of ethnicity."

Since those words were penned, the changing demographics that Gelb referred to have manifested themselves dramatically in the Asian American population. This segment, largely fed by immigration, has more than quadrupled. Diversity within the group has also expanded. Substantial concentrations of Asian Americans are now drawn from a broader range of nations.

In the eyes of many observers, the prospects for increased Asian American participation in the foreign-policy realm appear ripe. As Chang-lin Tien (1996), former chancellor of the University of California, Berkeley, remarked at the conference "Bridges with Asia: Asian Americans in the United States": "Asian Americans are well positioned to play a major role in foreign policy toward Asia." And, as an editorial in *Northwest Asian Weekly* (1995) declared: "Asian Pacific Americans have a natural role to play in development of U.S. foreign policy."

This chapter considers some of the complex factors needed to assess—at least as they pertain to Americans of Asian ancestry—the assumptions of Gelb, Glazer, Moynihan, and others. Also scrutinized is the validity of Tien's and the editorial writer's assertions. Items examined include the ways in which Asian Americans have been affected by the content of the United States' relations with Asian nations and the manner in which they have attempted to influence those policies. Some elements assisting and resisting effective advocacy and the role of Asian American organizations and individuals are analyzed. Responses to this activism are also explored.

This inquiry draws heavily on insights offered during a series of round-table discussions throughout the United States that focused on the interactions of Asian Americans with Asia. The individuals who took part represented a broad range of areas—government, law, business, academia, community organizing, social services, consulting, and journalism. Discussions were held in Chicago, Houston, Los Angeles, Seattle, and Washington, D.C.

A crucial fact to bear in mind at the outset is that considerable disagreement exists over the extent, feasibility, and desirability of Asian American involvement in the foreign-policy realm. There is no clear consensus about these matters. This is not necessarily the case for all ethnic groups. Among Jewish Americans, for example, while there may be disagreements about the appropriateness and impact of foreign-policy activism, there are few who deny that this involvement has been widespread and intense. The same is true to a considerable degree for Cuban and Greek Americans.

For Asian Americans, not only have different assessments been made of the extent of their involvement in U.S.foreign-policy concerns, but there has also been discord over the advisability of this involvement. Particularly for those individuals aware of and touched by the Asian American past, a prevalent paradigm posits the vulnerability of Asian Americans to the vagaries of foreign policies and to backlashes against those who seek to shape them. Where some people suggest a "natural" and "major" role for Asian Americans in influencing foreign policy, therefore, others warn of potential peril.

Asian Americans' efforts in the foreign-policy arena and responses to them are likely to be influenced by dramatic transformations in the United States and the global milieu. Especially compelling is the confluence of forces of change in at least three realms: 1) the size and composition of Asian American communities; 2) the role of Asia in the international system; and 3) American foreign-policy goals and the policymaking process.

CHANGES AND OPPORTUNITIES

Asian America

The explosion in the size and diversity of the Asian American population in the past generation has been extensively documented. Largely due to immigration, the Asian American population has grown since 1970 from 1.5 million to over 10 million. In 1997, approximately 60 percent of Asian American adults were foreign born. One-fourth of the nation's total foreign-born population came from Asia.

Those who predict enhanced foreign-policy activism by Asian Americans see a link between this activism and the changing size and demographics of the Asian American community. The assumption quite simply is that greater size means more political involvement and clout, including in the foreign-policy realm. In *The New Asian Immigration in Los Angeles and Global Restructuring,* Paul Ong, Edna Bonacich, and Lucie Cheng (1994a: 29) discuss this relationship: "As their numbers grow and their influence increases, Asian immigrants are not merely filling the positions that are being created as a result of restructuring. They are actively participating in the restructuring process. They are helping reshape the economic landscape by creating new and alternative ventures. And they have the potential to emerge as an important new political force, influencing legislation and policy on both the local and the international level."

At least two elements beyond the sheer size of the new immigration from Asia may influence foreign-policy activism. First, Asian America is now more diverse than ever before. As recently as three decades ago, Chinese Americans and Japanese Americans constituted the bulk of Americans of Asian ancestry. The countries from which recent immigrants have come in large numbers include Vietnam, Cambodia, South Korea, India, the Philippines, and other lands. Today, six Asian American groups—Chinese, Filipinos, Japanese, Koreans, Asian Indians, and Vietnamese—number more than half a million. Second, in comparison with the older Asian immigration, which drew heavily from poorer and less skilled sectors, the new immigrants are drawn from broader social strata, including a larger portion of highly trained, well-educated professionals.

The impact of these dramatic transformations can take several forms. With more immigrants from different countries, the number of nations involved with the United States that may generate interest and activism among Asian Americans has increased. Furthermore, with a substantial portion of Asian immigrants arriving with well-developed skills and high socioeconomic status, the capabilities of the communities that they are part of to engage in political enterprises are enhanced. This is true because the new immigration augments the prevailing tendency among some Asian Americans to develop rapidly advanced educational abilities and economic attainment. Research on political behavior suggests that gains in socioeconomic well-being are positively correlated with heightened political interest, participation, and effectiveness.

Asia on the Rise

A volume of the journal *Foreign Policy* (Halloran 1996), with a cover sporting a smiling Buddha with a laptop computer perched across his knees, carried the title: "The Rising East." A widely circulated flier for a conference in Boston, titled "Asia and the Pacific: The Promise and the Pitfalls," stated: "The importance of the new world of Asia and the Pacific is beyond question. But not every prospect pleases. In all its diversity the Asian and Pacific region presents huge challenges." A cover of *Newsweek* (1996) posed the question, "China: Friend or Foe?"; the special report inside was titled, "China on the Move."

Clearly, Asia is near the center of the international stage. Whether it is applauded or derided, feared or respected, the seemingly inescapable reality is that Asian nations are forces to be reckoned with. An article in the same volume of *Foreign Policy* commenced with a description of an ascendant Asia. "The evacuation [on December 20, 1999] of this last European enclave in Asia [Macao] will end 500 years of Western colonialism in the region. More importantly, it will register the opening of an age in which the Rising East will acquire the political, economic, and military power to rival that of North America and Western Europe. That power, much of which has already been accrued, will enable Asians to exert influence not only in their own region but throughout the world. They will become peers with Americans and

Europeans in the high councils where decisions are made on war and peace. Asians will not only play in the center court but, as a Malaysian scholar has put it, intend to 'have an equal say in writing the rules'" (Halloran 1996: 3).

Even Republican Senator Jesse Helms of North Carolina, who chairs the Senate Foreign Relations Committee and is an outspoken critic of many Asian governments, felt compelled recently to serve as a friendly host for a delegation of seven ASEAN leaders visiting his state, a delegation that included representatives from the Socialist Republic of Vietnam. After erecting roadblocks on the path toward full normalization of relations with Hanoi, Helms rolled out the red carpet. Of course, Helms's newfound preoccupation with Asia was not devoid of a few missteps. When accorded the task of introducing Benazir Bhutto, then the prime minister of Pakistan, to his colleagues, Senator Helms referred to her as "the distinguished prime minister of India."

The dual significance of the rise and restructuring of Asia for Asian Americans is that, beyond being dramatically shaped by these changes, Asian Americans may in turn influence the nature of those changes and American policy responses. According to Ong, Bonacich, and Cheng (1994b: viii): "As we see it, the new Asian immigration is not only a product of the restructuring of the Pacific Rim region, but also a force that is contributing to that restructuring. The region is experiencing large-scale growth in trade relations, in capital flows in both directions, and in accompanying political involvements. The movement of people is a concomitant of these flows and in turn plays an important part in them. Immigration, trade, investment, economic aid, political and military involvement all go hand in hand."

United States Foreign Policy:
Changing Roles and Processes

The passing of the Cold War, with its overriding emphasis on taming the Soviet Union, has ushered in a period of confusion and complexity. Fundamental assumptions about the international milieu and the role and position of the United States and other powers within it have been altered. Although the predominant role of the United States on a variety of international chessboards remains solid, the articulation of American foreign-policy goals is muddled, and the identification of putative allies and opponents is less distinct. In this period of complexity and flux, there are likely to be increased opportunities to define the United States' interests more broadly and to influence emerging policies by coupling interests with activism.

The convergence of changes in the global environment and the American foreign-policy agenda could signal, for example, movement away from the clear Eurocentric focus that has dominated the United States' experience as a superpower. Furthermore, the Cold War imperative to emphasize the primacy of security considerations may give way to more complex economic, political, and social interactions that may be the focus of developing relations with emerging Asian states. As issues and policies become more "intermestic," neither fully international nor domestic, the opportunities and motivations for activism may increase (Manning 1977: 306). Immigration, trade, and investment matters, for instance, blur the line between domestic and foreign policy and are near the top of the United States' Asian agenda.

The national-security state that defined the Cold War was marked by a tightly controlled foreign-policy–making process. Access points were limited; the roles of potential actors were circumscribed; and legitimate interests were narrowly defined. In the emerging structure, groups intent on influencing foreign relations, including Asian Americans, may find expanded opportunities to pry open the policymaking process and to inject their interests and perspectives.

In summary, the combined effects of recent transformations in the size and composition of the Asian American community, the expanded role of Asia in the world generally and its importance to the United States specifically, and the focus and structure of American foreign policy offer enhanced interest, opportunities, challenges, and critical scrutiny for Asian Americans intent on influencing foreign policy.

Foreign relations have played a major role in defining the destiny of Asian Americans. Consequently, their stake in the content of these relations has been substantial, and, generally speaking, their interest has been high as well. In the formulation of foreign policies toward Asian nations, however, Asian Americans, with some exceptions, have been pawns more than players.

ASIAN AMERICANS AND U.S.–ASIA RELATIONS

Linkages

History amply demonstrates that the well-being of Asian Americans has been inextricably linked to the role and influence of Asian nations and to the nature of the relationships between their adopted and ancestral homes. The size and composition of the Asian American community, as well as its legal standing, civil rights, and physical well-being, have all been coupled with events abroad.

The immigration of Asians to the United States has been significantly influenced by the nature of relations between the United States and Asian countries. When the United States has been a party to major Asian conflicts, it has contributed to dislocations that drive immigration. Many refugees from

Southeast Asia and immigrants from Korea, China, Hong Kong, and Taiwan have come from areas that have experienced political instability or the reality or serious threat of war.

When an Asian country has been deemed powerful, the treatment of the related nationality group in the United States has been affected, although it is difficult to generalize about whether that impact has been consistently positive or negative. The growing activism and expansionism of Japan in the early and mid-twentieth century, for example, had mixed results for the Japanese American community. The fact that the American government was slower and more reluctant to impose an outright exclusion on Japanese immigrants, compared with the Chinese, was largely a reflection of Japan's more formidable international position. As Japan became more aggressive, however, the government and people of the United States became more wary of the Japanese generally, and increasingly hostile toward Americans of Japanese ancestry specifically, culminating in the World War II internment.

From the early days of their settlement in America, Chinese Americans have been influenced by the relationship between the United States and China. As Ronald Takaki (1989: 268–89) has observed, "Chinese in America had realized for a long time how their situation here was tied to developments in China. The very political weakness of the Chinese government conditioned their treatment here and influenced the anti-Chinese immigration policies of the U.S. government. They supported the struggle for China's independence from foreign domination in order to free themselves in America. A strong China, they hoped, would mean greater protection and more rights for them here. . . . 'If you were Chinese-American, you certainly felt the fate of China was important,' recounted James Low. 'I remember the teachers would always complain, "China is weak, and look at the treatment we get here." ' "

Sucheng Chan (1991: 142) has also noted the relationship between Asian nations and the status of Asian Americans. "More than any other period of Asian American history, the years between 1941, when the United States joined the war against the Axis powers, and 1965, when a new immigration law ushered in a resurgence of immigration from Asia, were ones during which the fate of Asian Americans depended largely on the changing fortunes wrought by war. The lives of people whose ancestors came from countries that were U.S. allies during World War II improved, while those identified with the enemy were ripped asunder. Then as a hot war turned into a cold one and a defeated Japan became America's 'junior partner' in 'containing' communism, while China went Communist and became a feared enemy, the perception and treatment of Japanese and Chinese Americans flip-flopped. Well-educated Japanese Americans finally began to enter the mainstream, while some Chinese Americans were spied upon and on occasion harassed and deported."

Interest

In his often-cited adage, former Speaker of the United States House of Representatives Tip O'Neil proclaimed, "All politics is local." For several ethnic groups in America, however, a more appropriate maxim might be, "All politics is international." In their political activism, Cuban Americans, for example, generally reflect the primacy of foreign policy. Their preoccupation with the continuing hold of Castro in Cuba has largely defined their activities in both the foreign and local realms. Jewish Americans as well have tied much of their political involvement to an overarching determination to see that U.S. policies protect the safety and stability of Israel. Many Asian Americans share this preoccupation with homeland politics and U.S. foreign policy. This interest has often caused tension among and within Asian American communities.

The existence of generational differences regarding interest in foreign policy has been routinely identified by many Asian Americans, but with little agreement as to the direction and impact of those differences. Some individuals, for example, claim that first-generation immigrants have closer connections to foreign lands and, consequently, pay more attention to events abroad and external relations. Interest in these matters is said to wane with the passage of time as later generations of Asian Americans become more assimilated.

Accordingly, the fact that most Asian Americans are foreign born would suggest a heightened preoccupation with and passionate following of policies inside of and toward Asian homelands. A second-generation Chinese American in Houston, for example, noted, "My father coming in as an adult had strong anticommunist feelings. And when they opened a consulate in Houston, he said, 'No, I will never go to that place.' Whereas to me, I am an American, and that's just another governmental office here. So I think as far as trying to influence U.S. foreign policy to another country, MFN [most-favored–nation status] to me is no different from whether you're going to condemn France for nuclear testing. I mean, it's just another country" (Houston Roundtable 1995). Other individuals argue that first- and second-generation Asian Americans are so fully engaged in making a living and doing well in the United States that they devote little attention to matters involving foreign policy. "They are interested in making money," an Asian American woman in Seattle remarked (Seattle Roundtable 1995). Immigrants in particular, according to this view, regard foreign-policy involvement as something far removed from their principal daily concerns.

Generally speaking, with the passage of time and generations, immigrant communities expand their socioeconomic and other resources, which in turn enhances their ability to exercise political and policymaking clout. One may therefore discover a paradoxical dynamic at work. As interest diminishes, capabilities crucial for effective involvement grow. "The next generation will have the plus side of feeling more like Americans than immigrants," a Chinese American in Seattle noted. "But the minus side is that they will be a little less tied, less interested" (Seattle Roundtable 1995).

Activism

Prolonged stretches of sustained Asian American involvement in foreign policy have been rare. Activism has been uneven and episodic but not, as some contend, virtually nonexistent. Since the early days of their settlement in the United States, Asian Americans have occasionally turned their interest into activism.

In the early days of Chinese immigration, for example, the Chinese Six Companies lobbied hard to shape the 1868 Burlingame Treaty. Korean associations, which were principally religious, often attempted to steer the United States in the direction of curbing Japan's colonial appetite. In the Indian community, several associations included American support for the Indian independence struggle as part of their agendas. The Ghadar Party, for instance, was established with the struggle for Indian independence principally in mind. The Dimas Alang in the Filipino community played a comparable role in the Philippine independence movement.

More recent efforts have continued along similar lines. Thought (Taiwan independence) sympathizers in the United States have increased their visibility and organizational structure. They have selectively joined lobbying efforts to influence U.S. policy and have established national and regional offices.

A few years ago, considerable efforts were undertaken to see that the U.S. government granted Taiwanese President Lee Teng-hui permission to visit the United States. Newspaper advertisements in major daily newspapers throughout the United States were purchased to welcome President Lee. Voices of protest were raised opposing Lee's journey, as well. In an open letter to President Bill Clinton, a group of immigrant students from the mainland called for the withdrawal of Lee's visa, fearing that his visit would jeopardize the United States' two-decade-old "one China" policy.

More recently, the visit of Chinese President Jiang Zemin to the United States prompted activism from diverse sectors of the Chinese American community. Predictably, protesters greeted him at virtually every stop. Perhaps reflective of changing realities, however, many Chinese Americans on the streets and in letters and commentaries welcomed the Chinese leader and voiced their desire for strong, positive relations with China.

The Committee of 100 was established in 1990 soon after the events in Beijing's Tiananmen Square with the goal of promoting improved interaction between the United States and China. Several prominent Chinese Americans have lent their prestige to the organization, including Yo-Yo Ma, I.M. Pei, Oscar Tang, Chang-lin Tien, Shirley Young, and Henry Tang. At their annual conferences, held in Washington, D.C., registrants have met with members of Congress, senior government officials, and leading academics. Sessions have focused on topics such as "U.S.–China Relations into the Next Century—Constructive Engagement with China" and "U.S. Economic Policy in Relation to China."

Indian Americans have lobbied extensively on behalf of U.S. support for India. They have also spent some energy opposing what has often been perceived as a too-chummy relationship between the United States and Pakistan. Lately, this has meant marshaling opposition in Congress to the Brown Amendment. Pakistani Americans, on the other hand, have lobbied aggressively and with professional assistance for American aid to Pakistan.

Many recent activist efforts by Asian Americans have utilized imaginative technology, particularly in electronic communications. Many traditional communication instruments—letters, telegrams, faxes, and videos—were used by activists in response to the Tiananmen massacre. Additionally, protestors and their sympathizers took remarkably full advantage of what was then relatively new communications technology—namely, the Internet and electronic mail. A nationwide electronic service, the China News Digest, with more than 35,000 subscribers, was set up by Chinese American scholars and students after the Tiananmen experience. The Indian American community has deployed a similar service, called IndiaNet.

In describing instances of Asian American involvement such as those just mentioned, it is important not to lose sight of the fact that interest in foreign-policy matters may be high, but activism may be relatively low. The historical experience of Asian Americans amply shows that interest in foreign policy does not automatically translate into activism, and activism does not ensure success. This is true for many reasons and raises important questions about the causes of differentials in levels of political involvement, about the distribution of politically useful resources, and about feelings of alienation and vulnerability. Although they have been deeply affected by and interested in U.S. foreign policy, Asian Americans have often engendered further harsh treatment when they have attempted to alter its content.

BACKLASH: "ETHNICITY DETERMINES LOYALTY"

The growth of the Asian American community, as already noted, can contribute significantly to its potential political clout. On the other hand, the increase in size and activism may spur a backlash. Perceptions of Asian Americans as threats have repeatedly resulted in vigorous opposition. The specter of alleged treachery has been an easy fear to conjure up against Asian Americans. They have been viewed as perpetual foreigners and strangers. "The otherness of our faces," Vishakha Desai of the Asia Society has asserted, has been for some people a source of great trepidation (Los Angeles Roundtable 1995). Foreign-policy activism enhances these perceptions.

Charges of disloyalty and unreliability have served as convenient fronts for nefarious and narrow purposes. In 1942, for example, General John DeWitt, head of the Western Defense Command, maintained that ethnicity determines loyalty when he called for the internment of Japanese Americans. For many Americans, agitation for the removal of Japanese Americans was largely a convenient and ruthless response to economic gains made by Japanese Americans and a manifestation of long-held and deeply entrenched racism.

A Houston city councilman with a large Asian American constituency stated that he regularly encounters groups, particularly with roots in Taiwan, trying to influence U.S. policy on the Taiwan question. "I kind of resent that," he said, "quite frankly because people in this country, whether they're originally from the Republic of China or the People's Republic of China, I think they are basically Americans" (Houston Roundtable 1995).

Obviously, for some people, foreign-policy involvement is out of bounds for those who are "basically Americans." It is not enough for Asian Americans inclined to play an activist role simply to assert the legitimacy of their actions. While in a formal sense the right to act may be unimpeachable, acting on that right is a risky enterprise. In a dominant society that is suspicious of activists' true allegiances, aggressive actions, particularly against prevailing trends, tend to validate in many people's minds fears of divided loyalties.

A Chinese American man who once served as a State Department official said rather matter of factly, "Asians don't get to be Americans as easily as Greeks or Germans" (Seattle Roundtable 1995). In a similar vein, an Asian American woman in Houston observed, "When other groups express political opinions, they are viewed as coming from an 'American' perspective. When Asians express political opinions, they are first seen to be 'ethnic' opinions, because [if] you are Chinese, you are therefore speaking as an ethnic Chinese compared to an 'American.' [Or if you] are Indian, you therefore must be speaking ethnically rather than as an 'American'" (Houston Roundtable 1995).

Asian Americans, much like other ethnic groups active in the foreign-policy area, have sometimes been perceived as tools, unwitting or otherwise, of foreign entities. Cozy relationships between immigrant communities and foreign governments, particularly through local consulates, are common and arouse concern in some quarters.

Since much of the fear and trepidation prompted by Asian nations can easily be transferred to Asian Americans, one might argue—as a journalist did at a Los Angeles Roundtable discussion—that the proper strategy for Asian Americans would be to distance themselves from Asian affairs and U.S. policy (Los Angeles Roundtable 1995). Although the wisdom of this strategy is debatable, it arises partially from the belief that expanded Asian American activism on foreign-policy matters increases the likelihood of harsh backlashes. Given a host of factors, including historical experience, racism, and widely held suspicions about the appropriateness of this behavior, a likely accompaniment of foreign-policy activism will be an escalation of decidedly nasty consequences.

The tendency of many Americans and their government often to confuse activism and dissent with disloyalty may have a "chilling effect" on Asian Americans, dissuading them from even thinking about playing highly visible roles on the foreign-policy–making stage. Many Asian Americans, whether in communities that have been here for decades or days, have continued to struggle with how they are perceived. Identity issues can be complicated, and they are central considerations in decisions about participating in foreign-policy matters. Throughout the country, Asian Americans who are self-confident about their own commitment and identity as Americans nevertheless often become exceedingly anxious about perceptions of them as disloyal. According to a Chinese American man who served in the Defense Department, he had to be "very careful" when dealing with issues involving China. He felt that his impartiality and credibility were questioned by some of his colleagues. Asian Americans were particularly open to this suspicion "because they look different," he said (Seattle Roundtable 1995).

Many Asian Americans have challenged these sentiments. For instance, a Vietnamese woman in Chicago forcefully stated the case for involvement, "I would challenge that thinking [that it is disloyal to try to influence U.S. policies with one's homeland] because an individual like me, who has spent my life in Vietnam and here . . . , really feels a commitment to both countries. . . . I can imagine myself in a position advocating for policies that I think will be to the benefit of both, not only Vietnam. So I think that arguments that say you put the interests of another country ahead of your new country are just attempts to discredit a credible viewpoint that you bring to the table" (Chicago Roundtable 1995).

Asian Americans have responded to individuals who contest the validity of their foreign-policy involvement. In order to assess these responses, the forces that promote discord among Asian Americans and those that might bolster unity need to be identified. Some additional barriers to Asian American involvement and effectiveness should also be considered.

TEARING APART, COMING TOGETHER, AND IDENTIFYING BARRIERS

Centrifugal Forces

Important differences exist in the national origins, political affiliations, socio-economic status, cultures, and beliefs of Asian Americans. It is no wonder that opinions on foreign-policy matters reflect and, on occasion, have exacerbated this diversity. Differences that emerge within specific Asian American communities over foreign-policy matters reflect many factors, including generational differences, contending political allegiances, and regional variations.

Much of Asia has experienced animosities between and within nations. For Asian American immigrants, deep-seated differences often doggedly persist in the new world. Within the Vietnamese American community, for example, the war experience delineates rancorous political divisions. The debate within the Vietnamese American community over the United States' formal recognition of Vietnam reflected larger considerations tugging in different directions. The recognition imbroglio brought forward conflicting attitudes toward assimilation. Many of the immigrants of the older generation, who have strived to preserve their native languages, traditional norms and values, and established allegiances, were less inclined to dismiss the past and move on.

A fractious environment assuredly weakens political and policymaking influence. The persistence of myriad factors promoting potential disunity make the establishment and maintenance of unity around foreign-policy considerations more problematic for Asian Americans.

Whether a unifying Asian American consciousness partially expressed in political mobilization will emerge as the Asian American community "matures" is not clear. Greater unity, however, is more likely to arise in the domestic arena around distinctly Asian American issues rather than issues related to U.S. policies toward Asia. "[Among] Asian Americans, the trend is to move toward some kind of commonality," an Asian Indian woman in Chicago noted. "There is a common identity in being Asian Americans. However, when it comes to political activities, especially in foreign policy, this is where we all break. . . . Here is where all the coalition building kind of gets fragmented" (Chicago Roundtable 1995).

Centripetal Forces

Although it has been rare for Asian Americans from different homelands to unite toward common foreign-policy goals, there have been instances where support transcended individual ethnic communities. The long resistance to

Japanese imperialism early in the twentieth century at times brought together Chinese Americans and Korean Americans for shared purposes and mutual support. In the early 1940s, the Indian American and Korean American communities joined with Chinese Americans in calling for the repeal of the Chinese exclusion laws. A few decades later, young Asian Americans from diverse communities were drawn together partly to oppose the continued military involvement of the United States in Southeast Asia.

Although the development of a shared Asian American agenda, especially in the foreign-policy realm, has been difficult, one can discern circumstances that might promote unity among diverse Asian American communities. A long and sometimes troubled history and painful recent experiences demonstrate that Asian Americans, whatever their national origins, share a stake in the nature and tone of relations between the United States and a variety of Asian nations. In a fairly undifferentiated fashion, for example, Asian Americans have experienced prejudice and abuses triggered by the actions of foreign governments and tensions involving the United States. Despite its origins in the clearly differentiated domain of foreign and international politics, this treatment has been a broadly shared component of the collective Asian American experience.

On numerous occasions in recent times, for example, violence against individual Asians, regardless of their nationality, has been linked to hostilities and tensions involving a particular Asian nation. Consequently, actions such as the disturbingly familiar use of the widely accessible epithet "gook" to refer to all Asian Americans by those with lingering pain and hatred from the Vietnam experience, and the beating death of Vincent Chin, a Chinese American in Detroit, as a scapegoat for hatred directed at Japan and the sharp rise in anti-Asian American violence generally, are all unfortunate results of individuals too ignorant, lazy, or racist to be cognizant of differences.

Perhaps a succinct appraisal of the dynamic of Asian American political integration and segregation is that homeland and Asian experiences tend to divide Asian Americans, while shared American experiences provide opportunities to unite them. Furthermore, the emergence of a common identity among diverse Asian Americans may not be as vital to their well-being as one imposed from outside. To quote from Sucheng Chan (1991: xii): "Though it is often thought that these various groups are lumped together as 'Asian Americans' because they or their ancestors have all come from Asia, there is a more important reason for treating them as a collective entity: for the most part, the host society has treated them all alike, regardless of what differences might have existed in their cultures, religions, and languages, or in the status of their homelands in the family of nations."

As action and organization evolve on issues that elicit more unified responses, the prospects for coordination and activism on matters ensconced within the foreign-policy sphere are appreciably enhanced. Consciousness, net-works, and relationships forged in one policy area facilitate counterparts in others.

All of this suggests that foreign-policy activism by Asian Americans indi-vidually or collectively is especially called for when the consequences of policies impinge broadly on the welfare of Asian Americans. The reality for Asian Amer-icans of a partially shared fate establishes a foundation for a modicum of shared activism. The need for participation, however, does not always elicit concerted responses. Some formidable barriers stand in the way of successful advocacy.

Barriers to Participation

For decades, the political involvement of Asian Americans was restricted by severe limitations on immigration and naturalization. These structural impediments made it extremely difficult for Asian Americans to be active, especially when coupled with their weak sense of political efficacy. Individ-uals who carry around images of their own political vulnerability and ineffectiveness are disinclined to participate.

In addition, the desire of some Asian Americans to influence the for-eign-policy realm is complicated by the fact that several powerful Asian nations are ruled by communists. Although the Cold War in Europe has passed, in Asia the application by some Americans of the anticommunist imperative remains quite appealing. In the words of John Tateishi, "[Activism] translates very differently based on whether you are looking at a country that is communist or not" (Houston Roundtable 1995). At the very least, the range of positions that can be comfortably supported is circumscribed. Chi-nese Americans, for example, may be wary of advocating policies perceived as too tolerant of the communists. In contrast, staunchly anticommunist messages may be more widely embraced by politicians and policymakers.

Many Asian Americans are reluctant for various reasons to condone involvement in foreign-policy matters. For instance, Asian American associa-tions dedicated to promoting rapid assimilation—so-called Americanism—may be quite supportive of political participation by their members but still somewhat disinclined to approve of aggressive efforts to alter the shape of American foreign policy. For these associations, politics truly stops at the water's edge. During World War II, despite the wholesale internment of Americans of Japanese ancestry, organizations such as the Japanese American Citizens League were unwilling to advocate strongly against the policies of the U.S. government.

There is also some reluctance in sectors of the Asian American commu-nity to support foreign-policy activism because of the belief that domestic and local matters should be the principal focuses of political participation. Because of the scarce resources available to activists within the Asian American community, Asian Americans, according to this view, should prudently employ precious time and energy on behalf of concerns closer to home. A woman in Chicago, for example, lamented the Indian American community's apparent preoccupation with foreign policy. She argued that this activism prevented other, largely domestic, concerns such as affirmative action, education, and glass-ceiling issues from receiving adequate attention (Chicago Roundtable 1995).

A contrary view suggests that foreign-policy involvement generally enhances rather than diminishes attempts by Asian Americans to influence domestic policy. Demonstrations of interest and activism on foreign-policy issues may have spillover effects. Awareness and attention generated by foreign-policy concern and activism help in other struggles, including some that are fully ensconced in the domestic arena.

THE CASE FOR ASIAN AMERICAN ACTIVISM

Eloquent and effective advocates for Asian American involvement in influencing U.S. foreign policy can be found within Asian American communities. These individuals, while not oblivious to the often hostile reactions to this type of political activism, nevertheless are unapologetic about their right to participate. Furthermore, they are able to identify some contributions that Asian Americans can make to the development of responsive and responsible foreign policy. Here is a sampling of some of their views:

"I'm from Vietnam originally," said an Asian American woman in Chicago, "so to me, foreign relations are the heart of all the matters between the United States and Asia, because as a result of U.S. foreign policy we are here. I think it's really inevitable that the politics of the United States is based on interest groups, and as Asians we have our own interests and we should be able to exercise these interests in every sphere, including foreign relations. I think in the case of Japanese Americans, because of the negative experience during World War II, the leadership of that community may shy away from homeland issues, but I think for other communities who are recent immigrants, it is a very natural thing to talk about U.S. and homeland policies" (Chicago Roundtable 1995).

Another Chicagoan noted the unique knowledge and perspectives that certain Asian Americans can contribute to the policymaking process: "My view of America in this post–Cold War and complex international community is that we should be able to benefit from the presence of the people who are here. I think many of the mistakes that may have been made in the past in terms of foreign policy are based on a certain ignorance about those countries. And we need to take advantage of the people who have firsthand knowledge. They may have certain biases, but I think those biases need to be brought to the table with people who may have studied these issues academically but may have no first-hand experience of what it's like being a Third World person, what's it like being caught in the Cold War and having to play a certain role. Those experiences have to be brought to the foreign front so that they become part of the debate or solution or direction of policy" (Chicago Roundtable 1995).

Persons outside the Asian American community have also championed the right of Asian Americans to participate, to contribute their expertise and insight, and to present forcefully their concerns. In the main, Asian American activists welcome these sentiments. It should be noted, however, that at times politicians and others use these activists as tools for their own narrow political purposes. Chinese Americans, for example, are regularly summoned to Capitol Hill to engage in some erstwhile China-bashing. Many individuals who cheer on dissidents as they lambaste the Chinese government, such as Harry Wu, have not lifted a finger in support of human rights when the friendship of right-wing dictators and military juntas have been at stake.

Accompanying the activists drawn largely from nongovernmental ranks are a small number of Asian Americans in official capacities in the government. The identification and development of individuals in these positions can appreciably amplify the voice of Asian Americans in the foreign-policy–making process.

ASIAN AMERICANS IN FOREIGN-POLICY–MAKING

Asian Americans have seldom performed key foreign-policy–making roles. Instead, Asian Americans have been active principally on the policymaking periphery, working as consultants and helpers.

Asian American members of the U.S. House of Representatives and Senate have not been particularly aggressive in pushing Asian-related foreign-policy initiatives. This contrasts strikingly, for example, with the ample number of Jewish American and Greek American legislators who have routinely and aggressively focused on issues related, respectively, to Israel and the southern Mediterranean.

Asian Americans intent on influencing policy in the congressional arena must rely largely on non-Asian members of congress. This is not an insurmountable hurdle. The relative successes of other ethnic communities in the congressional arena have not fully relied on committed officeholders drawn solely from those communities. The vaunted Jewish lobby, for example, depends both on supporters who are Jewish and on a larger number of staunch and determined defenders who are not. For their part, Indian American lobbyists have effectively cultivated an impressive group of elected officials to advocate for foreign assistance to India. Former South Dakota Senator Larry Pressler, for example, regularly led the fight for this aid.

Long-time Washington, D.C., observers, while noting the increase in Asian Americans on Capitol Hill and in the administration, see little evidence of a particular proclivity by these individuals to be involved in the foreign-policy–making arena (Washington, D.C., Roundtable 1995). Although Asian members of Congress have been largely reluctant to press hard on Asian-related policy concerns, a growing crop of Asian American congressional staff could yield some pivotal players. On the executive side, as well, key individuals in departments such as State, Defense, and Commerce might influence the contours of foreign policy either directly or in alliance with Asian American organizations.

Except for Julia Chang Bloch and William Itoh, Asian Americans have not been well represented in ambassadorships to Asian countries. When asked to suggest reasons for this situation, some individuals note that Asian Americans of any generation have been suspected of potential disloyalty. One Asian American active in Washington, D.C., remarked that when she asked a high State Department official why an Asian American had not been appointed to a major Asian country, the response was, "It would be a conflict of interest" (Washington, D.C., Roundtable 1995).

CONCLUSION

Although Asian Americans are deeply influenced by American foreign policy, they have not consistently played major roles in shaping that policy. It is easy, as some suggest, to conclude that Asian Americans are in many ways responsible for their own plight and contribute to their status largely as pawns rather than players. This line of reasoning is certainly tempting, perhaps even self-satisfying, for those who have imposed and condoned some of the harsh and restrictive measures forced upon Asian Americans in the name of "military necessity" and national security. Although appealing to some people, these arguments are fundamentally flawed. For Asian Americans, their ability to influence foreign policy is determined not simply by how much they yearn to be heard, but also by whether they are allowed to speak. During the virulent Cold War years, for example, dissident voices in the Chinese American community against the prevailing anticommunist line were largely stifled. The history of the United States is fraught with evidence of the vulnerability of Americans of Asian ancestry. Asian Americans have been neither simply uninterested nor naive about the consequences of foreign policies on their status.

The harsh treatment of Asian Americans has retarded widespread activism in at least two ways. First, many Asians in America have been consciously and systematically denied access to the political process. Second, those who have attempted despite formidable barriers to influence foreign policy and to advocate for policy alternatives have become even more vulnerable because of their activism. Asian Americans have experienced firsthand the prodigious capacity of the government and powerful forces in the public to combat dissent and silence opposition.

The legacy of responses to the linkage between Asian Americans and U.S. policies toward Asian nations, therefore, does not invite optimism about the prospects for activism in the foreign-policy realm. On the other hand, transformations in the size and makeup of the Asian American community, coupled with the burgeoning importance of Asia, raise the stakes and the possibilities of expanded Asian American involvement. These modifications have also arisen in an environment undergoing significant alterations in the focus and framework of American foreign policy. The opportunities accompanying these changes, despite the forces tugging differentially at the Asian American community and the formidable barriers to participation, may prove to be irresistible.

The growing importance and confidence of several Asian countries may influence the self-esteem and internal efficacy of Americans of Asian ancestry, which in turn may contribute to positive political and psychological consequences. The pride, interest, and self-assurance of a rapidly growing Asian American population may be tied to the ascent of their ancestral homes. As Evelyn Hu-DeHart has stated, "Because for so long we [Chinese Americans] were a maligned minority, when we see our motherland getting stronger internationally and more respected, it strengthens our position here" (Houston Roundtable 1995).

On the other hand, the rise of Asia, coupled with a stronger, more active Asian American community, has in recent times revived several familiar paranoid reactions. Myriad aspects of the controversies involving political contributions by Asians and Asian Americans, principally during the 1996 elections, offer ample evidence that many individuals in politics and the media are prepared to invoke swiftly and often irresponsibly a darker and more damaging side of the so-called Asian connection.

In summary, the cumulative effects of profound changes and the persistence of certain continuities in the Asian, American, and Asian American experiences do not allow for easy predictions about the course of Asian American activism on foreign-policy concerns. Perhaps the pull of the past and the persistence of powerful opposition will discourage activists. Or, recalling Glazer and Moynihan's (1975: 23–24) formulation as cited at the beginning of this chapter, the growth and maturation of the Asian American community will mean that "foreign policy will be affected in diverse and profound ways."

■ REFERENCES

Chan, Sucheng
1991   *Asian Americans: An Interpretive History.* Boston: Twayne Publishers.
Chicago Roundtable
1995   Tape recording. Asia Society, November 18.
Gelb, Leslie H.
1997   "Foreword." *Defining the National Interest: Minorities and U.S. Foreign Policy in the 21st Century. Conference Report.* New York: Council on Foreign Relations.
Glazer, Nathan, and Daniel P. Moynihan, ed.
1975   *Ethnicity: Theory and Experience.* Cambridge, Mass.: Harvard University Press.
Halloran, Richard
1996   "The Rising East." *Foreign Policy* 102 (spring): 3–21.
Houston Roundtable
1995   Tape recording. Asia Society, November 4.
Los Angeles Roundtable
1995   Tape recording. Asia Society, November 15.
Manning, Bayless
1977   "The Congress, the Executive and Intermestic Affairs." *Foreign Affairs* 55 (January): 306–24.
Newsweek
1996   "China on the Move." April 1.
Northwest Asian Weekly
1995   "Editorial," December 9–15.
Ong, Paul, Edna Bonacich, and Lucie Cheng
1994a "The Political Economy of Capitalist Restructuring and the New Asian Immigration." In *The New Asian Immigration in Los Angeles and Global Restructuring,* ed. Paul Ong, Edna Bonacich, and Lucie Cheng. Philadelphia: Temple University Press, 3–35.
1994b "Preface." In *The New Asian Immigration,* ed. Ong, Bonacich, and Cheng, vii–xi.
Seattle Roundtable
1995   Tape recording. Asia Society, November 17.
Takaki, Ronald
1989   *Strangers from a Different Shore: A History of Asian Americans.* Boston: Little, Brown and Company.
Tien, Chang-lin
1996   Keynote address. "Bridges with Asia: Asian Americans in the United States." National Conference, Asia Society, May 2–4, New York.
Washington, D.C., Roundtable
1995   Tape recording. Asia Society, November 7.

6

EXCLUSION
AND
INCLUSION

Immigration and American Orientalism

NEIL GOTANDA

I. INTRODUCTION

In 1995, immigrants reemerged as a focal point of national domestic political dispute. Proposition 187 in California, directed at undocumented aliens and illegal immigration, was debated amid heated anti-immigrant rhetoric. Opponents charged that Proposition 187 was a racist initiative. In response, proponents claimed that the proposition was an effort to control "illegal" not "legal" immigrants; the United States had lost control of its borders, and Proposition 187 was an effort to reestablish control of those borders. Proposition 187 and the political issue of the immigrant as a racial question thus became a crucial part of the debate.[1]

With the overwhelming passage of Proposition 187 by California voters, the issue of immigration was moved to the center stage of American politics. In Washington, the debate over illegal immigration was expanded into a "reform" proposal that included drastic and dramatic changes in several key areas of domestic and immigration law. Those changes addressed both legal and illegal immigration. These efforts in Congress addressed several domestic areas, especially welfare and immigration. The bipartisan welfare legislation passed in 1996 marked a dramatic shift in national policy. Instead of a federal program that established on a national basis basic minimum guidelines, the responsibility for welfare and health care was shifted back to the states, which would receive block grants of funds. As part of the welfare legislation, federally mandated benefits and medical care for large numbers of "legal" immigrants were ended. (For a summary, see Ellen G. Yost 1997.)

These efforts at the federal level to devolve to the states power over immigrants were only partly successful. Unlawful immigration was targeted in the new legislation, with major penalties and restrictions imposed on the "illegal immigrant." The drastic step of allowing states to exclude undocumented children from elementary and secondary education was blocked. Also defeated was the call for dramatic cuts in the total number of immigrants from states with large populations of non-white immigrants, such as California and Florida.

As in past campaigns against immigrants, these congressional actions carry within them overlapping, and even contradictory, distinctions about citizenship, ethnicity, border geography, and race. To sort through this confusing overlay of social, political, and legal categories, this essay uses the evolving idea of American Orientalism. That concept includes as a crucial element a distinct understanding of race—a socially constructed category linked to physiognomy—applied to persons of Asian ancestry. In addition to including a notion of race, American Orientalism has developed through a definition and redefinition of the Orient—a cultural and ideological location related to, but distinct from, geographical Asia. American Orientalism also includes a complex reworking of Americanness through the mechanisms of ethnicity and the legal category of citizenship.

This essay outlines how persons of Asian ancestry have been treated within the confines of what can be seen as an expanded understanding of immigration law. Immigration law is usually taken to mean the study and application of federal statutes governing entry into the United States and naturalization—that is, crossing U.S. borders and becoming an American citizen. Such a narrow legalistic view of immigration law constricts our ability to examine fully the situation of the immigrant. Immigration is a concept that has been tied integrally to our shifting geographical position in the world, to notions of being "American" as well as technical conceptions of citizen versus alien. Using the concept of American Orientalism allows other non-legal considerations to be factored into an examination of immigration law and Asian Americans.

The American Orientalist treatment of the person of Asian ancestry is illuminated through analysis of the American tradition of racial categorization. The process of racial categorization gives race a social and legal context grounded in the ability to define and demark substantial groups of population based on their membership in a legally recognized group—a racial category. Available within those confines are the outlines of emerging American Orientalism, marked by a deeply embedded and historically dense received racial practice, overlaid and intertwined with the questions of ethnicity, citizenship, and geography. Immigration legislation affecting persons of Asian ancestry has long avoided direct mention of race. At the same time, legislation affecting immigrants and immigration at the state and federal levels, as well as court decisions interpreting and applying those enactments, have all involved considerations that go toward constructing American Orientalism.

II. AMERICAN ORIENTALISM AND RACIAL CATEGORIES

Orientalism

For persons of Asian ancestry, the constructed social categories of race and ethnicity are infused with the long-established tradition of European Orientalism. In discussing "Orientalism," Edward Said's influential 1979 critique of European literary and scholarly interest in the Orient, Lisa Lowe asserted that:

> Said defines the phenomenon [of Orientalism] as the body of occidental representations of the oriental world which both constitute the Orient as Other to the Occident and appropriate the domain of the Orient by speaking for it. Orientalism is a discourse, Said argues, which is on the one hand homogenizing—the Orient is leveled into one indistinguishable entity—and on the other hand anatomizing and enumerative—the Orient as an encyclopedia of details divided and particularized into manageable parts. The discourse manages and produces information about an invented Other, which locates and justifies the power of the knowledgeable European self. (Lowe 1991: 3, fn3)

Lowe argues in her analysis of Orientalism, *Critical Terrains* (1991), that Orientalism is neither monolithic nor stable, but historicized and contextual. Her work explores French and British Orientalisms. Lowe's most recent book, *Immigrant Acts* (1996), is a pioneering study of American Orientalism.

American contact with the Orient has focused on East and Southeast Asia—from Korea and Japan through China, the Philippines, and Vietnam—rather than on the Middle East, India, and China, which occupied Europe's attention, according to Said and Lowe.

Under the approach described by Lowe, Orientalism homogenizes and flattens all differences between and among the people and countries of Asia into a single "Orient" and "Oriental." An example of this homogenizing from current popular culture would be the ease by which American audiences accepted the transposition of Puccini's opera *Madame Butterfly* into wartime Saigon in the Broadway musical *Miss Saigon* and into revolutionary China in David Henry Hwang's *M. Butterfly.*

The American Orientalist constructs the Orient and Orientals as the external and foreign Other who define America and Americanness. Under an Orientalist analysis, our American national identity is thus invested with the Otherness of the Orient. The American racial peculiarity is that the Orientalist impulse to homogenize all East and Southeast Asians into a category of Oriental coincides with our domestic understanding of such racial categories as "black" and "white." While they are related, the Orientalist racialized impulse has a genealogy that is distinguishable from that of the "black"–"white" racial categorization.

Racial Categories

The American racial tradition has been most highly developed in the domestic context for persons of African ancestry. In the nineteenth century and for most of the twentieth century, however, the process of racial categorization never has been fully extended in American practice to persons of Asian ancestry. To explore the nature and meaning of this partial racialization, this study uses a reification model of racial categories—that is, racial categories such as "black" and "white" are the reified form of more specific and concrete forms of economic and social subordination. Historically, this approach finds the early origins of American understanding of the "white" and "black" racial categories in the early colonial era (Gotanda 1991, 1980).

In the seventeenth century, as slavery took hold as the dominant labor form for the plantation economy, the category of "Negro," within its own logic of social construction, went from a descriptive term to a category legitimating enslaveability. Some early efforts to legitimate slavery held that the enslaved were wartime captives or non-Christian heathens. Calling the enslaved captives or heathens "Negroes" was a mere description and not central to those legitimating ideologies. By the end of the seventeenth century, the idea that "Negroes" could be enslaved superseded these other legitimations. The racial category was itself a reification of the status of enslaveability. The category of "Negro" was transformed into a vehicle of legitimation.

Using this concept of the racial category as a reification of relations of subordination, we can examine the ideology of the social practice of race. In particular, this methodology allows extension of the analysis to Asians in the nineteenth and twentieth centuries. In this examination of immigration statutes, we study three ideological characteristics of the "African American," or "black," racial category as practiced at the end of the nineteenth century: domestication, erasure of national origin, and scientific naturalization of race. Each of these characteristics as practiced and applied to the "African American" category is sufficiently similar to the treatment of Asians in the United States to justify describing Asians as an American racial category.

The first characteristic, and the one most significant for Asians, is that race is a domestic American category that is associated with domestic relations and situations. Foreign considerations play a secondary role in formulations of the "black" racial category.

The opposing racial category to "black" was "white"—meaning a white American. The social practice of American racial categorization took place within American borders. The social categorization, and hence social identity, of slaves and former slaves was not "Yoruba," "Hausa," or even "African," but "Negro" or "black." Thus, the identity of whiteness was constructed around the otherness of the Negro, but within the American nation.

This construction of domestic Otherness was very different from the Orientalist construction. The Orientalist tradition looked to construction of national identity by posing an external Orientalized Other—located in the Orient and embodied in the Oriental. This conflict between the domesticating impulse of racialization and the foreign Otherness of Orientalism goes to the heart of conflicting constructions of Asian Americans, as well as to the heart of conflicts of identities among Asian Americans.

The second common practice of racialization is the erasure of prior social identities, such as tribe, nation, language group, and other ethnic identifications. As it evolves through history, the racial category supersedes the claims of culture, ethnicity, and nationality. Thus, the "Negro" or "black" category supersedes, and even denies, language-group and tribal membership. For Asians, the vast and profound differences between the parts of the enormity of geographical Asia are all conflated into a single "yellow" or "Asian" category.

A third practice is that the racial category is "naturalized" as a biological or self-evident scientific category. Much of the history of modern anthropology embodies efforts to invent a science that will legitimate white supremacy. For Asians, the "yellow," or Asiatic, race as a biological or anthropological division becomes the unspoken premise of discussion.

Such a discussion takes as common sense or as scientific truth that a category such as "mongolian," "Oriental," or "yellow" has already been determined. No explanation or justification is necessary for the boundaries of the category, only a discussion or argument over the characteristics of the Asian race. The traits that are assigned to the Asian racial category emerged in the nineteenth century and are now familiar: foreignness and unassimilability.

III. *PEOPLE V. HALL*

Reviewing historical legal statements about persons of Asian ancestry provides further insight into American Orientalism. An especially useful case for such study is the 1854 California Supreme Court decision in *People v. Hall* (4 Cal. 399 1854). That decision, which came early in the history of modern immigration from Asia to the United States, reviewed the murder conviction of a "free white citizen" where the witnesses were Chinese. The historical context of this case is the widespread use in the years before the Civil War of state statutes that excluded testimony of blacks against whites. The California Supreme Court faced the immediate but accidental issue of how to apply the statute to the testimony of a Chinese.

The *Hall* case can be seen as a discussion about excluded foreigners that articulates an understanding of a "pre-racial" period in which Chinese were completely foreign. Under review was the applicability of a statute that stated, "No Black, or Mulatto person, or Indian, shall be allowed to give evidence in favor of, or against a white man." While the statute made no mention of Chinese, the California Supreme Court concluded that the statute did apply to this group and excluded the witness's testimony. Of interest are the court's several theories to explain how Chinese were to be included as either "Indian" or "black."

In its decision, the court did not use history in its traditional sense of describing and thus accommodating a new arrival—Chinese—to the California racial scene. Rather, history was invoked through a linguistic and scientific review of Columbus's use of the term "India" and the migration of indigenous peoples across the Bering Strait. Using a scientific discursive framework, Chinese were related to Indians and therefore included in the scientized category of "American Indian."

In a different discursive mode, the court used a historical legislative-language analysis to analogize application of the statute to Chinese as if they were non-whites. This came through a generalized discussion that the term "black" in the statute was intended to be a generic descriptor for all non-whites since it went beyond the term "Negro" found in other statutes. Chinese could only be accommodated to the statute by analogizing the excluded Chinese foreigners to subordinated non-whites. The comparison for Chinese was only by analogy. Chinese were available for comparison as non-whites because they were self-evidently not white. Yet Chinese were not "really" blacks or Indians. In this analysis and in other language in the text of the opinion, there was no sense that Chinese were a part of American or Californian society. This was not an argument that Chinese were a domestic non-white race whose presence was to be contested. Chinese were not treated as another racial minority, similarly situated to slaves or free Negroes. Instead, the Chinese were foreigners, mere unwelcome visitors upon our shores.

Later Supreme Court cases from the 1890s reflected efforts to accommodate Chinese as a racialized minority, not to exclude them as totally foreign. By the end of the century, four decades of Chinese in California had provided the social context for Chinese to be "raced." This social process of "racing" had produced a subordinated, non-white racial minority. This "raced" Chinese occupied distinctive racial positions with identities different from "black" and "white." Of special importance was a dimension of "foreignness" as part of the racialized Chinese identity.

This reading of *People v. Hall* creates a complex set of interactions among race, Americanness, immigration, and the U.S. border. On the one hand, immigration becomes more than the simple act of changing geography and crossing a fictitious line. The Chinese in *People v. Hall* were different legal persons from the Chinese in later cases. Chinese in these two periods may have a similar status as "legal" immigrants, but their racial treatment differs sharply. Further, what appears to be a simple line between "American" and "foreigner" becomes confusing when, in the later cases, the "raced" identity of a Chinese includes being identified as a "foreigner." The irony is that this occurs when the Chinese are assimilated into America as "raced" Americans.

The pervasiveness of these understandings of Asians can be seen in the 1897 comments of Justice Harlan's dissent in *United States v. Wong Kim Ark* (169 U.S. 649 1898: 731):

> After some years' experience . . . the Government of the United States was brought to the opinion that the presence within our territory of large numbers of Chinese laborers, of a distinct race and religion, remaining strangers in the land, residing apart by themselves, tenaciously adhering to the customs and usages of their own country, unfamiliar with our institutions and apparently incapable of assimilating with our people, might endanger good order, and be injurious to the public interests.

The context of Harlan's dissent was his objection to the interpretation of the Fourteenth Amendment that any person born within U.S. borders was a U.S. citizen. The characteristics of foreignness and unassimilability are treated by Harlan as fixed attributes that can never be lost, no matter how many generations have lived in the United States and how much assimilation has taken place. His dissent reflected and reproduced attitudes that have been used and reused to justify both exclusion and expulsion of Asians from the United States. While his comments contributed to the construction of the American understanding of Chinese, they were similar to statements directed at every Asian immigrant group.

IV. ASIAN IMMIGRATION AND ASIAN EXCLUSION

Chinese Exclusion

After a decade of intense agitation against Chinese, Congress passed the first Chinese Exclusion Act in 1882. The confusing pattern of Asian exclusion can be seen in the early history of these laws directed at Chinese. An initial version providing for a twenty-year suspension of Chinese immigration was vetoed by President Arthur. Within one month, Congress passed a new measure with a ten-year suspension period, which Arthur signed (22 *Statutes at Large* [hereafter *Stat.*] 58). Against a background of continuing anti-Chinese agitation and widespread violence against Chinese throughout the West, additional restrictive measures soon followed.

An 1884 law limited use by Chinese of reentry certificates issued to them by the U.S. government (23 *Stat.* 115). In 1888, the Scott Act was passed, which unilaterally abrogated all outstanding certificates of reentry issued to Chinese (25 *Stat.* 504). Some 20,000 Chinese who had returned to China to visit were affected by the act. Chinese exclusion was renewed for another ten years in the Geary Act of 1892 (27 *Stat.* 25), which also established a requirement that Chinese have a certificate of residence. The immigration suspension was renewed in an open-ended provision in the Chinese Exclusion Act of 1902 (32 *Stat.* 176), then made permanent in 1904 (see Hutchinson 1981; Daniels 1988).

These statutes were the first stage in the emerging system of restrictive regulation of immigration, which culminated in the national-origins–quota program of the Immigration Act of 1924. Under the quota system, an annual maximum number of immigrants was established, and that number was divided into national quotas based on the number of persons of that national ancestry residing in the United States in 1890, with the minimum nominal quota of one hundred persons per year (Daniels 1988: 150).

Immigration from Japan increased in the latter part of the nineteenth century, led in part by labor contractors recruiting workers for Hawaiian plantations. While Japan's growing international stature provided a basis for diplomatic resistance to direct exclusion of Japanese immigrants, pressure for exclusion resulted in the Gentlemen's Agreement of 1907. Under the agreement, Japan "voluntarily" limited the number of Japanese coming to the United States, Hawaii, Mexico, and Canada (Hutchinson 1981: 431).

Borders and Geographical Exclusion

Efforts to exclude Asians continued through the early decades of the twentieth century. The "barred-zone" provision of the 1917 immigration law was primarily directed at Asian Indians, characterized as the "Hindu" problem (Act of February 15, 1919: 39 *Stat.* 874). This provision, which remained in effect until 1952, prohibited immigration by natives from an area much larger than India. The barred zone, defined by latitude and longitude, was a geographical area that included South Asia from Arabia through Southeast Asia and islands in the Indian and Pacific Ocean, but excluded the American possessions of the Philippines and Guam. Not included in the barred zone were China and Japan, already subject to the Chinese Exclusion Act and the Gentlemen's Agreement (Hutchinson 1981: 432).

This use of a geographical area, inscribed upon the South, East, and West Asian subcontinents, is notable for the absence of national, racial, and ethnic conditions. Congress's choice of a set of lines on the Earth's surface can be seen, in modern terms, as a set of conditions that do not discriminate on the basis of race, ethnicity, or national origin.[2] This pre-figuration of modern antidiscrimination considerations is not an accident. Immigration law reflects congressional experimentation with these color-blind forms of categorization and exclusion.

This geographical form of exclusion, introduced in the 1917 Asiatic Barred Zone, was reproduced in 1952 in the Asia Pacific Triangle. As part of the 1952 Immigration and Nationality Act (commonly known as the McCarran–Walter Act), a new zone was created that included the countries from India to Japan and the Pacific Islands north of Australia. A small, exclusionary quota from this area was established (66 *Stat.* 163). It was not until the modern 1965 immigration act that the geographical basis for exclusion was abandoned.

National Origin Quotas and Ethnicity

Another form of Asian exclusion came in the Immigration Act of 1924. Aimed at Japanese and supported by those unhappy with even the limited numbers of Japanese entering under the Gentlemen's Agreement, a provision of the 1924 act barred aliens who were ineligible for citizenship. Because Japanese and other Asians were barred by the racial limitation on naturalization, they were totally excluded from immigration (Daniels 1988: 150).

The Japanese exclusion provisions were part of a broader program of immigration control. The 1924 act consolidated a major immigration "reform" in which the flow of immigrants was based on the immigrants' country of origin and was limited to a quota determined by the number of persons of that particular national origin already in the United States. Since the largest number of immigrants were from England and Northern Europe, those countries had the largest quotas. There was a clear preference for the "whitest" of the Europeans under the quota system.

The Racial Bar to Naturalization

The racial bar to naturalization dated from the first naturalization statute passed in 1790, which limited naturalization to "white persons" (Act of March 16, 1790: 1 *Stat.* 103). After the Civil War, the law was amended by adding an exception to allow the naturalization of African Americans (Hutchinson 1981: 53). For Chinese, however, the exclusion acts, beginning in 1882, had specifically stated that Chinese were ineligible for citizenship.

This statutory racial bar to naturalization had been applied to immigrants from East Asia and South Asia, but without consistency. The naturalization cases in the lower courts were a maze of contradictory rulings and justifications (Haney López 1996). The matter was not clarified until the early 1920s, when the U.S. Supreme Court issued a series of opinions in which the constitutionality of the bar was upheld as applied to Takeo Ozawa—an American-educated, culturally assimilated Japanese immigrant—and Baghat Singh Thind, an Indian who was a World War I veteran.[3]

These opinions had multiple results. Not only did they provide clarification of who was "white" under the naturalization statutes, but they also established the basis for upholding a series of state statutes that had differentially treated Asians by using the status "alien ineligible for citizenship." States in the West, as part of the continuing campaign against Chinese, Japanese, and then Indians, had passed "alien land laws" seeking to prevent members of these groups from owning land. In *Terrace v. Thompson,* the U.S. Supreme Court in 1923 upheld as constitutional California's versions of laws that barred "aliens ineligible to citizenship" from owning land (263 U.S. 197).

This euphemism, "aliens ineligible to citizenship," was the language adopted in the Japanese-exclusion provisions of the 1924 immigration law. Rather than granting Japan its token quota of one hundred immigrants as provided under the main provisions of the 1924 law, the exclusion provision added another chapter to Asian exclusion from America.

V. REPEAL OF ASIAN EXCLUSION

Beginning in 1943, the U.S. Congress substantially modified the exclusionary laws restricting immigration from Asia. The first and most important of these statutes was the Magnuson Act of 1943, passed in the middle of World War II. The Magnuson Act is known as the statute that repealed the Chinese Exclusion Acts. However, because the structure of exclusion of Asians included several different devices, overturning the Chinese Exclusion Acts was more complex than a simple repeal of a law or of laws (Act of December 17, 1943: 57 *Stat.* 600). Addressing Chinese, Indians, and Filipinos, these changes had little practical effect on the lives of immigrants, because exclusion was replaced with token immigration quotas. The significance of the acts repealing Asian exclusion is found in the arena of racial ideology rather than in its quantitative impact upon immigrants.

The Magnuson Act of 1943 was composed of three sections. The first section repealed those portions of the Chinese Exclusion Acts that had specifically named Chinese as barred from immigration into the United States. To replace total exclusion, the second section of the Magnuson Act established a token racial quota for Chinese entry. The third section allowed Chinese to become naturalized American citizens, which bypassed another of the Asian exclusion mechanisms.

After the end of World War II, the Magnuson Act was followed by passage of the Act of July 2, 1946, allowing Indians and Filipinos to become naturalized citizens and establishing a small quota for Indian immigration (60 *Stat.* 416). As a companion to the declaration of Philippine independence, a presidential proclamation on July 4, 1946, provided an immigration quota for the newly independent Filipinos (60 *Stat.* 1353). The Act of August 9, 1946, allowed the Chinese wives of U.S. citizens to enter the United States outside the Chinese quota, in the same manner as had the European wives of American citizens (60 *Stat.* 975). Finally, the Act of August 1, 1950, allowed Guamanians to become naturalized citizens as part of legislation that established self-rule for Guam (60 *Stat.* 384).

These statutes together repealed Asian exclusion but differed in significant aspects from earlier immigration legislation. By all accounts of the deliberations leading up to passage of the Magnuson Act, the impetus for repeal of the Chinese Exclusion Acts came from our wartime foreign policy (see Riggs 1950; Daniels 1988; Hutchinson 1981). After repeal, the annual quota for Chinese was around one hundred. The establishment of the nominal entry quota, and allowing a small number of Chinese to become naturalized citizens, had little immediate economic or social impact domestically. The traditional considerations in analyzing immigration legislation—international trade, investments, industrial labor—were barely affected. Given this nominal economic impact, these acts would have to be seen as of minor import under traditional economic approaches. Examining these immigration laws as elements of racial ideology suggests that they are of much greater interest and significance.

It was the conflicting political and racial ideologies of World War II that generated the impetus for the repeal of Asian exclusion. In the Pacific, Japanese propaganda emphasized anti-Asian laws and polices of the United States, e.pecially the exclusionary acts. In the battle for moral superiority among the Allies, the American position was further undermined by its racially discriminatory domestic policies. The ideologies supporting racially discriminatory policies can be seen reproduced in the structure of the repeal acts and the racial and ethnic character of past Asian exclusion statutes.

American Foreign Policy

At the beginning of America's involvement in the Pacific War, Chinese and Asiatic exclusion had been a central part of immigration policy for more than sixty years. Yet within a few years, the repeal acts significantly altered these policies. The relative ease of passage of the repeal acts was the result of the ideological struggles generated by the war (Dower 1986: 164–170; Riggs 1950).

In both the Pacific and Europe, the military campaigns were accompanied by clashing racial ideologies. The American war effort was marked by an emphasis on reestablishing the American social and political identity in opposition to Nazi ideas of Aryan racial supremacy and the Japanese calls for pan-Asian unity against white imperialists.

Japanese war publicists' efforts directed toward China and India emphasized America's racially discriminatory immigration and naturalization policies. The Japanese could justifiably note that the exclusion acts of the 1880s and 1890s had been aimed at Chinese, the "barred-zone" law of 1917 had been aimed at Indians, and the 1924 immigration law had included sections whose purpose was to cut off even the limited Japanese immigration allowed under the Gentlemen's Agreement. The Japanese also publicized the fact that Chinese and Indians were ineligible to be naturalized as American citizens under the 1790 statute (Act of March 26, 1790: 1 *Stat.* 103).

American propaganda, on the other hand, emphasized democracy, freedom, equality—values that opposed the tyranny and despotism ascribed to the Axis powers. The American position was that the Allied powers fought to further these lofty-sounding goals. When placed in the international arena, these principles suggested independence for colonized peoples and international equality and respect for all nations.

When these principles of international equality were applied to American domestic concerns, however, their suggestion that all peoples—and hence all races—should be treated with equality and respect was in conflict with U.S. racial policies and immigration laws. Foreign-policy concerns over issues of race led toward a position of legal racial equality—a position that the American government was not yet ready to embrace unequivocally.

Domestic racial policies were considerably different from the international principles of equality. In the early 1940s, local statutes and legal decisions throughout the country supported racial segregation in nongovernment employment and housing; in public areas, such as government buildings; and in public accommodations, such as hotels, restaurants, and local transportation. Further, there was tolerance of private violence aimed at African Americans as well as of violence directed at other non-whites.

The U.S. laws and court decisions therefore provided a solid basis for Japan to claim to nationalists throughout the Pacific that America and its European Allies offered Asians only second-class participation in their alliance. In December 1942, a long Tokyo broadcast stated, "The Chungking authorities must certainly know that Chinese are rigidly prohibited from emigrating to the United States and that this ban on Chinese immigration was established in the later portion of the last century after a campaign of venomous vilification of the character of the Chinese people. . . . The Chinese are rigidly excluded from attaining American citizenship by naturalization, a right which is accorded to the lowliest immigrant from Europe. . . .

"It is meaningful, indeed, that for decades the United States and the British Empire have been traditionally discriminating against the Chinese and all other Asiatics in [all their other] domains, and it is only after they have become hard-pressed in the present war, after they have become desperate, they use their allies to serve their ends. . . . Far from waging this war to liberate the oppressed peoples of the world, the Anglo-American leaders are trying to restore the obsolete system of imperialism by which they hope to prolong their iniquitous exploitation of the best portions of the earth" (Riggs 1950: 161).

To respond to at least some of this racial propaganda, proposals that would have had little chance of success before the war began to gain in credibility. With the support of the Citizens Committee to Repeal Chinese Exclusion, the effort ended in success with the passage of the Magnuson Act in 1943. Fred Riggs (1950: 131) concludes his study of the repeal of the Chinese Exclusion Acts with the observation that the argument with the widest appeal and the greatest weight was that the repeal would support the war effort. He argues that this was particularly true "in weakening the opposition and winning at least acceptance if not support from pressure groups and Congressmen who might otherwise have rejected the proposal."

Race and Foreign Policy

A possible interpretation of this conflict between foreign policy and domestic policy is that it was an early preview of the concerns that surfaced around the landmark 1954 Supreme Court decision in *Brown v. Board of Education* (347 U.S. 483 1954). Mary Dudziak (1988) has written a study of the foreign-policy influences on *Brown*. Dudziak used as her framework of analysis the influential suggestion of Professor Derrick Bell that civil-rights progress occurs when there is an interest convergence between white Americans and black Americans, and that progress ends when their interests diverge (Dudziak 1988). She concludes that Bell's interest-convergence hypothesis is supported by the history of *Brown*. Similarly, John Hayakawa Torok (1996) has examined the repeal of the Chinese Exclusion Acts and concluded that Bell's interest-convergence analysis is applicable.

When viewed as an ideological conflict over the period from 1943 to 1964, one can see this as a chapter in the continuous debate over racial segregation over two decades. The debate included the Supreme Court decision in *Brown v. Board of Education* in 1954, with the tension between foreign and domestic policy being resolved only with the passage of the Civil Rights Act of 1964 (78 *Stat.* 241), the Voting Rights Act of 1965 (79 *Stat.* 437), and the Supreme Court's enforcement of public-school desegregation.

By the end of the 1960s, it was possible for our international position to be consistent with our domestic racial politics—formal racial equality was the legal position within the United States as well as our official international position.

Repeal of the Asian Exclusion Laws

Efforts to address Chinese exclusion thus referred to a number of these exclusionary devices. Section One of the Magnuson Act referred to fifteen different enactments dating from 1882. Crafting the repeal of the Chinese Exclusion Acts required reference to this entire patchwork set of laws.

Simple repeal of the Chinese Exclusion Acts, without more, would have eliminated the reference to Chinese in the statutes. But because Chinese were still barred from naturalization, they would have been excluded by the "aliens ineligible to citizenship" clauses of the 1924 act. Such a repeal would have been more insulting than helpful in the Pacific propaganda war. Chinese would still have been barred from becoming both citizens and legal immigrants. As Riggs points out, that would have promoted the Chinese to the same legal level as the enemy Japanese, hardly a foreign-policy triumph (Riggs 1950: 39).

In order to address all of these considerations, the final version of the Magnuson Act not only included repeal of the sections that barred Chinese, but also granted Chinese the right to become citizens and provided a quota for Chinese under the 1924 act. This quota, however, differed from the European national-origin quotas in that *all* persons of Chinese ancestry, regardless of the country of birth or origin, were included in the quota. This distinction set the Chinese quota apart from European quotas.

The actual campaign for repeal of Chinese exclusion was relatively short, but it occurred at a moment when wartime pressures made Congress especially receptive to the campaign. It was also marked by leadership from an ad hoc pressure group called the Citizens Committee to Repeal Chinese Exclusion (Riggs 1950: 39).

On October 11, 1943, President Roosevelt issued a special appeal to Congress, using many of the committee's arguments and emphasizing the foreign-policy aspects of the repeal. Within ten days, the House passed the Magnuson bill, and on December 17, the president approved repeal of the Chinese exclusion laws (Riggs 1950: 38).

In the course of the campaign, several other proposals that were discarded by Congress in favor of the Magnuson Act had attempted to extend the repeal of Asian exclusion to other named Asian groups, or even to repeal the racial bar to naturalization entirely (Hutchinson 1981: 478–80). The broad-based repeal efforts were rejected in favor of an ad hoc group-by-group process.

In July 1946, a combined set of statutes and presidential proclamations granted the Philippines independence and opened up Filipino and Indian immigration. With independence, Filipinos were granted quotas, and the bar to naturalization was lifted. Indians were removed from the "barred zone," granted a quota, and allowed to become naturalized. The quotas, however, were similar to the Chinese quota, applying to all persons of Filipino or Indian ancestry, regardless of their place of origin (Riggs 1950: 38). Another step in easing the Chinese quota came in the August 9, 1946, placing of Chinese wives of U.S. citizens on a non-quota basis. The rule was gender-specific to "Chinese alien wives of American citizens" (Act of August 9, 1946: 60 *Stat.* 975). In 1950, Congress provided for self-rule for Guam and granted citizenship to natives and most residents of Guam; it also lifted the racial barrier to naturalization (Act of August 1, 1950: 64 *Stat.* 384).

VI. ORIENTALIZED ETHNICS AND RACIAL IDEOLOGY

The repeal acts operated on a country-by-country basis. Chinese had been excluded by name, and the repeal acts provided for quotas and lifted citizenship barriers on a similar country-by-country basis. Current usage is to call these nominally national-origin descriptions "ethnic" categories. Following current popular usage, "ethnic" invokes the names of the modern Asian nation-states to describe immigrants from Asia and their descendants: Chinese are from China, Filipinos are from the Philippines, and so forth (Espiritu 1992). This usage of ethnicity is an Orientalized and racialized usage.

An important way in which current popular discussion of "race and ethnicity" has developed is to use ethnicity as if it were a neutral descriptive term without normative content. In discussions of race and gender, the phrases color-blind, race-neutral, and gender-neutral are terms that describe a particular manner of speaking in which race or gender is regarded as nonnormative.

Hidden in most popular references to ethnicity is the assumption that any such discussion is "ethnicity-neutral." Under an ethnicity-neutral approach, Chinese are "just another ethnic group," like Irish or Italians. This assumption is unjustified. Examination of the quota provisions of the Asian exclusion repeal acts shows that Chinese and Indians in these statutes were treated differently from European immigrants. Racialized aspects of ethnicity continue as hidden attributions to Orientalized ethnic categories.

The quota established for Chinese in the Magnuson Act was a worldwide quota. Any person of Chinese ancestry, regardless of where the person was born, was included within the category. This differed from other national-origin quotas under the 1924 law. Under those definitions, nationality of the immigrant was determined by country of birth, not by ancestry. This approach was repeated in the quota for India, also using the "worldwide" quota formulation for "all persons of races indigenous to India" rather than the definition applicable to other national-origin quotas. The language used to explain the quota for India explicitly invokes biological race. The statutory language includes the terms "blood of a race indigenous to India" and "one-half Chinese blood."

The "Chinese" and "Indian" ethnic categories as used in these Asian exclusion repeal statutes are Orientalized through differentiating Asian immigrants from immigrants from elsewhere in the world. This particularized "Othering" of Asia is an important element of making Asian ethnic categories into Orientalized ethnic categories. These ethnic descriptors are also racialized. We have seen how the Orientalized ethnic category of "Chinese" is functionally also a racial category.

Orientalized ethnic categories are "racialized" in the repeal statutes in two ways. Each individual ethnic category is treated as if it were a naturalized "racial" category like "black," "white," and "yellow." Thus, Chinese become scientifically naturalized into a biological or anthropological group via bloodlines of descent. The descriptor "Chinese" can apply to all persons whose ancestry can in some fashion be traced back to China, whose history and complexity are not discussed.

This racialized treatment of Chinese denies or erases a number of significant possibilities. Geography of national origin is erased, because communities self-identified as Chinese have existed for centuries outside of the borders of the nation-state of China. It denies juridical citizenship, because a person of Chinese ancestry from Indonesia who carries an Indonesian passport is still considered ethnic Chinese. It erases national culture, because the American-born, Harvard-educated, fourth-generation Chinese American, with no direct knowledge of China or Chinese national culture, is considered ethnically Chinese. Finally, all cultural and national-minority distinctions within China are similarly erased into a single, monolithic Chineseness.

The second moment of racialization occurs as the Orientalized traits of foreignness and unassimilability are biologically naturalized into attributes of the Chinese ethnic category. These attributed traits of foreignness and unassimilability, described by Harlan in the late nineteenth century, continue today.

These Orientalized, racialized ethnic categories are "Orientalized ethnics." The Asian exclusion repeal acts reveal the construction of these ethnic and racial variations. Both the Asian racial category and the Orientalized ethnic can be seen in the Asian exclusion laws and their repeal. Together, these are crucial aspects in the construction of American Orientalism. For persons of Asian ancestry in America, the powerful social dynamics of American Orientalism and American "black"–"white" racial categorization have created multiple and ambiguous identifications and identities.

VII. MODERN TRANSFORMATIONS

Immigration legislation after World War II was marked by mixed efforts to move away from the legacy of Asian exclusion. In 1952, the McCarran–Walter Act removed the "white persons" racial criterion for naturalization; it also abolished the Asiatic Barred Zone but replaced it with the Asia Pacific Triangle (66 *Stat.* 163). Preceding the McCarran–Walter Act were two Supreme Court decisions in 1948 that struck down discriminatory state legislation that had focused on Japanese Americans. Alien land laws passed at the state level in the early twentieth century barred aliens ineligible for citizenship, and Japanese in particular, from owning or leasing land. The alien land laws had been approved by the Supreme Court as constitutional. *Oyama v. California* struck down presumptions used to enforce California's Alien Land Law (332 U.S. 633 1948). In *Takahashi v. Fish and Game,* the court struck down California's prohibition on issuing commercial fishing licenses to persons ineligible for citizenship (334 U.S. 410 1948). These court decisions on domestic matters coincided with international developments in racial politics.

During the post–World War II era, domestic politics had become slowly sensitized to the deeply felt injustices of racial segregation and discrimination against African Americans. In foreign policy, international Cold War considerations were framed by the ongoing conflict in Korea amid the growing rivalry between the United States and the Soviet Union over influence among the decolonized newly emerging nations. As a result, a significant sentiment developed to abolish the racial barrier to naturalization. Given its origins under slavery, this barrier was perceived as a racist provision whose abolition would be of symbolic importance. Viewed in this light, the elimination of the barrier can be seen as part of the slow developments in the legal arena leading to the landmark Supreme Court decision in *Brown v. Board of Education,* which declared unconstitutional racially segregated public schools (347 U.S. 483 1954).

Just as the competition between the United States and Japan had hastened the repeal of the Chinese exclusions laws during World War II, emerging Cold War concerns provided a important backdrop for American racial policies. Eliminating racial barriers to naturalization removed an important contradiction in the American self-image as the defenders of equality and democracy.

Sentiments against racial and ethnic discrimination played a part in the debates leading up to passage of the McCarran–Walter Act. Unfortunately, most antidiscrimination proposals to amend the McCarran–Walter Act were defeated in committee and on the floor of Congress. After initial passage by Congress, the measure was vetoed by President Truman, in part because of its anti-Asian biases. Both houses of Congress then voted to override Truman's veto. Among the important steps taken in the complex measure was the removal of the racially restrictive criteria for naturalization and the abolition of the Asiatic Barred Zone.

The modest progressive step of removing the racial bar to naturalization, however, was offset by a number of exclusionary measures, including the replacement of the Asiatic Barred Zone with the Asia Pacific Triangle.[4] Congress imposed upon this new Asia Pacific Triangle a sharply limited national-origin quota. A total quota of two thousand visas was allocated for the entire nineteen-country area, including 185 for Japanese, 100 for Koreans, 100 for Chinese, and 100 for Indians (Hing 1993: 40, 247).

This geographically based exclusion was complemented by the imposition of a racialized-descent basis for the quota instead of a nationality–place of birth approach. The quotas followed the approach taken during the earlier repeal of Chinese and Indian exclusion. The 1952 law similarly imposed descent-based quotas on persons from within the Asia Pacific Triangle. As noted earlier, these descent-based quotas create racialized ethnic categories.

President Truman's veto was largely motivated by dissatisfaction with Congress's failure to replace the national-origins system with some alternative that did not appear so clearly preferential to Europe. He noted that the national-origin–quota system's disguised preference for northern Europeans contrasted with the explicitly exclusionary Asia Pacific Triangle provisions. The passage of the McCarran–Walter Act over Truman's veto meant that the abolition of the national-origin–quota system would wait for more than a decade. Truman appointed a special Commission on Immigration, which, after a year of study, recommended abolition of the national-origin–quota system and proposed quotas without regard to national origin, race, creed, or color (Hing 1993: 39). In was not until 1965 that President Johnson was able to secure passage of the program proposed by President Kennedy in the year before his assassination.

Kennedy's vision of a system oriented toward skilled immigrants and encouraging family reunification was only partly fulfilled, because the 1965 law included these elements along with a nation-based allocation of visas. For immigrants from outside the Western Hemisphere, the basic visa allocations were the same regardless of the size of the country, and they were implemented through a number of specialized "preference" subcategories. These complex provisions had a number of varying effects.

The formal language of the 1965 law did not use national-origin quotas; nor did it specify an Asian Barred Zone or Asia Pacific Triangle. As a result, there was a dramatic rise in the number of immigrants from Asia. Yet, both national quotas and geography still dominated the application of immigration law. The large numbers of applicants in certain countries seeking to emigrate to the United States resulted in the reestablishment of yet another form of nation-based quota. These countries were predominantly in Asia. The waiting period for the backlog of applicants from some countries in Asia stretched back several years. These backlogs were specific to each country and the type of preference—family, special skill, and so on—sought by the applicant. As a result, it was Asians seeking to emigrate from specific countries who faced the greatest obstacles (Hing 1993: 38–41).

The 1965 act marked the culmination of the efforts to eliminate the explicit use of racial devices to exclude Asians. All named racial barriers were eliminated from the U.S. immigration laws. The use of geographical markers to surround Asia and exclude immigrants from those areas was abandoned. The use of national-origin quotas crafted to favor northern European immigrants was ended. Nevertheless, familiar themes of immigration have repeated themselves. Even with immigration preferences supposedly based on equal treatment for all nationalities, significant obstacles emerged for immigrants from Asia.

VIII. CONCLUSION

The 1990s have seen a marked shift toward greater restrictions on immigration. California's Proposition 187 was followed by significant anti-immigrant activity in Congress. Legislation proposed, but not passed, by Congress would have drastically reduced family immigration as well as certain categories of employment-related immigration. Important provisions of federal welfare legislation, crime legislation, and anti-terrorist legislation were aimed at aliens. The Illegal Immigration Reform and Immigrant Responsibility Act of 1996 (IIRAIRA) was the principal congressional enactment on immigration. Its provisions expanded the grounds for excluding and deporting aliens and substantially narrowed the availability of discretionary relief. The IIRAIRA sharply limited administrative court review and eliminated federal-court judicial review of a wide range of agency decisions.

Taken together, these laws are an important move away from the positions taken in the 1965 act. Instead of welcoming immigrants as valuable contributors to America and recognizing that America has a special role to play as a refuge for those seeking asylum, IIRAIRA and related laws on aliens adopted a summary, punitive posture toward non-citizens. Less clear is whether the new legislation begins a new phase of Asian exclusion. On its face, there are few of the blatantly anti-Asian provisions of past years. However, the complexities of IIRAIRA and interpretive regulations will take years to implement and understand; thus, stronger conclusions must await the actual operations of the new laws. Looked at most generously, the alien and immigrant legislation of the 1990s withdrew the American welcome, with strong suggestions of hostility toward non-white immigrants and aliens.

The turn away from direct exclusionary measures by Congress is part of the broad shift away from the use of legislation and administrative agencies to promote racial subordination. In other areas of racial jurisprudence, especially in the Supreme Court's affirmative-action decisions, the emphasis has been on color-blind approaches. Those court decisions direct racial politics and policies away from government into nongovernmental decision making and the even more diffuse realms of cultural politics.

For Asian Americans, sorting through this new direction of racial politics into private conduct and political and popular culture is best carried out through a continuing examination of American Orientalism. As an analytical framework, American Orientalism makes possible an understanding of how the United States has treated, and continues to treat, immigrants of Asian ancestry differently from other immigrants. Asian Americans of widely varying family ancestries in the United States live in varied conditions and face different treatment as a result of those ancestries. Further, understanding the treatment and conditions facing Asians in America includes a domestic as well as an international context. Foreign-policy analyses of Asia have traditionally ignored the interaction of domestic racial and ethnic politics.

Recognizing the differences among Asian nationalities and ethnicities, but also appreciating how these ethnicities have been racialized under American Orientalism, lays the groundwork for the possibility of an Asian American politics. Yet the pervasive acceptance of Orientalist understandings by America means that such a politics carries the basis of its own self-destruction.

The most recent barrage of American Orientalism has come through the controversy over campaign donations from Asia and Asians. It may be premature to predict the long-term impact of the recurrent media references to Chinese, Japanese, or Indonesian attempts to "buy" American politicians through unlawful campaign donations. But the negative impact of those images was immediate, and there is little to suggest that this impact will be transitory and short-lived. The stereotyped images that surfaced during the campaign-donation controversy are extensions of old-fashioned Orientalism in popular culture.

It is easy to overlook the depth of the roots of American Orientalism in immigration laws and the court decisions that sustained and produced that Orientalism. Critique and criticism of stereotypes in popular culture are an insufficient basis for an anti-Orientalist politics. Without a thorough examination of Orientalist impulses in such fundamental structures of American culture as our legal system, we will never be able to remove the pervasive influence of Orientalism on American politics and culture.

■ NOTES

1. There is a large body of literature on Proposition 187. See generally José C. Villareal (1996); Gerald Neuman (1995); and Kevin Johnson (1995).

2. The language of modern antidiscrimination civil-rights legislation typically forbids discrimination on the basis of race, color, national orgin, and sex. See, for example, Title VI and Title VII of the Civil Rights Act of 1964.

3. *Takao Ozawa v. United States,* 260 U.S. 178 (1922); *United States v. Third,* 261 U.S. 204 (1923).

4. Act of June 27, 1952, Public Law 414, 66 *Statutes at Large* 163, Section 202; Bill Ong Hing (1993: 38).

■ REFERENCES

California Supreme Court
  1854   *People v. Hall* (4 Cal. 399).
Daniels, Roger
  1988   *Asian American: Chinese and Japanese in the United States Since 1840.* Seattle: University of Washington Press.
Dower, John W.
  1986   *War Without Mercy: Race and Power in the Pacific War.* New York: Pantheon Books.
Dudziak, Mary
  1988   "Desegregation as a Cold War Imperative." *Stanford Law Review* 41 (November): 61–120.
Espiritu, Yen Le
  1992   *Asian American Panethnicity: Bridging Institutions and Identities.* Philadelphia: Temple University Press.
Gotanda, Neil
  1991   "A Critique of 'Our Constitution is Colorblind.'" *Stanford Law Review* 44 (November): 1–68.
  1980   "Origins of Racial Categorization in Colonial Virginia: 1619–1705" (unpublished ms. on file with author).
Haney López, Ian F.
  1996   *White by Law: The Legal Construction of Race.* New York: New York University Press.
Hing, Bill Ong
  1993   *Making and Remaking Asian America Through Immigration Policy: 1850–1990.* Stanford, Calif.: Stanford University Press.
Hutchinson, E. P.
  1981   *Legislative History of Immigration Policy 1798–1965.* Philadelphia: University of Pennsylvania Press.
Johnson, Kevin
  1995   "An Essay on Immigration Politics, Popular Democracy, and California's Proposition 187: The Political Relevance and Legal Irrelevance of Race." *Washington Law Review* 70(July): 629.
Lowe, Lisa
  1991   *Critical Terrains: French and British Orientalisms.* Ithaca, N.Y.: Cornell University Press.

1996 *Immigrant Acts: On Asian American Cultural Politics.* Durham, N.C.: Duke University Press.

Neuman, Gerald

1995 "Aliens as Outlaws: Government Services, Proposition 187, and the Structure of Equal Protection Doctrine." *UCLA Law Review* 42 (August): 1425–52.

Riggs, Fred W.

1950 *Pressures on Congress: A Study of the Repeal of Chinese Exclusion.* New York: King's Crown Press.

Torok, John Hayakawa

1996 "Asians and the Reconstruction Era Constitutional Amendments and Civil Rights Laws." In *Asian Americans and Congress,* ed. Hyung-Chan Kime. Westport, Conn.: Greenwood Press.

U.S. Statutes at Large

1790 Vol. 1, p. 103. *Act of March 26, 1790.*

1882 Vol. 22, p. 58. *Chinese Exclusion Act of 1882.*

1884 Vol. 23, p. 115. *Act of July 5, 1884.*

1888 Vol. 25, p. 504. *Scott Act of 1888.*

1892 Vol. 27, p. 25. *Geary Act of 1892.*

1902 Vol. 32, p. 176. *Chinese Exclusion Act of 1902.*

1919 Vol. 39, p. 874. *Act of February, 15, 1919.*

1924 Vol. 43, p. 153. *Immigration Act of 1924.*

1943 Vol. 57, p. 600. *Magnuson Act of 1943.*

1946 Vol. 60, p. 416. *Act of July 2, 1946.*

1946 Vol. 60, p. 1353. *Presidential Proclamation of July 4, 1946.*

1946 Vol. 60, p. 975. *Act of August 9, 1946.*

1950 Vol. 64, p. 384. *Act of August 1, 1950.*

1952 Vol. 66, p. 163. *McCarran–Walter Act of 1952.*

1964 Vol. 78, p. 241. *Civil Rights Act of 1964.*

1965 Vol. 79, p. 437. *Voting Rights Act of 1965.*

U.S. Supreme Court

1898 *United States v. Wong Kim Ark* (169 U.S. 649).

1923 *Terrace v. Thompson* (263 U.S. 197).

1954 *Brown v. Board of Education* (347 U.S. 483).

Villareal, José C.

1996 "District Court Holds Provisions of California's Proposition 187 Concerning Classification, Notification and Cooperation of State and Federal Agencies and Denial of Primary and Secondary Education to Illegal Immigrants Preempted by Federal Law." *Georgetown Immigration Law Journal* 10 (spring): 545–98.

Yost, Ellen G.

1997 "International Legal Developments in Review: 1996, Immigration and Nationality Law." *International Lawyer* 31 (summer): 589–98.

7

ASIAN AMERICANS AT THE INTERSECTION OF INTERNATIONAL AND DOMESTIC TENSIONS

An Analysis of Newspaper Coverage

SETSUKO MATSUNAGA NISHI

INTRODUCTION

When the Supreme Court of the United States upheld the constitutionality of the World War II ouster from the West Coast and incarceration in concentration camps of more than 110,000 Japanese Americans (two-thirds of whom were American citizens) solely on the basis of their descent—without charges or trial—Justice Robert M. Jackson warned, "The principle . . . lies about like a loaded weapon ready for the hand of any authority that can bring forward a plausible claim of an urgent need" (*Korematsu v. United States* 1944). More than a half-century later, the "loaded weapon" precedent in the law of *Korematsu* has yet to be challenged successfully, and evidence abounds that Asian Americans—regardless of the number of generations they have lived in the United States—are characterized by many as "foreign"; that is, as outsiders identified with their ancestral nations and often held accountable in America's conflicts with those countries.

Listen to the perpetrators of violent assaults against Asian Americans: "Go away gooks" was the message left on a Vietnamese Catholic church set on fire and vandalized by three white teenagers in DuPage, Illinois, in March 1994. In another case, upon being arrested, also in 1994, a white man in Sacramento, California, said that he had stabbed an Asian American man "to defend our country." Leaving a party in Fairmont, Pennsylvania, in October 1994, an Indian American student was assaulted by a group of Caucasian men throwing beer and yelling, "Go home, . . . you f---ing Asian sh-t; go home, foreigner."

Also in October 1994, in San Francisco, an intoxicated white man hit an Asian American man at his place of business with a glass bottle, threatening, "I'm not gonna leave, you f---ing gook or Jap or whatever you are. I'm gonna smash your windows and smash you! Go back to wherever you came from." More than half of the racially motivated incidents reported against taxi drivers in New York City were allegedly perpetrated by police officers, who were said to use such words as: "Go back to China," "F---ing Orientals," "Go back to Pakistan," and "This is not f---ing Pakistan" (National Asian Pacific American Legal Consortium 1995: 10).

Notable in the words of these perpetrators of anti-Asian American violence is a potent linkage between the presumed foreignness of their victims and a hated enemy. Typically, the perpetrators make no differentiation by specific ethnicity.

Sadly, these obscene acts have been on the rise, according to the National Asian Pacific American Legal Consortium (1995). The Consortium's most recent audit, while acknowledging serious underreporting, indicated a 35 percent increase in reported hate crimes against Asian Pacific Americans in 1994 over the previous year.

As grave as these violent indicators may be, more disturbing and revealing of the ubiquitous nature of the characterization of Asian Americans as "foreign" are the slips made even by national public figures who say they know better. After mimicking the third-generation Japanese American Judge Lance Ito with a caricatured Japanese accent on the nationally syndicated Don Imus radio show, New York's Senator Alphonse D'Amato apologized, saying, "You shouldn't stereotype people. Because I understand a little about this" (Weiss 1996: 50).

At the workplace, much of the imagery of Asian Americans has a more subtle connection to their foreignness. Underlying the frequently reported "glass ceiling" limiting equal-employment opportunity for Asian Americans (U.S. Commission on Civil Rights 1992: 131–36) are such stereotypes as: "passive, quiet, short, humble, clannish, reserved, submissive, and sneaky," which are combined with "diligent, smart, well organized, motivated, well educated, and family-oriented" and, importantly, problems with English. Some illustrative employee comments are: "Talk slowly and precisely to people with foreign accents. Don't trust groups that tend to be quiet [Orientals]"; "I get impatient with cultures that cannot express themselves in the English language. The Chinese do not write documents with proper grammar. I feel I should not have to be subjected to reading these"; "I have to work extra hard to work with an Asian female in my group and at understanding their [Asians'] contributions. They are very quiet and will do any task I ask without question, so I have to make sure I go out of my way to get their feedback. This is frustrating because I prefer to work with forthright people who tell me what's on their mind"; and "They seem to work too much as a team" (Fernandez 1991: 140).

Indeed, facility with the English language is a major symbolic indicator of American identity—along with "trying to get ahead" and "treating all equally"—and affects public attitudes toward cultural minorities (Citrin, Reingold, and Green 1990: 1132–33). For Asian Americans, who often report being subjected to discrimination because of their accents (U.S. Commission on Civil Rights 1992: 137–39), language complaints appear to have become the symbolic substitute for nativism. Striking in the co-workers' comments are what were probably the most pervasive images of Japan during the war (Dower 1986) and the basis of the racist beliefs according to which Japanese Americans were exiled to camps—sneaky, not to be trusted, quiet, won't say what's on their minds, unquestioning obedience to authority.

Asian Americans—visible as a racial minority and seemingly forever perceived symbolically as foreign—are vulnerable targets at the intersection of international and domestic tensions. This paper analyzes how U.S.–Asian tensions, particularly when linked to domestic strains, put Asian Americans at risk for anti-Asian sentiments and behavior. The thesis to be developed is that 1) for most Americans, conflicts between the United States and an Asian country as covered by the media provide a reservoir of potentially negative images of a foreign country and its people; 2) since Asian Americans are viewed as a racially distinct minority-status group regardless of specific ancestry, they tend to be generically identified with the depicted characterizations of any Asian country; and 3) when Americans view their own material well-being threatened by those whom they perceive as foreign, there is a ready store of negative imagery to support their hostility against Asian Americans.

Impressionistic and anecdotal accounts of the effects on Asian Americans of U.S.–Asian country conflicts as triggered by domestic tensions are many. For example, Ronald Takaki's analysis "Who Killed Vincent Chin?" (1989: 23–29) is a thoughtful consideration of how Japan came to be scapegoated for the decline of the Detroit automobile industry, as well as of the historic and cumulative buildup in the media of Asian Americans as foreigners, aliens, criminals, and brutes at the same time that our educational institutions failed to include their contributions in America's development. And, of course, there is a large body of literature on the racist rationalization for the catastrophic incarceration of Japanese Americans during World War II (e.g., Commission on Wartime Relocation and Internment of Civilians 1982; tenBroek, Barnhart, and Matson 1954). But still not examined systematically are the social processes by which a population group in the United States identified by national ancestry is affected by international conflicts between these countries and the United States. This paper seeks to contribute some thoughts on these processes as well as empirical data that connect images of U.S.–Asian country conflicts and Asian Americans in newspaper coverage.

Theoretical Concerns: Social Processes of Discrimination and the Role of the Press

This paper takes as its theoretical context the cumulative social processes that lead to racial/ethnic discrimination; a brief overview of these processes is provided. Although the focus of the study is mainly on a component of the first process—that is, the reservoir of racist ideology, beliefs, and stereotypes—our two case studies, of the press coverage of the Pearl Harbor anniversary and of Asian Americans and race relations in 1991–92, concern the entire sequence of processes.

The first process is the exposure to and incorporation from a reservoir of racist ideology, beliefs, and stereotypes. Our present concern lies with 1) residuals of U.S. military involvement in Asian countries; 2) legacies of historical exclusionary movements, such as the "yellow peril" campaigns in the nineteenth-century and early-twentieth–century United States; 3) continual reinforcement of these images in the entertainment media, popular literature, and the print and electronic news media; and 4) the failure of the educational system to provide alternative, more accurate depictions of Asian Americans and of their ancestral countries.

The second process is the perception of competition or threat from the racial/ethnic group for scarce and valued objects, such as jobs, education, housing, real estate, and consumer and labor markets.

The third process is the occurrence of a triggering event or condition, such as downsizing and other indicators of economic downturn; the fiftieth anniversary of Pearl Harbor or Hiroshima; the Rodney King verdict; and changes in affirmative action.

The fourth process is the attribution of blame for the negative event or condition to the racial/ethnic group or to the foreign country with which the group is identified.

The fifth process is the removal of constraints against discriminatory actions toward members of the racial/ethnic group. This could be a matter of loss of social control as exercised by individuals, by legitimated authorities, or by both.

And the final process is perpetration of a racially discriminatory action. As we observed in opening this paper, these varied actions can be overt, intended, and violent; unintended regressions of speech or behavior revealing latent racism; or institutionalized behavior of even manifestly benign practices that maintain categorical racial inequality.

The specific empirical focus of this inquiry is the analysis of how newspaper coverage links U.S.–Asian country conflicts and Asian Americans. While there is substantial understanding about the function of newspapers in providing wanted information (Shibutani 1966; Gans 1979), relatively little is known about how the press ultimately influences the actions of people. The "agenda-setting" function of the press in the formation of public opinion and beliefs is relevant here. Essentially, the proposition is that what people consider to be America's important social problems is directly related to the amount of press coverage given to those issues (Holz and Wright 1979: 208–209). Relatedly, sociologists have been interested in the role of the media in the social construction of reality—that is, in the framing of accounts of social issues such as race relations (Hartmann and Husband 1974; Warren 1972)—and in the socialization of racial attitudes (Hur and Robinson 1978). News coverage makes occurrences public events and matters of public concern; furthermore, news coverage "shape[s] the notions of the general characteristics" of all instances of an event, such as a riot (Tuchman 1978: 190).

Or, as Mark Fishman (1980: 5–11) puts it, "News organizes our perception of a world outside our firsthand experience." In the manufacturing of news—or "newswork," as he calls it—"themes" are the "organizing concepts" relating diverse instances, providing the basis: 1) for sorting and selecting related items as newsworthy; 2) for choosing an order of presentation; and 3) for placing articles on common themes near one another. Once established, themes need to be replenished through a search for fresh incidents to report. Thus, we investigate what we hypothesize as thematic linkages, the connections in news coverage of U.S.–Asian country conflicts and Asian Americans. As Herbert Gans (1979: 37) has noted, and as acknowledged in the regional roundtable discussions that preceded the conference for which this paper was prepared, Americans pay relatively little attention to foreign news except as it is relevant to American interests. In sum, the central research question here is: how does news coverage contribute to the effects on Asian Americans of the intersection of international and domestic tensions?

Data Sources

For this research, the primary database source was DNEWS, the City University of New York's on-line search system for newspapers. However, for the case study of the coverage of the fiftieth anniversary of Pearl Harbor, we used NEXIS/LEXIS in order to access the complete text of the articles. DNEWS provides abstracts of articles from twenty-eight newspapers (see Appendix A for a list) nationwide, including five African American weeklies, covering the years 1989 to the present. Searches can be done by subject, key word, date, and newspaper source. Information is also available on authors' names and type of item (news, commentary, feature).

U.S.–ASIAN COUNTRY TENSIONS

Coverage of Asian Countries

Our first task was to analyze trend data on coverage of U.S.–Asian relations, operationalized as the number of articles about each Asian country (Japan, China, Vietnam, Korea, India, Philippines, Cambodia, Pakistan, and Taiwan) in each year (1989–95) in order to see the relative importance given to each country. As is apparent in Table 7-1, except in 1989, the year of China's Tiananmen Square uprising, Japan received an overwhelming amount of news coverage as compared with the eight other Asian countries included in the study. Clearly less attention was paid to China than to Japan, but China also received a conspicuously greater amount of coverage than the seven remaining countries. Also to be noted is the steady rise in the number of articles on China since 1992. Articles on Korea reached a peak in 1994 at the time of the death of President Kim Il Sung in July while North Korea was in the midst of heightened tensions with South Korea over the nuclear-proliferation issue.

TABLE 7-1

Number of Articles About Asia by Country and Year, 1989–95

	1989	1990	1991	1992	1993	1994	1995	Total
Japan	2,910	4,002	3,873	4,443	4,051	3,656	4,826	27,761
China	4,696	2,237	2,045	2,120	2,640	2,881	3,290	19,909
Vietnam	859	868	1,032	1,227	868	868	1,062	6,784
Korea	647	818	759	866	985	1,936	777	6,788
India	756	882	850	646	678	650	770	5,232
Philippines	572	674	649	412	196	173	284	2,960
Cambodia	694	615	435	325	522	135	98	2,824
Pakistan	326	551	189	287	281	215	415	2,264
Taiwan	165	232	263	366	283	248	332	1,889

Source: DNEWS

Sources of Tension

We posited as indicative of sources of tension in relations with the United States: 1) economic and trade issues; 2) issues of democracy, including human rights and free elections; and 3) war and residuals of U.S. military involvement. For each of the three categories of issues, we then developed a set of the key words that we found to be most effective in including relevant articles and excluding irrelevant articles. Though the selection of the key words in DNEWS was admittedly arbitrary, the key words' uniform use for each year and each country enabled us to look at trends over time and to make comparisons among countries. The issue categories and key words we used were:

1) *Economy*—trade, economic policy, foreign investment, joint ventures, U.S. corporations, or economic conditions;
2) *Democracy*—human rights, democracy, protests, political leadership, martial law, or election;
3) *War*—war, military, missile, arms, or weapon.

For the peaks in the trend lines, we used the article abstracts to identify the specific events being covered.

Table 7-2 presents the number of articles about each of the nine Asian countries for each of the three types of issues that are sources of tensions between the United States and Asian countries over the seven-year period 1989–95. The number of articles varies greatly by country—for example, a hundred times more articles about these issues were written about Japan and

TABLE 7-2

Number of Articles by Country, Type of International Tension, and Year, 1989–95

Country and Category	1989	1990	1991	1992	1993	1994	1995	Total
Japan								
Economy	886	1,269	1,035	1,477	1,351	1,214	1,405	8,637
Democracy	288	177	135	197	315	121	95	1,328
War	224	268	374	192	164	263	960	2,445
China								
Economy	402	357	592	623	715	1,171	691	4,551
Democracy	2,564	724	623	397	441	754	701	6,204
War	316	141	189	213	179	174	169	1,381
Vietnam								
Economy	35	57	68	74	146	269	90	739
Democracy	32	46	41	29	34	24	36	242
War	486	523	710	953	524	316	629	4,141
Korea								
Economy	118	134	138	164	121	133	105	913
Democracy	153	106	123	149	31	60	63	685
War	104	91	195	239	538	1,193	184	2,544
India								
Economy	56	49	56	62	66	109	180	578
Democracy	244	157	306	82	71	61	63	964
War	100	108	42	53	44	41	44	432
Philippines								
Economy	34	38	31	35	28	31	37	234
Democracy	69	51	25	164	4	15	33	361
War	147	228	346	49	10	25	27	832
Cambodia								
Economy	10	1	11	10	4	5	4	45
Democracy	42	39	64	36	226	6	4	417
War	364	340	245	125	108	47	14	1,243
Pakistan								
Economy	7	9	9	7	18	8	21	79
Democracy	53	165	19	43	61	29	30	400
War	113	123	58	67	62	57	74	554
Taiwan								
Economy	34	58	64	117	103	66	51	493
Democracy	41	33	31	45	15	22	48	235
War	4	7	13	61	11	15	31	142

Source: DNEWS

China than about Taiwan. Immediately catching the eye as one scans the table is the relative prominence given to economic issues pertaining to Japan as compared with all the other countries except Taiwan, even though the number of articles is very small for that country. The rise in 1992 and subsequent decline in the number of articles regarding Japan and economic issues is closely related to the degree of tension in trade relations with the United States. The fiftieth anniversaries of Pearl Harbor and of the atomic bombing of Hiroshima and Nagasaki account for the peaks in the number of war-related articles in 1991 and 1995. The link in public attitudes between the wartime imagery rekindled by the commemoration of Pearl Harbor and trade competition will be analyzed later.

For Vietnam, Korea, the Philippines, and Cambodia, the residual concerns of U.S. military involvement are clearly indicated in the relative attention given to issues in the "War" category as compared with the "Democracy" and "Economy" categories. In 1992, the MIA (missing in action) issue gained prominent attention, then declined as Hanoi cooperated in the search for and return of the missing, leading ultimately to the end of the U.S. economic embargo in 1994. (Note the rise in the number of articles regarding the economy in that year.) We have already mentioned the increase in 1993 and spurt in 1994 of war-related articles regarding Korea as concerning worries about nuclear proliferation in North Korea and the death of President Kim Il Sung; news coverage of that country's economic and democracy issues is evenly scant over the seven years under study. The decision to require the withdrawal of American armed forces accounted for the 1991 surge in war-related articles on the Philippines, and the 1992 peak in democracy-issue articles dealt with the Aquino / Ramos election. For Cambodia, 1989 shows the largest number of articles about war-related issues, with a steady decline through 1995. This was a period of considerable debate about U.S. policy toward the Khmer Rouge, the sending of covert arms to the non-communist Cambodian resistance, and the negotiations for a truce among Cambodia's warring factions. The spate of articles on democracy issues in 1993 had to do with the United Nations–sponsored elections and a warning from the United States to the Khmer Rouge not to seize parts of the country in the wake of the vote.

The elections of 1989, in which the Nehru–Gandhi dynasty struggled to retain power, gained prominence in the news coverage of India, but it was the 1991 assassination of Prime Minister Rajiv Gandhi during a campaign appearance, perpetrated by a woman with explosives strapped to her back, that received the greatest amount of attention. The war-issue articles about India in 1989–90 concerned nuclear weapons and ballistic-missile development; the country's withdrawal from Sri Lanka; and its conflict with Pakistan. As for

Pakistan, the 1990 candidacy of Benazir Bhutto gained prominent coverage, as, to a lesser degree, did the 1993 election. Except for the 1990 election, the Pakistani issues that got the most press were war-related, involving the border conflict with Afghanistan in 1989 and, in 1990, U.S. anxiety about Pakistan's nuclear-weapons capabilities, which raised questions in Congress about continuing aid to that country.

We have already noted the relatively greater attention that was paid to economic issues pertaining to Taiwan as compared with each of the other countries, besides Japan. The peak in war-related issues in 1992 concerned the lifting by President Bush of the decade-long ban on the sale of F-16 jets to Taiwan.

What we have established thus far concerning newspaper coverage of tensions between the United States and Asian countries are the following: 1) Japan has gotten by far the largest amount of coverage, except in 1989, the year of Tiananmen; 2) China is clearly more prominently featured than the other countries in the study, besides Japan; 3) of the issues we have posited as indicative of tensions in relations with the United States, economic concerns are given major prominence only for Japan and Taiwan; 4) events related to U.S. military concern receive more coverage than economic and democracy issues for Vietnam, Korea, the Philippines, and Cambodia; and 5) the democracy-related issue of free elections, especially as it concerns U.S. military interests, was given much attention for India and Pakistan as well as for Cambodia and the Philippines.

Earlier, we noted that Americans pay relatively little attention to foreign news unless it is linked to their self-interest. Thus, although a reservoir has been built up of images of the foreigner or the "Other"—that is, the "not us"—through the interaction of individual and collective memories of wartime experience (directly in military conflict with Japan, Korea, and Vietnam, and peripherally with other Asian countries) and through current experience and depictions in the media, these images are not necessarily acted on. This storehouse of images—some of which may be contradictory—may be drawn from when triggered by events that are construed as threatening to Americans' self-interest and linked to these images. We consider two such events in some detail. The first, a case study of which immediately follows, is the fiftieth anniversary of Pearl Harbor, which coincided with mounting trade conflicts between the United States and Japan and with job loss in the United States. The second, which follows the section on the press coverage of Asian Americans, is the hostile explosion in American race relations in 1991–92, as epitomized by the riots in South Central Los Angeles in which Korean American stores were targeted, and by the rising anxieties concerning the fallout on Asian Americans from Japan-bashing.

In addition to its relevance to our theoretical interest in the linkage between international and domestic strains as affecting Asian Americans, several other considerations influenced our decision to study the press coverage of the Pearl Harbor commemoration. One was the preponderance of attention that newspapers paid to Japan relative to other Asian countries; another was the symbolic significance of Pearl Harbor. Regrettably, only a summary of our findings can be presented in this paper.

THE PEARL HARBOR ANNIVERSARY

Pearl Harbor as a Defining Event

In the view of many scholars (Dower 1986; Deutsch 1995; Portier 1993; Watanabe and Imperiale 1990), Pearl Harbor was the defining event that imprinted a lasting image of Japan and the Japanese in the American consciousness. The image may, of course, become latent and fade with time and with the shifting of attention to other matters. However, I believe that this imagery—which often takes the form of virtually indelible, emotionally weighted verbal and visual symbolism—becomes a part of a reservoir of beliefs and sentiments that are ready to be called forth as relevant issues are confronted. John Dower (1986: 13–14), in his moving analysis of the racism that permeated the views on each side of the Pacific during World War II, observed:

> [The] racist ways of thinking which had contributed so much to the ferociousness of the war were sublimated and transformed . . . [but not] dispelled. They remain latent, capable of being revived by both sides in time of crisis and tension. . . . These patterns of thinking also were transferred laterally and attached to new enemies of the cold-war era: the Soviets and Chinese Communists, the Korean foe of the early 1950s, the Vietnamese enemy of the 1960 and 1970s, and hostile third-world movements in general. The patterns persist, even as specific circumstances change.

Indeed, Robert Deutsch (1996), during a fascinating series of focus-group discussions held across America, found the metaphor of Japan as wartime enemy to be the vivid and emotional base for contemporary attitudes toward Japan—that is, "We got them [Japan] in '45, they got us in the '80s. We're still at war" (Deutsch 1996: 3). Summarizing, Deutsch (1996: 6–7) characterizes American views of Japan as ambivalent, triggering feelings of unease about the lost American Dream. He identifies an American "reasoning pattern" about Japan: 1) "Everything to them (the Japanese) is business";

2) "They are always preparing for the future"—"strategizing," "never laid back," "think long-term"; 3) "They are capable of anything"—"family... intact," "well-educated... children trained in math and science"; and 4) "We must be on guard, they always have a hidden agenda." Deutsch continues his report of the words of his focus-group participants: "We bombed them to smithereens and look what they have achieved"; "Japan is extremist and fanatical. They [the Japanese] are willing to suffer, like we are not. They prefer death to surrender. That's not American business, that's not American, that's not human"; "Because Japan is capable of anything, they [the Japanese] are an unknown quantity"; "Japan is out to get back at us."

In particular, "the correlation between World War II and present day commerce is made," Deutsch (1996: 8–9) continues, quoting his discussants: "That's what Japan does;... invade and conquer." In connection with "invader," Deutsch notes the frequent use of the terms "'sneaky' (unfair) and 'aggressive' (seeks to annihilate its competitors)." Pearl Harbor is used to "prop up" the metaphor as expressed in such phrases as: "Then as now, America was caught unprepared"; "Their kamikaze loyalty to the emperor has been replaced by loyalty to Toyota. Now they use Toyota instead of battleships, but they are still fighting a war... without any compassion or mercy"; and "They took our lives in 1941. In 1981, they took our livelihoods."

It is not just the language of the ordinary American that links Pearl Harbor and Japan's economic competitiveness. Anne Portier (1993) has done a quantitative and qualitative analysis of the American press's creation of the image of Japan as a "pseudo-event" in the crucial period of December 1991 to April 1992. A series of events converged: the Pearl Harbor anniversary, massive layoffs in the auto industry, President Bush's visit to Asia, Japanese political leaders' humiliatingly critical comments about the United States, and the presidential-election campaign. As Portier (1993: 366, 376–81) points out, "the boom in Japan bashing" took place when a reduction in trade balances actually was occurring. So what were the elements from which the "imaginary alternative" of Japan was constructed? First was the stereotyping of "the Japanese," particularly in contradictory and opposite dichotomous terms as compared with the United States. Second was the linking of two logically unrelated facts to suggest a connection, such as the press coverage of the Pearl Harbor anniversary and President Bush's trip, which inaccurately joined the wartime conflict of the past with present economic tensions and projected a "prejudice of distrust." And last, depicting Japan's weakness functions as an effort to regain self-confidence in American society.

From our perspective, we view the fiftieth anniversary of Pearl Harbor as signficant because it recalled the emotional imagery of Japan during World

War II during a period of heightened political—and press—attention to economic tensions with that country. Using NEXIS/LEXIS, we undertook a thematic analysis of articles appearing in the *New York Times* during 1991 that pertained to Pearl Harbor, focusing on how they treated issues that related to contemporary tensions in U.S. relations with Japan. Our inquiry also looked at the treatment of Japanese Americans in connection with Pearl Harbor, our thesis being that when international (U.S./Asian country) and domestic tensions intersect, Asian Americans are vulnerable to negative treatment. The 1991–92 period was one of unprecedented press attention to this population, given the explosion of tensions between African Americans and Korean American storekeepers during the riot that followed the Rodney King verdict and the release of a major report on Asian Americans by the U.S. Commission on Civil Rights.

The Fiftieth Anniversary and Japanese Americans

Our inquiry into the press coverage of the anniversary began with the idea that Pearl Harbor was a defining event in American history and that coverage of the event would yield rich evidence of residue from World War II affecting contemporary perceptions of Japan and the Japanese—and, remarkably, Japanese Americans.

We can only summarize here our thematic analysis of the *New York Times* coverage of the fiftieth anniversary of the Pearl Harbor attack. We found that: 1) controversy continues regarding a number of historical issues, including who/what caused the war, whether Roosevelt and Churchill knew beforehand that Japan was going to attack, and whether Japan intended to perpetrate a sneak attack; 2) Americans and Japanese continue to have apparently irreconcilable constructions of the war, especially of moral accountability for the "sneak attack" on Pearl Harbor and atrocities committed in Asia by Japan, and/or the atomic bombing of Hiroshima and Nagasaki by the United States; 3) Japan's current economic expansion, especially as it affects job loss in the United States, is discussed analogously to Japan's wartime expansionism; and 4) the wartime incarceration of Japanese Americans is depicted as a wrong for which the United States rightly has apologized, and the valorous service of Nisei soldiers has been acknowledged, but this has not assuaged the residual concerns of Japanese Americans about continuing racism against Asian Americans.

Nearly half of the articles linking the Pearl Harbor commemoration with contemporary issues concerning the Japanese refer to Japanese Americans. This in itself is a significant connection, regardless, ironically, of the patently positive tone of these references. Most of these articles mention the camps in which Japanese Americans were incarcerated and refer to the injustice involved. Some note the service of Japanese Americans in the highly decorated 442nd Regimental Combat Team and in the Pacific Theater, even characterizing that service as especially valorous in light of the military prejudice and special dangers the servicemen confronted. Despite these major themes, it is notable that President Bush's apology to Japanese Americans is juxtaposed in the news to his refusal to apologize for the U.S. atomic bombing of Hiroshima and Nagasaki. Or, alternatively, the acknowledgment by Americans of its "mistakes" is presented as a contrast to Japan's rationalizations for Pearl Harbor. Clearly, the incarceration of Japanese Americans is a major component in the residual issues of World War II as covered by the press. Thus, integrally linked to the press's construction of World War II history is the incarceration of Japanese Americans as an aberrant act of wartime hysteria for which the United States has apologized and paid restitution. Nevertheless, the press notes the continuing anxiety among Japanese Americans about the fiftieth anniversary's effects on Asian Americans.

We conclude that the anniversary articles demonstrate that closure has not yet been achieved regarding Pearl Harbor, and that there is an active residue of emotion-laden war-related imagery in the American consciousness. The metaphorical symbolism of Pearl Harbor and associated attitudes were revitalized during the fiftieth-anniversary period, gaining new strength as they were transferred to economic and trade competition between the United States and Japan—possibly near its peak at the time of our case study (see Portier [1993], which comes to the same conclusion). Thus, the meaning of Pearl Harbor came to reside not only in the gut and memories of those old enough to remember, but also in Americans who believed that their livelihoods had been gutted by Japan's—"sneaky" and "unfair"—economic "warfare." Japanese Americans, seared by the violations of their constitutionally protected civil rights in the crisis of war, continue to be wary of the racism that they see becoming generalized against Asians and Asian Americans. It is our view that the wartime imagery about Japan and the Japanese—including Japanese Americans—was added to the collective reservoir of racist beliefs to be drawn from when reacting to perceived threats from racial outsiders.

TREATMENT OF ASIAN AMERICANS IN THE NEWS

How are Asian Americans depicted in the news? For this analysis, we return to the DNEWS database of article abstracts.

TABLE 7-3

Number of Articles on Asian Americans by Ethnicity and Year, 1989–95

	1989	1990	1991	1992	1993	1994	1995
Jpa. Ame.	140	112	112	129	55	58	99
Chi. Ame.	49	29	32	39	46	40	71
Kor. Ame.	9	33	44	87	61	49	42
Vie. Ame.	5	11	11	18	16	26	25
Fil. Ame.	12	8	7	14	14	14	14
Ind. Ame.	1	1	3	1	7	4	1
Pak. Ame.	0	0	1	3	2	1	2
Tai. Ame.	3	0	1	0	0	0	1
Asi. Ame.[a]	277	411	585	580	524	425	475
Total[b]	469	549	732	738	635	526	635

Source: DNEWS

[a]"Asi. Ame." stands for articles found using "Asian Americans" as the key word.

[b]"Total" shows the sum of articles by ethnicity, plus "Asi. Ame." articles not included under specific ethnicity.

Trends in Coverage by Ethnicity

Table 7-3 provides an overview of press coverage of Asian Americans based on our analysis of trends in the number of articles by specific ethnicity over the 1989–95 period.

What is immediately apparent on inspecting the table is the disproportionate amount of press attention given to Japanese Americans relative to other Asian American groups until 1993. (That year reflects the aftermath of the outburst of conflicts between African Americans and Korean American merchants in Los Angeles.) This high level of press coverage is not directly related to the percentage of Japanese Americans in the population; for example, in 1990, Japanese Americans constituted 11.6 percent of the Asian American population, but 58.0 percent of the articles about Asian Americans, as classified by specific ethnicity, were about Japanese Americans. Also of note is the number of articles found when "Asian Americans" was used as the key word (from which we have removed those classified under a specific ethnicity as a key word); such articles constituted three-fourths or more of the total, except in 1989, when the proportion was just under 60 percent. In 1989, we find the largest number of articles on Japanese Americans during the seven-year period of study; this is due to the passage of the so-called Reparations Bill at the end of 1988. The 1992 peak for coverage of Japanese

Americans, we believe, was triggered by the increased press attention to trade tensions at the time of President Bush's visit to Japan. The relatively large amount of coverage of Chinese Americans in 1989 is connected, we believe, to the heavy press coverage of Tiananmen Square. For Korean Americans, the peak was 1992, the year of the Los Angeles riots. By 1994 and 1995, the trends of decline in coverage of Korean Americans and rise in coverage of Chinese Americans are evident. We interpret these findings to indicate the kind of thematic linkage between stories that Fishman (1980: 5–11) identified—that is, in our inquiry the connection between articles on U.S.–Asian country tensions and those on Asian Americans. Though it could not be done for this paper, it would be feasible and useful to establish the relative influence of international tensions and other factors on press coverage of Asian Americans. For now, we must content ourselves with the conceptual link.

Coverage of Asian Americans by Subject

In addition to examining the relative attention paid to Asian Americans by ethnicity and the likely link between this and the United States' international concerns with their countries of origin, we wanted to investigate how the American press construes Asian Americans. For this, we compared the number and proportion of articles about Asian Americans with the number of articles about the total population by all 990 subject descriptors used in the DNEWS database system. For each subject, we calculated the ratio of the proportion of articles on that subject in the Asian American articles relative to the total population articles, which we call the "ratio of subject emphasis." For example, the subject descriptor "aliens" picked up 51 Asian American articles, or 0.87 percent of the total Asian Americans articles. The same descriptor, "aliens," picked up 4,431 articles relating to the total population, or only 0.10 percent of all the articles in the database having to do with the total population. Thus, the ratio of subject emphasis ("aliens") in the articles about Asian Americans and those about the total population was 8.47:1. In other words, the subject of "aliens" was covered proportionally eight-and-a-half times more frequently in articles about Asian Americans than in articles concerning the total population.

We then arrayed the top one hundred subject descriptors by this ratio of subject emphasis, excluding those subjects that brought up fewer than ten articles about Asian Americans. Since the number of articles on a subject is also an important indicator of the press's depiction of Asian Americans, we constructed an index combining the ratio of subject emphasis with the number of articles. We call this the "index of attention." The results are presented in Appendix B.

Predominance of the Depiction of Asian Americans as a Racial Minority

The startling result is that Asian Americans are treated in the press overwhelmingly through subjects that clearly depict them in their racial or ethnic minority-status characterization. Whether measured in terms of relative subject emphasis or number of articles, this finding is incontrovertible. The disproportionate subject emphases, in order, are: Reparations (97.8:1), Concentration Camps (52.4:1), Race Relations (20.8:1), Race (17.4:1), Languages (17.2:1), Cultural Relations (16.1:1), Censuses (14.5:1), Emigration (14.0:1), Prejudice (13.1:1), Immigration (12.8:1), Riots (12.1:1), Citizenship (12.1:1), and Aliens (8.5:1). The subjects with the largest number of articles, in order, are: Race, 370; Race Relations, 362; Immigration, 210; Discrimination, 184; Editorials, 158; Prejudice, 152; International Relations, 127; Life (as in Social Life and Customs, Families and Family Life), 124; Crime, 116; Demonstrations and Protests, 116; Emigration, 115; Riots, 109; and Social Conditions and Trends, 109.

Model Minority

What of the "model-minority" characterization of Asian Americans? Our subject search under "Awards and Honors" found only 31 articles on Asian Americans, which, surprisingly, was the same ratio (1.02:1) as that for articles on this subject about the total population; we did, however, find 93 articles under "Students," more than twice (2.3:1) the proportion for the total population. We also found greater relative coverage of entrepreneurism-related subjects both in the number of articles and in the ratio of emphasis (in parentheses): Entrepreneurs, 41 (4.4:1); Small Business, 48 (3.7:1); Corporate Culture, 10 (2.9:1); Commercial Fishing, 11 (2.8:1); Business Community, 15 (2.4:1); Retail Stores, 60 (2.3:1); International Trade, 57 (1.8:1). On the other hand, we found 116 articles about Asian Americans under "Crime," which was nearly three times (2.9:1) the proportion of coverage of the subject in articles on the total population. Other related subjects were Crime Prevention, 11 (1.7:1); Law Enforcement, 27 (1.6:1); and Criminals 22 (1.3:1), all of which were given somewhat heavier emphasis in the articles about Asian Americans. Thus, the subject emphases in press coverage of Asian Americans present them disproportionately in connection with entrepreneurship and as students—as well as in connection with crime—and more so than in connection with Awards and Honors.

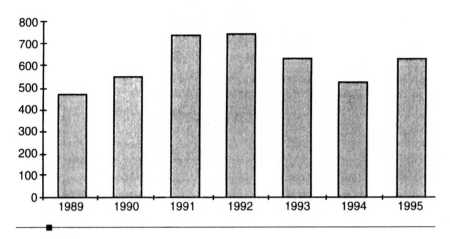

FIGURE 7-1

Number of articles on Asian Americans by year, 1989–95. *Source:* Table 7-3

ASIAN AMERICANS AND RACE RELATIONS:
JULY 1991 THROUGH JUNE 1992

In view of the overwhelming amount of press treatment of Asian Americans in connection with the subject of race relations, we decided to take a closer look at July 1991 through June 1992—the twelve months surrounding the Pearl Harbor anniversary. The years 1991 and 1992 saw the largest number of articles on Asian Americans (see Figure 7-1) and, among these, on the subject of race relations (see Figure 7-2) in the 1989–95 period of the DNEWS database.

Furthermore, this was the period of dramatic shifts in coverage of specific Asian American ethnic groups, as evident in Table 7-3, from the conspicuous predominance of attention to Japanese Americans in the years prior to and including 1991 to the dramatic rise in attention paid to Korean Americans in 1992, following the riots in Los Angeles at the end of April. In February 1992, the release of the U.S. Commission on Civil Rights' major report "Civil Rights Issues Facing Asian Americans in the 1990s," accompanied by the full force of the commission's public-relations staff, contributed to press attention. By 1994, and even more clearly by 1995, attention to Korean Americans had subsided, and Japanese Americans and Chinese Americans assumed their pre-1992 positions of prominence in newspaper coverage. We believe that this is related to thematic news linkage with American interest in international-policy tensions between the United States and Asian countries.

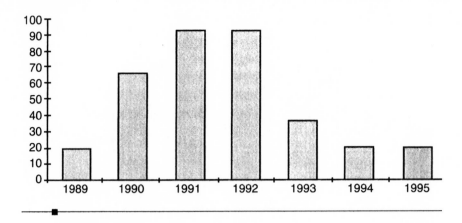

FIGURE 7-2

Number of articles on Asian Americans and race relations by year, 1989–95.
Source: DNEWS

Attention to race-relations issues in the articles about Asian Americans in the 1991–92 period is patently heavier compared with the 1989–95 total DNEWS period. This is documented in Appendix C, which compares the subject coverage for the 1991–92 period and the total DNEWS years of 1989–95. Using the percentage of articles about Asian Americans on a subject in the DNEWS years, we calculated the expected number of articles on that subject in the 1991–92 period. Our results are presented in Appendix C and are arrayed in the order of relative subject emphasis.

We next calculated a ratio of the actual number of 1991–92 articles on a subject relative to the expected number of articles according to its proportion in the total number of DNEWS articles about Asian Americans. Table 7-4 ranks these results for subjects that had more than one-and-a-half times the proportion of expected articles.

Clearly, the July 1991 to June 1992 period intensified press attention to race-relations issues pertaining to Asian Americans, as well as to their entrepreneurial presence in urban areas and, interestingly, to cultural distinctions and international trade. The originating question of this study concerned the nature of the connection—the bridge—between international and domestic tensions as experienced by Asian Americans. We had proposed that domestic strains, such as economic competition for jobs or markets and racial tensions in urban areas, when linked to Asian Americans, would draw on the reservoir of images of Asians associated with international conflicts, regardless of specific ethnicity. Thus, we examine the characterization of Asian

TABLE 7-4

Ratio of Subject Emphases of Pearl Harbor Year (7/91–6/92) to DNEWS Period (1/89–12/95) in Articles About Asian Americans

Riots	3.84	Urban Areas	1.88
Prejudice	2.61	International Trade	1.87
Race	2.43	Culture	1.80
Race Relations	2.40	Emigration	1.79
Harassment	2.36	Entrepreneurs	1.73
Cultural Relations	2.19	Retail Stores	1.65
Small Business	2.07	Language	1.52

Source: Appendix C

Americans in the press during the crucial twelve-month period surrounding both the Pearl Harbor commemoration and the Los Angeles riots, one an international and the other a domestic source of tension. Other than the obvious linkage in time, we wanted to know what other connections we could establish in the data.

In this task, we looked first at the number of articles about Asian Americans by subject and month of appearance (see Appendix D). The subjects that had the largest number of articles were: Race Relations, 125; Race, 124; Riots, 59; Prejudice, 56; Discrimination, 38; Immigration, 33; and Emigration, 29. It is apparent that many articles have multiple subject classifications. On examining the abstracts of the articles classified under the subject "Riots," we decided to focus on those that also covered the issues of Race, Race Relations, Prejudice, and Discrimination, as well as on those that covered Immigration and Emigration. Thus, we downloaded the articles about Asian Americans that appeared when we used the subject-search key words "Race Relations," "Race," "Prejudice," and "Discrimination." We found 217 items, which constituted the basis of our thematic analysis.

Only a summary of the findings are presented here; the details of the thematic analysis will be presented elsewhere. The dramatic focus was on the conflicts between African Americans and Korean Americans: 130 articles were found on the subject, constituting 59.9 percent of the total 217 articles. Articles regarding Japan and Japanese Americans numbered 38, or 18.1 percent; those regarding Asian Americans generally and discrimination numbered 34, or 15.7 percent; and those regarding other specified Asian American ethnic groups in locales east of California numbered 17, or 7.8 percent (two articles are counted twice, under both the Japanese American and Asian American categories).

African American–Korean American Conflict

The article titles and abstracts available in the DNEWS database provide, on the one hand, a contrapuntal account of escalating conflict between African Americans and Korean American merchants, and on the other, conciliatory efforts by public officials and community leaders leading up to the explosion of hostility in the burning and looting of an estimated 2,000 Korean American–owned stores during the Los Angeles riots in April 1992. The narrative of the buildup of tensions is dramatic. The following is a sampling of the article headlines:

DIARY OF A WAR OF ATTRITION IN VOLATILE URBAN DISPUTE
COMPTON JUDGE WON'T MOVE SOON JA DU TRIAL
BLACKS WON'T END KOREAN STORE BOYCOTT
MELTING POT OF BLACKS, KOREANS BOILS OVER
TRUCE IS CALLED IN BLACK-KOREAN CONFLICT
DU CONVICTED: KOREAN GROCER FACES 16 YEARS
BLACK, KOREAN CLERGY MEET
BLACKS SEEK TO CHANNEL ANGER OVER SENTENCE
LOS ANGELES PUSHES RACIAL-TRAINING PLAN FOR STORE OWN-
     ERS IN BLACK AREAS
RAPPER'S NUMBER CHILLS BLACK–KOREAN RELATIONS
KOREAN GROCER CODE SEEKS TO EASE TENSION
BLACK–KOREAN ALLIANCE BLAMES THE SYSTEM
BLACK–KOREAN HOSTILITY FUELED FLAMES OF RIOT

This sampling of headlines is illustrative of the contrapuntal juxtaposition of themes of "conflict" and "conciliation," which we found in our more systematic content analysis of themes. Surprisingly, themes of conciliation were present in at least a third of the articles leading up to the riot and even more often in the aftermath of the conflagration. Involving both the Los Angeles political leadership and the leadership of the African American and Korean American communities, numerous efforts at cooling and improving interpersonal relationships are reported. However, our search for themes of what we called "remedy"—that is, of dealing with the underlying causal factors of the relative absence of African American entrepreneurs and the disproportionate presence of Korean American merchants in urban ghettos—yielded very little press attention. Though triggered by the Rodney King verdict, the rampage of destruction was obviously an expression of much more than anger at the criminal-justice system. Visible and considered "outsiders" because of their racial and cultural distinctiveness and foreign origin,

Korean Americans became the most accessible major target of the frustrations of African Americans and Latinos in South Central Los Angeles.

Anti-Japanese and Anti-Asian American Hostility

Far overshadowed by the outburst of violence against Korean Americans, articles about Japanese Americans made up only 18 percent of the total number of articles about Asian Americans pertaining to race relations in the July 1991 through June 1992 period. Despite this, the number of articles about Japanese Americans on all subjects in the total years of 1991 and 1992 was considerably higher than the total number of articles about Korean Americans (see Table 7-3). It was only in 1993 that any Asian American group received more press attention than Japanese Americans. In that year, we found only 55 articles using the key word "Japanese American," as contrasted with 61 using "Korean American." Even in 1992, there were 129 articles about Japanese Americans, compared with 87 articles about Korean Americans. In 1994, Japanese Americans were again getting more press coverage than Korean Americans, and in 1995 both Japanese Americans and Chinese Americans were receiving increased press attention, while coverage of Korean Americans declined. According to our thesis, this relative amount of attention to specific Asian American groups, as well as to Asian Americans in general, is heavily affected by thematic linkage to press interest in issues of U.S. concerns with their countries of origin, especially as linked to domestic concerns.

Relations between the United States and Japan were particularly tense during the July 1991 through June 1992 period. Not only was the fiftieth anniversary of Pearl Harbor at hand, but economic conflicts, especially with President Bush's less-than-successful trade mission to Japan, were reflected in a rising momentum of Japan-bashing. How were these reflected in press coverage of Japanese Americans and Asian Americans?

The overarching theme in the 38 articles on this subject is anxiety about the fallout from Japan-bashing not only on Japanese Americans, but on all Asian Americans. Not quite a third—that is, twelve—of the items are related to the Pearl Harbor anniversary; relatedly, five were connected with the annual remembrance by Japanese Americans of Executive Order 9066, which set into motion their wartime removal and imprisonment; five concerned the Commission on Civil Rights report, which not only documented blatant violence and the institutionalized discrimination of the glass ceiling, but also warned against the spillover onto Asian Americans of the rising animosity against Japan (an additional item notes that the Michigan Commission on Civil Rights issued a similar report, which was particularly significant because of the state of the Detroit auto industry); several articles refer to the effects of the trade war with Japan on Asian Americans in specific locales—that is, in New Hampshire and the District of Columbia; and seven articles cite the general rise in anti-Japanese American and anti-Asian American sentiment as linked to the economic conflict between the United States and Japan.

Specific anti-Japanese incidents are cited as related to increasing racism against Asian Americans: the killing of an overseas Japanese businessman and the controversy surrounding the sale of the Seattle Mariners to Japanese interests. One article reported a lawsuit charging that a Japanese-owned advertising agency discriminated against American-born employees.

We found only two items that could be construed as at least positive in direction. One was an item in an African American newspaper reporting a poll showing that most African Americans view Japan favorably, despite strains; the other urged that Kristi Yamaguchi's winning of Olympic gold medals provided an opportunity to "heal the wounds" of Japanese Americans.

The last abstract we found regarding Japanese Americans and race relations in the DNEWS database for the July 1991 through June 1992 period was the following:

BIG THREE WILL GET A WARNING ON BASHING THE JAPANESE

Members of the National Network on Anti-Asian Violence will be in Metro Detroit to mark the 10th anniversary of the death of Vincent Chin, who was killed in what is widely believed to be a racial attack. The group will speak with Big Three automakers about Japan bashing [*Detroit News*, June 19, 1992].

Asian Americans and Discrimination

We now look at the remaining newspaper coverage of Asian Americans and race relations—that is, articles other than those concerning the Korean American–African American conflict and the anti-Japan and anti–Asian American connection. When those articles were excluded, 34 articles about Asian Americans and race relations remained, or about 16 percent of the total 217 articles.

The underlying theme of these articles is that, although progress has been made by Asian Americans, prejudice and discrimination continue and may be increasing. Several articles decry the rise in racism, including hate crimes against Asian Americans. In one article, a Houston judge is quoted as apologizing for his "racially insensitive" remarks. Stereotypes of Asian Americans, including the "model minority," "Asian gangs," "Asian immigrants on welfare," and those related to the "bamboo ceiling"—"passive, self-effacing, lacking management skills"—are referred to in five articles.

Institutionalized discriminatory patterns are the subject in six articles. Three items cover a Federal Reserve Board study finding that African Americans and Hispanics are denied home mortgages more frequently than whites and Asian Americans of the same income level. The increasing attention of realtors to the growing Hispanic and Asian American markets is the focus of another article. While these articles report favorable treatment of Asian Americans, an article on the savings-and-loan bailout indicates that Asian Americans, along with other minorities, are shortchanged.

With regard to protesting against institutionalized employment discrimination in the protective services, two articles report the inclusion of Asian Americans, along with African Americans and Hispanics, in settlements of lawsuits with the Los Angeles City Council and El Monte, California. Another item reports on a Chinese American woman who won an employment-discrimination suit. Despite the large number of Asian Americans in the employment of the city of San Francisco, few are being promoted to major positions, says another article.

Several articles report the presence of Asian Americans, along with other minorities, at a conference on "environmental racism."

Some of the proposals for dealing with prejudice and discrimination found in the articles are: fight stereotypes, protest being scapegoated and invest in American workers, train children against anti-Asian bigotry, and change the civil-rights agenda to include Asian Americans and other minorities.

The Geographical and Ethnic Spread of Anti–Asian American Hostility

Of the 217 total articles, 17, or 7.8 percent, were about locations east of California and did not pertain mainly to Korean Americans and Japanese Americans. The subjects covered included tension between the police and Cambodians in Reeves, Massachusetts; resentment by older residents of the increasing presence and political competition of Asian Americans, who say they have revitalized dying neighborhoods in Flushing, New York; the fear engendered among Asian Americans by the massacre of nine Buddhists in Phoenix, Arizona; accusations of police racism for allowing a naked fourteen-year-old "Asian boy" to remain with the serial killer Jeffrey Dahmer, who later murdered him in Milwaukee, Wisconsin (four articles); the violent killing of Jim Ming-hai Loo by Robert Piche in Raleigh, North Carolina; the rise in Asian American–white tensions after the stabbing death of an eighteen-year-old white person by a Chinese–Vietnamese American restaurant worker in Philadelphia; the disparaging remarks of Boston City Councilor Albert "Dapper" O'Neil about Vietnamese immigrant businessmen, urgings for an apology, and his refusal to give one (six articles), and a story contrasting O'Neil's remarks with the struggle of a Vietnamese refugee family to come to the United States, become naturalized, and establish themselves through hard labor in Boston; and, finally, a vigil on the steps of the Massachusetts State House commemorating the 1982 killing in Detroit of Vincent Chin, who was mistaken for Japanese, and calling for multiracial unity to combat hate crimes in the Boston area.

Apparent in these articles is that anti–Asian American hostility is nationwide and that those considered outsiders coming into an area are particularly vulnerable. It appears also that the press is very attentive to racist behavior among political celebrities.

We undertook this analysis of Asian Americans and race relations as portrayed in newspapers from July 1991 through June 1992 because we found that this was the predominant focus of press interest in Asian Americans in the total 1989–95 DNEWS database. We believed that our theoretical interest in the connections between and among international tensions, domestic strains, and Asian Americans would be well served, because this period included two events of major consequence—that is, the Pearl Harbor anniversary and the Los Angeles riots.

The conflict between African Americans and Korean American merchants in urban ghetto areas has a story of its own, involving a complex set of reasons why these immigrants establish themselves in those areas and African American entrepreneurs are few (see Waldinger 1989; Kim 1981; Min 1993). In addition, cumulative circumstances lead up to such hostile outbursts (Smelser 1963). However, our interest is in the press's depiction of the event—especially the image the press portrayed of Asian Americans, in this case Korean Americans. In the press coverage of the buildup to the riots, it is clear that Korean American merchants were disproportionately targeted because they are resented by many of the residents of South Central Los Angeles as culturally different outsiders—that is, immigrants or foreign newcomers—who are making a living in their neighborhoods and yet are often perceived to be rude and suspicious.

Unexpected to us was the amount of attention given to conciliatory efforts by the mayor and other officials, as well as by community leaders from both sides—glaring failures in light of the subsequent catastrophic destruction of Korean American businesses during the riot. It is our view that efforts to develop understanding and respect between groups—such as appealing to their shared Christianity and common experience of American racism—

may be significant in the long run but require sustained investment in the development of ongoing means of communication and structures for joint action. Fundamentally, however, unless the underlying categorical inequalities by race are addressed—in employment, housing, criminal justice, small-business loans, municipal services, and so on—the potential for friction in race relations will remain chronic and endemic. Asian Americans such as the Korean American merchants—like the Jews before them—are accessible scapegoats to bear the brunt of anger born of accumulated frustration.

Interestingly, Korean American merchants are not depicted as the passive recipients of either racial violence (they are armed and shoot) or institutional neglect (they demonstrate for more equitable police and fire protection and relief for riot damage). Furthermore, they are pictured as responsive to the complaints of their market: the merchants developed a Code of Behavior for dealing with customers and announced a willingness to hire African Americans and train some in their small businesses. The visit to the riot scenes and promises of aid from South Korean political leaders and the South Korean government's sending a delegation to Los Angeles to seek reparations for riot damages, however, probably reinforced the image of Korean Americans as foreigners identified primarily with their native country.

Related to our case study of newspaper coverage of the Pearl Harbor anniversary is our look at the press coverage of the linkage of anti-Japanese and anti–Asian American hostility. While the sensational news of escalating animosity as well as of efforts to cool relations between African Americans and Korean Americans captured the largest share of attention under the subject "Race Relations," Japanese Americans continued to receive more coverage generally than any other Asian American group. Regarding race relations and Japanese Americans, the major themes are the continuing memory of their wartime treatment and concern about the fallout on all Asian Americans of Japan-bashing. The case study of the Pearl Harbor anniversary concluded that Pearl Harbor as a metaphor for sneakiness in gaining advantage was alive and well, and that this wartime characterization of the Japanese was being revitalized in the contemporary economic conflict between the United States and Japan. Like scarred wounds, collective memories of Pearl Harbor—and of the degradation set in motion by Executive Order 9066—are very present among Japanese Americans. Now, however, the reservoir of wartime imagery of the Japanese enemy—which was categorically applied to Japanese Americans as untrustworthy and took away their freedom during World War II—has been stirred to new life in economic and trade conflicts with Japan. It is spilling over into racially based manifestations of anti–Asian American hostility as well as the more subtle institutionalized forms of discrimination such as the so-called bamboo ceiling.

As depicted in the press, discrimination against Asian Americans continues, but progress has been made. Stereotypes persist, as do the blatant racism of violent hostility and the structured and institutionalized patterns maintaining the inequality of Asian Americans. However, the picture of Asian Americans is mixed—for example, they are portrayed as advantaged along with whites in getting home loans as compared with African Americans and Hispanics of the same income; as shortchanged along with African Americans and Hispanics in the savings-and-loan bailout; and as included with African Americans and Hispanics in employment-discrimination lawsuits for equitable inclusion in protective services.

As the Asian American population has become increasingly diversified, both ethnically and geographically, what Joann Lee (1996) calls new "hot spots" of anti–Asian American animosity have appeared outside the Pacific states and the urban centers where they have been historically concentrated. A common theme appears: newcomers are competing economically and politically with those already established, and they are resented.

In the 1991–92 press coverage of Asian Americans and race relations, we saw the portrayal of the African American–Korean American merchants' escalating conflict explode in the spectacular race riot triggered by the Rodney King verdict. We also saw Japanese Americans presented as worried about the Pearl Harbor anniversary and weighted with the painful memories of wartime incarceration, while the official civil-rights fact-finding agency, in a major study, warned against the fallout on Asian Americans of Japan-bashing. While recognizing progress, the continuing anti–Asian American hostility in bias crimes, as well as in police conduct and statements of political leaders, is depicted as nationwide. Of the greatest significance to our thesis, however, is that newspapers have paid attention to Asian Americans primarily as linked to race, race relations, prejudice, and discrimination (domestic tensions), and to the residual effects of the war with Japan, now revitalized as "economic warfare" (international tensions), perceived as affecting the well-being of Americans—that is, employment and competitiveness.

SUMMARY AND CONCLUSIONS

Connecting Images of U.S.–Asian Country Conflicts and Asian Americans: The Role of the Press

This chapter examined the press coverage of U.S.–Asian country conflicts and of Asian Americans and identified linkages between them. We theorized that: a) press coverage of conflicts between the United States and Asian countries contributes to a reservoir of blatantly negative images of these for-eign countries and their people; b) because Asian Americans are seen as a racially distinct minority status group regardless of specific ancestry, they tend to be generically associated with the more prominently depicted char-acterizations of any Asian country; and c) when Americans view their own material well-being threatened by those whom they perceive as foreign, there is a storehouse of negative imagery to support their animosity toward Asian Americans. Thus, this study has sought to increase understanding of the social processes by which a group identified by ancestry with Asian countries is affected by international conflicts between the United States and these countries. What are the cumulative social processes that lead to racial or ethnic discrimination? In particular, what is the role of the press?

We were guided in our inquiry by an interest in the functions of the press in "agenda-setting" issues and framing their accounts, as well as in the formation of racial attitudes. Empirically, what we looked for were thematic linkages—the connections in news coverage of U.S.–Asian country conflicts, domestic concerns, and Asian Americans. Our central research question was: how does news coverage contribute to the effects on Asian Americans of the intersection of international and domestic tensions?

By using DNEWS, the on-line newspaper database in the City Univer-sity of New York system, we examined the titles, subject descriptors, and ab-stracts of newspaper articles in 28 newspapers nationwide from January 1989 through December 1995. For the case study of the Pearl Harbor commem-oration, we used NEXIS/LEXIS in order to look at the full text of the articles.

U.S. International Tensions with Asian Countries:
Issues of the Economy, War, and Democracy

In the study of the press coverage of Asian countries and of sources of international tension between the United States and these countries, we found the following: 1) Japan received an overwhelming amount of press attention, except in 1989, the year of Tiananmen Square; 2) China got the next largest amount of press—far more than other Asian countries—and coverage of economic issues was rising; 3) only for Japan and Taiwan (with a very small number of articles) were economic issues more prominent than war- and democracy-related sources of tension; 4) U.S. military concerns were most prominent in press attention to Vietnam, Korea, the Philippines, and Cam-bodia; and 5) the democracy-related issue of elections, especially when linked to American military interests, were featured for India, Pakistan, Cambodia, and the Philippines. Japan, in particular the economic concerns, was of overriding interest in the press in the years under study, though the rising trend of coverage of economic issues regarding China augurs a major shift in the future. The residue of war and military conflict continues to attract press interest, resonating with the collective memories of the many Americans who saw military service in those countries and keeping the issues alive.

Pearl Harbor: Still the Defining Event and Metaphor for Economic Competition with Japan

In our thematic analysis of the *New York Times* articles about the anniversary of Pearl Harbor, we found that: 1) historical controversies continue concerning who and what caused the war, whether Roosevelt or Churchill knew beforehand about Japan's plan to attack, and whether Japan intended to perpetrate a "sneak" attack; 2) contemporary Americans and Japanese have differing constructions of moral responsibility for the "sneak" attack on Pearl Harbor, atrocities committed in Asia by Japan, and the atomic bombing of Hiroshima and Nagasaki by the United States; 3) Japan's current economic expansion is depicted as paralleling its expansionism in the war; and 4) the wartime treatment of Japanese Americans is considered a wrong for which the United States has apologized, and the United States has recognized the distinguished service of Nisei soldiers, but Japanese Americans continue to have concerns about anti–Asian American racism.

We conclude that closure regarding Pearl Harbor has not been accomplished and that war-related images of Japan continue to be vital in the American consciousness. The symbolism of Pearl Harbor and related emotions have gained renewed force in their transfer to the economic and trade competition with Japan, blamed by many for America's economic decline.

Press Attention to Asian Americans and International Issues

Our examination of the DNEWS database found that Japanese Americans got a disproportionate amount of coverage, except in 1993, when a somewhat greater number of articles were written about Korean Americans in the aftermath of the Los Angeles race riots and when attention to Japanese Americans dropped to its lowest point in the seven-year period under study. Our thesis guided us to examine the ups and downs of coverage of Asian Americans of specific ethnicity as significantly linked to news coverage of United States international tensions with their countries of origin. Indeed, we found that in 1989—the one year in which the number of articles on China exceeded by far those on any other Asian country, including Japan—a larger number of articles appeared about Chinese Americans than in any other year until 1995, when American trade interests in China were prominently connected to human-rights concerns. The rise in the number of articles on Japanese Americans in 1992, we believe, was related to the peak of press attention to trade tensions between the United States and Japan—sensationalized in the image of President Bush getting sick on the Japanese prime minister's lap. Thus, in our case study of the newspaper treatment of Asian Americans in the July 1991 through July 1992 period, we looked at this connection more closely.

Portrayal of Asian Americans as a Racial Minority

An unexpectedly strong finding in our analysis of the subjects through which Asian Americans are treated in the press was that they are depicted primarily in their racial or ethnic minority circumstances. Disproportionately—as compared with articles on the total population—the top fifteen subjects of Asian American articles concerned: Race Relations, Reparations, Race, Concentration Camps, Immigration, Prejudice, Emigration, Cultural Relations, Riots, Discrimination, Aliens, Languages, Neighborhoods, Culture, and Demonstrations and Protests.

Regarding the "model-minority" characterization, our search under "Honors and Awards" found only 31 articles; the proportion of articles on that subject was the same for Asian Americans and for the total population. The 93 articles about Asian Americans found under "Students" were twice the proportion as that for the total population. Entrepreneur-related articles appeared relatively more frequently for Asian Americans than for the total population—but so did crime-related stories.

Asian Americans and Race Relations: 1991–92, a Critical Year

We selected July 1991 through June 1992 for a closer look at the press coverage of Asian Americans and race relations because of two crucial events—the fiftieth anniversary of Pearl Harbor and the outburst of African American hostility against Korean Americans in Los Angeles—indicative of international and domestic conflicts, respectively. Korean American merchants were targeted by African Americans because they were perceived as outsiders—foreigners—who were making a living in their neighborhood and yet were seen as prejudiced toward them. Conciliatory efforts by officials as well as by leaders of both communities were given press attention along with stories of mounting tensions. But we found very little attention to the inequalities in employment, housing, criminal justice, small-business loans, municipal services, and so on. Nor did we find much attention paid to the reasons that Korean American merchants are in those neighborhoods and that black entrepreneurs are so few. Korean Americans were not portrayed as passive victims of either racial violence or institutional neglect; some were armed and were galvanized in demonstrations and were responsive to the complaints of their market, shown by their development of a code of conduct toward customers.

Japanese Americans also were covered prominently by the press in connection with race relations because of the Pearl Harbor anniversary, which evoked and revitalized for some the imagery and emotions of the war and their wartime incarceration. Significantly, the rising trade tensions with Japan, which peaked with President Bush's visit to Japan, elicited the greatest concern about anti–Asian American hostility. The wartime images of Japan as the enemy, recollected in the fiftieth anniversary of Pearl Harbor, were transferred to the current economic conflict with Japan. Japanese Americans, having been considered untrustworthy and imprisoned on the basis of their ancestry during the war, were depicted as particularly anxious about the effects of Japan-bashing on Asian Americans—as the U.S. Commission on Civil Rights study cautioned.

The newspaper articles characterized Asian Americans as having made progress against discrimination, although violent hostility may be increasing and institutionalized discrimination, such as the bamboo ceiling, continues. And as the Asian American population has become more diverse and geographically less concentrated, new trouble spots of anti–Asian American resentment have come into the news with a common theme: newcomers— foreigners—are competing economically and politically with those already established, and they are resented.

We found that the press has paid attention to Asian Americans mainly as connected to race, race relations, prejudice, and discrimination (domestic tensions), and to the residual effects of the war with Japan, now brought to life in "economic warfare" (international tensions), thought by many Americans as threatening their well-being.

At the Intersection of International and Domestic Tensions

Our analysis of newspaper articles has substantially supported our thesis that, in its agenda-setting function, the press focuses public attention selectively on international issues relevant to domestic concerns, and that this adds to and stirs the reservoir of images of Asians available to Americans in their relations with Asian Americans—identified by their Asian country origins and generalized as a racial minority group. We have documented that the major coverage of economic conflict with Japan, to which the wartime imagery of the Japanese has been transferred, is thematically linked to domestic concerns with the lagging economy. Other connections have been identified but are not systematically documented in this paper: for example, issues of democracy such as human rights and free elections are frequently connected to economic considerations, as are the residual effects of war (for example, the MIA issue and the opening of the market in Vietnam). The racial characterizations of Asian wartime enemies—not just from World War II against the Japanese, but also from combat in Korea and Vietnam—often appear in hate speech accompanying violence as well as in the stereotypical beliefs underlying the more subtle institutionalized forms of discrimination against Asian Americans.

The newspaper portrayal of Asian Americans disproportionately in their racial-minority status was unexpectedly strong. They are frequently depicted as resented outsiders—foreign newcomers—competing for employment, business opportunities, and political power, and as victims of this resentment in racial violence .

Thus, Asian Americans today are at the intersection of international and domestic tensions—shown in the press primarily in their racial-minority and perceived–foreigner/outsider status. Ironically, at this juncture, many Asian Americans are also actively shaping and traversing the bridges between domestic and international concerns with their actual or assumed bicultural capabilities. Regrettably, this is not news.

APPENDIX A

List of Newspapers in the DNEWS Database at City University of New York

Afro American	*Christian Science Monitor*	*Michigan Chronicle*
American Banker	*Denver Post*	*New York Times*
American Muslim Journal	*Detroit News*	*San Francisco Chronicle*
Amsterdam News	*Detroit News/Free Press*	*St. Louis Post Dispatch*
Atlanta Constitution	*Guardian*	*Times-Picayune*
Atlanta Journal Constitution	*Houston Post*	*USA Today*
Boston Globe	*Journal and Guide*	*Wall Street Journal*
Call & Post	*Los Angeles Sentinel*	*Washington Post*
Chicago Defender	*Los Angeles Times*	*Washington Times*
Chicago Tribune		

APPENDIX B

Relatively Most Frequent Subjects of Articles About Asian Americans by Number of Articles, Ratio of Subject Emphasis, and Index of Attention, 1989–95

Subject[a]	Number of Articles	Ratio of Subject Emphasis[b]	Index of Attention[c]
Reparations	69	97.84155	6,751.07
Concentration camps	63	52.38885	3,300.50
Race relations	362	20.77917	7,522.06
Race	370	17.40920	6,441.40
Languages	25	17.24317	431.08
Cultural relations	84	16.14912	1,356.53
Censuses	12	14.47748	173.73
Emigration**	115	13.98198	1,607.93
Prejudice	152	13.07876	1,987.97
Immigration	210	12.80636	2,689.34
Riots	109	12.09002	1,317.81
Citizenship	14	12.05046	168.71
Aliens	51	8.47052	432.00
Community centers	10	7.99065	79.91
Population	41	7.61380	312.17
Diplomatic recognition	13	6.21247	80.76
Culture***	67	5.85396	392.22
Discrimination	184	5.61948	1,033.98
Veterans	34	5.26113	178.88
Neighborhoods	84	4.77329	400.96
Americans abroad	11	4.69566	51.65
Activists**	23	4.57228	105.16
Entrepreneurs	41	4.42038	181.24
Festivals	88	4.09346	360.22
Small business	48	3.74921	179.96
Language	28	3.38363	94.74
Demonstrations and protests	116	3.37814	391.86
Reporters**	14	3.35935	47.03
Corporate culture	10	2.89740	28.97
Crime	116	2.85410	331.08
Commercial fishing	11	2.75445	30.30
			(continued)

Source: DNEWS

[a]Subjects with *, **, and *** were used from 1993, 1992, and 1991, respectively. Subjects with fewer than ten articles were excluded.

[b]Ratio of subject emphasis: Percentage of all articles about Asian Americans divided by percentage of all articles about total population.

[c]Index of attention: Number of articles multiplied by ratio of subject emphasis.

Subject[a]	Number of Articles	Ratio of Subject Emphasis[b]	Index of Attention[c]
Human rights	28	2.62100	73.39
Families and family life	52	2.60385	135.40
Business community	15	2.40398	36.06
Curricula	17	2.39674	40.74
Life	124	2.30527	285.85
Students	93	2.30089	213.98
Voter behavior***	11	2.26760	24.94
Retail stores	60	2.26385	135.83
Performing artists	12	2.19957	26.39
Social conditions and trends	109	2.18047	237.67
Shopping centers	17	2.16565	36.82
Harassment	27	2.06317	55.71
Urban areas	34	1.95133	66.35
Indictments	18	1.89729	34.15
Philanthropy	10	1.85609	18.56
Magazines	17	1.81898	30.92
International trade	57	1.78421	101.70
Journalism	21	1.76807	37.13
Religion	27	1.70913	46.15
Crime prevention*	11	1.67605	18.44
Suburban areas	13	1.67259	21.74
Law enforcement	27	1.60880	43.44
Conferences	50	1.58519	79.26
Writers	34	1.56976	53.37
Organizations	37	1.55991	57.72
Social services	16	1.54366	24.70
Conventions	29	1.47320	42.72
Museums	18	1.46682	26.40
International relations	127	1.43008	181.62
Diplomatic consular services	12	1.42142	17.06
Disasters	10	1.40420	14.04
Older people	20	1.39448	27.89
Marketing	26	1.38605	36.04
Criminals	22	1.33619	29.40
Personal profiles	100	1.31818	131.82
Politics	58	1.24878	72.43
Schools	78	1.23262	96.14
Law	39	1.20803	47.11
Editorials	158	1.16279	183.72

(continued)

Subject[a]	Number of Articles	Ratio of Subject Emphasis[b]	Index of Attention[c]
Political dissent	11	1.12811	12.41
Litigation	30	1.08242	32.47
Visual artists	28	1.06059	29.70
Fund-raising	18	1.03193	18.57
Industry profiles	11	1.02291	11.25
Awards and honors	31	1.02186	31.68
Competition	15	0.97795	14.67
Buildings	35	0.97560	34.15
Bombings	16	0.95569	15.29
Volunteers	10	0.94545	9.45
Area planning and development	54	0.92638	50.02
Clergy	14	0.88454	12.38
School boards	14	0.87993	12.32
Gambling	13	0.84921	11.04
Housing	28	0.83674	23.43
Fatalities***	23	0.81167	18.67
Food	31	0.79742	24.72
Children and youth	40	0.78904	31.56
Behavior	19	0.78728	14.96
Settlements and damages	14	0.74327	10.41
Research	34	0.73975	25.15
Investigations	45	0.71341	32.10
Company profiles	17	0.71263	12.11
School administration	12	0.68560	8.23
Television	66	0.61275	40.44
Criminal sentences	14	0.59926	8.39
Statistics	24	0.54573	13.10
Weapons	14	0.52497	7.35
Income	14	0.49016	6.86
Investments	17	0.45781	7.78
Arrests	11	0.45246	4.98
Appointments and personnel changes	36	0.45201	16.27
Health	24	0.32891	7.89
Travel	10	0.32851	3.29
Armed forces	12	0.32752	3.93
Cartoons	10	0.23199	2.32
Finance	14	0.19482	2.73

Subjects of Articles About Asian Americans by DNEWS Period (1/89–12/95) Compared with Pearl Harbor Year (7/91–6/92)

Subject[a]	DNEWS Period		Pearl Harbor Year		
	Number	Percent	Number	Expected Number	Actual Percent
Reparations	69	1.173	9.73	7	0.843
Concentration camps	63	1.071	8.88	10	1.204
Race relations	362	6.288	51.04	125	15.060
Race	371	6.152	52.31	124	14.940
Languages	25	0.425	3.53	5	0.602
Cultural relations	84	1.428	11.84	26	3.132
Emigration	115	1.954	16.22	29	3.494
Prejudice	152	2.583	21.43	56	6.747
Immigration	210	3.569	29.61	33	3.976
Riots	109	1.852	15.37	59	7.108
Aliens	51	0.867	7.19	1	0.120
Population	41	0.697	5.78	0	—
Culture	67	1.139	9.45	17	2.048
Discrimination	184	3.127	25.94	38	4.578
Veterans	34	0.578	4.79	5	0.602
Neighborhoods	84	1.428	11.84	10	1.204
Activists	23	0.391	3.24	0	—
Entrepreneurs	41	0.697	5.78	10	1.204
Festivals	88	1.496	12.41	15	1.807
Small business	48	0.816	6.77	14	1.686
Language	28	0.476	3.95	6	0.723
Demonstrations and protests	116	1.971	16.36	13	1.566
Crime	116	1.971	16.36	19	2.289
Human rights	28	0.476	3.95	1	0.120
Families and family life	52	0.884	7.33	8	0.964
Life	124	2.107	17.48	11	0.120
Students	93	1.581	13.11	11	0.120
Retail stores	60	1.020	8.46	14	1.687
Social conditions and trends	109	1.852	15.37	22	2.651
Harassment	27	0.459	3.81	9	1.084
Urban areas	34	0.578	4.80	9	1.084
International trade	57	0.969	8.04	15	1.807
Journalism	21	0.357	2.96	3	0.361
Religion	27	0.459	3.81	5	0.602

Source: DNEWS

[a]Subjects are in order of ratio of subject emphasis. Only the top 50 subjects were used for this analysis. Subjects with fewer than 20 articles in the 1989–95 DNEWS period were excluded.

APPENDIX D

Number of Articles About Asian Americans by Subject and Month in the Pearl Harbor Year (7/91-6/92)

Subject[a]	1991						1992						Total
	7	8	9	10	11	12	1	2	3	4	5	6	
Reparations	0	0	2	0	1	0	0	0	2	1	1	0	7
Concentration camps	0	0	1	0	0	3	0	5	0	0	1	0	10
Race relations	2	17	8	18	9	10	3	6	3	2	31	16	125
Race	3	17	8	18	9	10	3	6	3	2	31	16	126
Languages	0	0	3	0	0	1	0	0	1	0	0	0	5
Cultural relations	3	2	5	1	3	1	0	3	2	4	2	0	26
Emigration	3	4	5	3	1	1	1	2	2	2	5	0	29
Prejudice	1	4	5	2	1	10	1	9	11	3	1	8	56
Immigration	3	4	5	3	1	1	1	2	2	2	6	3	33
Riots	0	0	0	0	0	0	0	0	0	0	50	9	59
Aliens	0	0	1	0	0	0	0	0	0	0	0	0	1
Population	0	0	0	0	0	0	0	0	0	0	0	0	0
Culture	1	1	1	1	2	1	0	3	1	2	2	2	17
Discrimination	3	2	1	7	2	1	1	7	6	2	2	4	38
Veterans	0	0	0	0	0	2	0	1	0	2	0	0	5
Neighborhoods	0	1	0	2	0	0	4	1	0	0	1	1	10
Activists	0	0	0	0	0	0	0	0	0	0	0	0	0
Entrepreneur	0	1	2	0	1	0	1	1	0	0	0	4	10
Festivals	2	1	1	2	0	0	2	2	2	1	2	0	15
Small business	2	2	0	1	1	0	0	0	0	0	3	5	14
Language	0	0	0	1	1	0	1	1	1	1	0	0	6
Demonstrations and protests	0	1	0	0	0	1	0	0	1	0	6	4	13
Crime	0	2	6	1	2	0	1	2	0	1	1	3	19
Human rights	0	0	0	0	1	0	0	0	0	0	0	0	1
Families and family life	2	1	2	0	0	1	0	1	0	1	0	0	81
Life	3	1	2	0	0	1	0	2	0	2	0	0	11
Students	0	0	4	1	1	1	0	1	2	0	1	0	11
Retail stores	1	1	0	2	1	1	1	3	1	0	3	0	14
Social conditions and trends	3	2	6	0	1	1	2	1	1	1	1	3	22
Harassment	0	1	0	0	0	0	0	5	3	0	0	0	9
Urban areas	1	0	1	0	0	0	0	2	0	0	3	2	9
International trade	2	0	0	0	2	1	4	3	1	0	2	0	15
Journalism	1	0	0	0	0	1	0	1	0	0	0	0	3
Religion	0	1	0	1	0	1	0	0	0	0	0	2	5

Source: DNEWS

[a]Subjects are listed in order of ratio of subject emphasis. Only the top 50 subjects were used for this analysis. Subjects with fewer than 20 articles in the 1989–95 DNEWS period were excluded.

■ NOTE

Acknowledgment: This paper was prepared with the counsel of Joann F. J. Lee, Queens College, and the assistance of Yoshio Shibata and Masami Tamagawa, The Graduate School, The City University of New York.

■ REFERENCES

Citrin, Jack, Beth Reingold, and Donald P. Green
  1990 "American Identity and the Politics of Ethnic Change." *Journal of Politics* 52:
         1125–1154.
Commission on Wartime Relocation and Internment of Civilians
  1982 *Personal Justice Denied.* Washington, D.C.: Commission on Wartime Relo-
         cation and Internment of Civilians.
Deutsch, Robert D.
  1995 "American Mythologies of Japan." Vienna, Va.: EBR Consulting, Inc.
  1996 "Images of Japan." Transcript, *ABC News Nightline* (April 15).
Dower, John W.
  1986 *War Without Mercy: Race and Power in the Pacific War.* New York: Pantheon
         Books.
Fernandez, John P.
  1991 *Managing a Diverse Work Force: Regaining the Competitive Edge.* Lexington, Ky.:
         D.C. Heath.
Fishman, Mark
  1980 *Manufacturing the News.* Austin: University of Texas Press.
Gans, Herbert J.
  1979 *Deciding What's News: A Study of CBS Evening News, NBC Nightly News,
         Newsweek and Time.* New York: Pantheon Books.
Hartmann, P., and C. Husband
  1974 *Racism and the Mass Media.* Totowa, N.J.: Rowan and Littlefield.
Holz, Josephine R., and Charles R. Wright
  1979 "Sociology of Mass Communications." *Annual Review of Sociology* 5: 193–217.
Hur, K.K., and J.P. Robinson
  1978 "The Social Impact of 'Roots.'" *Journalism Quarterly* 55: 14, 19, 83.
Kim, Illsoo S.
  1981 *The New Urban Immigrants: The Korean Community in New York.* Princeton,
         N.J.: Princeton University Press.
Korematsu v. United States
  1944 No. 22 (October Term).
Lee, Joann F.J.
  1996 "Reflections on Asian Americans and News Coverage." Paper presented at
         the annual meeting of the Association of Asian American Studies (May 31),
         Washington, D.C.

Min, Pyong Gap

    1993   "Korean Immigrants in Los Angeles." In *Immigration and Entrepreneurship*, ed, Ivan Light and P. Bhachu. New York: Transaction Books.

National Asian Pacific American Legal Consortium

    1995   *1994 Audit of Violence Against Asian Pacific Americans: Anti–Asian Violence, A National Problem* Washington, D.C.: National Asian Pacific American Legal Consortium.

Portier, Anne

    1993   "American Mass Media and Japan: Exotic Traveling from Pluralism to Imaginary Alternatives." *Current World Leaders* 36: 363–86.

Shibutani, Tamotsu

    1966   *Improvised News: A Sociological Study of Rumor.* New York: Bobbs-Merrill.

Smelser, Neil J.

    1963   *Theory of Collective Behavior.* New York: Free Press.

Takaki, Ronald

    1989   "Who Killed Vincent Chin?" In *A Look Beyond the Model Minority Image: Critical Issues in Asian America,* ed. Grace P. Yun. New York: Minority Rights Group, U.S.A.

tenBroek, Jacobus, Edward N. Barnhart, and Floyd W. Matson

    1954   *Prejudice, War and the Constitution: Causes and Consequences of the Evacuation of the Japanese Americans in World War II.* Berkeley: University of California Press.

Tuchman, Gaye

    1978   *Making News: A Study in the Construction of Reality.* New York: Free Press.

U.S. Commission on Civil Rights

    1992   "Civil Rights Issues Facing Asian Americans in the 1990s." Washington, D.C.: U.S. Commission on Civil Rights.

Waldinger, Roger

    1989   "Structural Opportunity or Ethnic Advantage? Immigrant Business Development in New York." *International Migration Review* 23: 48–72.

Warren, D.I.

    1972   "Mass Media and Racial Crisis: Study of the New Bethel Church Incident in Detroit." *Journal of Social Issues* 28: 111–31.

Watanabe, Paul, and Laura E. Imperiale

    1990   "The Past as Present: United States–Japan Relations and the Politics of the Toshiba Scandal." *Business in the Contemporary World* 2: 84–94.

Weiss, Philip

    1996   "The Senator Cannot Help Being Himself." *New York Times Magazine* (March 3).

8

INVENTING

THE

EARTH

The Notion of "Home" in

Asian American

Literature

LUIS H. FRANCIA

> To us already,
> a birthplace is no longer home.
> The place we were brought up is not either.
> Our history, rushing to us
> through fields and hills, is our home.
>
> *Ko Won, Korean poet*

Home. Where is it? Is it always where the heart resides? As we approach the end of the millennium, glimpse the shiny new roofs of an emergent global village, and as 100 million refugees of different nationalities live outside their own borders, we need to rethink this question, which is now invested with more urgency than ever before. From the emblematic figure of the Wandering Jew to the late–twentieth-century Vietnamese boatperson, ideas of "home" have always played a central and essential role in the ways that we imagine the world or, more specifically, in the ways that we imagine relating to it. The world may still not be home writ large, but home is usually the world writ small. It is not surprising, then, that the idea of home remains fundamental to all cultures, with its empowering, utopian allure. I refer not to the nation-state—a human, though not often humane, construct that localizes and concentrates political power in an artificial entity known as "government"—but to the cherished ideal, a specific site anointed as the matrix and nourisher of a particular culture. In mythic terms, there is the Original Home—a Christian Eden, a Muslim al-Janna, a Buddhist Nirvana—from which separation, painful exile, and the inevitable fall from grace become an anguished prelude to recurring attempts to once again be embraced by it. Without home as a bedrock concept, a culture can teeter on the edge of dissolution, driven there by the specter of amorphousness. Perhaps one of colonialism's most disabling, traumatizing effects has been its ability to undermine the subjugated culture's views of its homeland as a sacrosanct site by subverting traditional notions of national and ethnic character, often replacing these with the colonizer's own. "Imperialism," as Edward Said once wrote, "is the export of identity" (Said 1990: 38).

This is the age of migration: whether we refer to the East Indian merchant booted out of Uganda, the political activist exiled from Iran, or the Hutu refugee fleeing Rwanda's turmoil, the planet has come to resemble a giant terminus. In addition, the accessibility of almost every part of the world, and the rapid advances in communications, render traditional demarcations old-fashioned, seemingly irrelevant, inevitably resulting in changes in age-old cultural patterns. In the case of diasporic communities, attempts to preserve traditions are bound to be selective and mutative, resulting in hybridization—anthem of both the forward-looking rootless immigrant and the ever-increasing number of "internationalists," believers not just in the inevitability of multiple cross-border alliances but in their desirability.

And so when Filipino carolers reenact a favorite Yuletide ritual in the high-rise apartments of Manhattan, or when Chinese dragon dancers parade vigorously in Chinatown during lunar-year celebrations, the fires of a shared past are stoked, and images of home are resurrected. And yet, while the remembered rituals, the songs, and the routines may be the same, the context remains a world removed, figuratively and literally, from the source, cut off from the umbilical matrix. If home remains the primordial, archetypal locus of innocence, then indeed one, having left it, can never return.

In her preface to a collection of short Asian Pacific American[1] fiction, *American Eyes,* Lori M. Carlson (1994: xi) states, "Is home the place that keeps the ways of another, more ancient homeland, or is it where new replaces old?

In a nation where Asian-Americans can change from black haired to blond, from cooking stewed pig's knuckles to craving fast-food hamburgers, from speaking pidgin to uttering standard English, where is home? Is home where we are different or where we learn to be the same?"

Postcolonial global migrations, the continuing shifts in the racial composition of American society, and the growing emphasis on Asia and the Pacific Rim are prodding different Asian Pacific American communities to refashion their ideas of home, particularly in the area of culture. It is not surprising, then, that in Asian Pacific America's creative literature a consistent theme has been the imaginative, and often painful, rethinking of what and where home is. Displacement and the malaise of spiritual, if not physical, exile, it seems to me, constitute part of the Asian Pacific American's core condition.

With families, tribes, and even nations fragmented, with the flow of ideas and capital now possible through cyberspace—a global economy no longer just idle talk but a vivid, even unsettling reality—a Hmong teenager in Minneapolis or a Vietnamese fisherman in Texas may well ask, What is home? Where is it? If the frontier keeps moving, where then do we locate it? Since the conventional ways of conceptualizing home no longer suffice, what cultural modes would best express—and symbolize—the Asian Pacific American's peculiar situation? In this country, precisely because it is largely an immigrant society, the concepts of home (and of homeland) continually mutate, being as varied as the immigrant communities themselves. In this sense, "American" becomes a synonym for "new" or, better still, for hybridity— much to the dismay of those who would forever anchor views of America to antique notions of a narrowly viewed past.[2]

And yet, America as a concept that is all-embracing has its seemingly distinctive features subsumed—"undermined" might be a more accurate term—by intricately linked, homogenizing consumerism and pop culture. One constant of rapidly evolving globalization is the seeming triumph of capitalism, an extended version of American laissez-faire. This model, based on the classic role of a freewheeling, income-generating consumer, offers little emotional weight or comfort to people who have traditionally been marginalized. If the substitute for home is simply capital, where the strength of citizenship is proportionate to purchasing power, then "home" loses its meaning. And so what Asian Pacific Americans have done to strategize their survival beyond the physical is to create enclaves within America, to render a wide-open, deeply ambiguous notion/nation ethnic-specific, thereby not merely paying homage to but reconstituting ancestral memories in the American here and now. If identity politics have become an arena where irrational passions—and even calculated ones—are played out, it is partly as a reaction to the intrusive assertions of a profit-margin–loving center, and partly out of a sense that specific histories must be rescued from the oblivion of marginality.

In the process, of course, these distinct, and distinctive, communities have come to represent clear markets for increasingly aggressive corporations. Witness, for instance, AT&T's marketing approach to the Filipino community in the United States, believed to have an estimated annual spending power of $13 billion. To tap into that market, the giant telecommunications firm uses a weekly radio program that is broadcast in the United States and the Philippines, in addition to newspaper ads and TV commercials that feature prominent Filipino Americans. One of its most successful promotional efforts is "Klub Pilipino," a program that rewards people whose average monthly long-distance bill to the home country meets an agreed minimum with perks associated with culturally significant events and activities (Cacas 1995: 15–16). Clearly there is money to be made in redemptive, and even fake, nostalgia.

In rethinking, remembering home, the question of physical space is in many ways the least problematic aspect. In a series of Asia Society-sponsored roundtable discussions held in 1995 in various cities, including Chicago, Seattle, and Los Angeles, the question of home, among other issues, was discussed. It was clear that the participants' feelings toward America as home were, to say the least, ambivalent. For a young, female Japanese American professor in Los Angeles, home was an issue intimately tied up with gender. Though her father had lived in the United States for many decades, he insisted on his primacy as a Japanese man; gender had privileged him in the land of his birth in a way that is not possible in the Los Angeles metropolitan area. For a septuagenarian Korean man in Seattle, it was a question of generation. He remarked on how he often tells his grandchildren, "No matter how long you have lived here, [though] you are second-generation, you are still Korean." He went on to state, "I think this is my home, but culturally, emotionally, my home is over there." Even though he had lived in this country for four decades, and likely would stay for the rest of his life, he was perpetually looking back, as if he wanted to make sure he had not strayed too far from his place of birth.

In some instances, the simple, experiential notion of home that we assume is universal never even existed, as in the case of a Vietnamese Chinese woman in Chicago. She pointed out how, although she had been born and raised in Vietnam, she had never been accepted as Vietnamese by the Vietnamese, who regarded her home as China, a place she had never ever visited. She noted, "The problem is, Chinese from other countries don't recognize me as Chinese. They say you are Vietnamese." And in the Midwestern environment of Chicago, those feelings of displacement, of deracination, were both reinforced and ameliorated. The feelings were reinforced because in Chicago people automatically assumed she was from someplace else; ameliorated because if she was not going to be at "home" anywhere, then this society was a better one to participate in, for part of its defining characteristic was that it was made up significantly of people "from somewhere else."

Her situation underscores the fragility of one's status as a minority: whether we speak of Japanese Americans, Korean Americans, Filipino Americans, or any of the other distinctive groups that make up the Asian Pacific American spectrum of the American rainbow, we must acknowledge how strongly ideas of home are tied to concepts of ethnicity and race. As a Filipino professional living in Seattle put it, his own rule of thumb is wherever "I will be accepted because of my color, because of my diction, because of my accent . . . that will be home for me." As he spoke of often feeling ill at ease even though he has lived in the United States for fifteen years, the desire to be back in the Philippines (where his ethnicity would never be an issue and where the reflexive, almost daily experiences, of self-definition would considerably diminish, if not totally disappear) was palpable in these concerns.

It should be apparent by now that the seemingly simple concept of home is not, for in an era in which hybridity, whether transgressive or evolutionary, has increasingly become a prominent, even desirable, feature of the postcolonial order, the idea of home has come to stand as a reconfiguration of many other issues crucial to societies all over the world. I need only mention the volatility in the Middle East, the "troubles" in Northern Ireland, and the demented impulse toward ethnic cleansing in Bosnia for this to become immediately clear. Such reconfiguration, or the portraiture of such reconfiguration, is explored most imaginatively in literature. Textbook history informs us about movements and dates and heroes and villains, but it does not, cannot, decipher the language and history of the ordinary heart. This is best left to the artists, poets, and fictionists.

If we are to understand and appreciate the ways in which Asian Pacific Americans, straddling the confluence of East and West, conceptualize America and the different countries of Asia from which they or their forebears came, then we need to have more than a passing familiarity with their creative literature—indeed, with any of their cultural expressions.

How is America as home, mythical or real, seen, felt, thought of, by Asian Pacific American writers? Is it burden or benediction? Transitory or terminal? All of the above? And correspondingly, how do the "strangers from a different shore," to use Ronald Takaki's poignant phrase, think of that shore? In Carlos Bulosan's searingly vivid, semiautobiographical work of fiction, *America Is in the Heart*, the narrator Allos, quoting his brother Macario on America, says impassionedly, "America is not bound by geographical latitudes. America is not merely a land or an institution. America is in the hearts of men that died for freedom; it is also in the eyes of men that are building a new world. America is a prophecy of a new society of men: of a system that knows no sorrow or strife or suffering. America is a warning to those who would try to falsify the ideals of freemen" (Bulosan 1991: 189). Yet the America outside the heart emphatically resisted such idealizing impulses, maintaining a cold, racist demeanor toward Allos and his fellow *manong,* where "every hour was a blow against the senses, dulling all impulses toward decency" (Bulosan 1991: 137). Their lives were ever in danger because to be a Filipino in California, in America, "was a crime" (Bulosan 1991: 121).

More than three decades later, as the narrator in Maxine Hong Kingston's classic *The Woman Warrior* recounts her growing up, America becomes both a fabled and a feared place, inhabited by barbarians and ghosts, a stronghold of patriarchy (almost as much as the China her mother portrays), where she attempts to reconcile her American and her Chinese female sensibilities: "Walking erect (knees straight, toes pointed forward, not pigeon-toed, which is Chinese-feminine) and speaking in an inaudible voice, I have tried to turn myself American-feminine" (Kingston 1989: 11). The reconciliation of two distinct modes of being "feminine" is surely synecdochic, a gendered gateway to a unitary sense of self.

The America we see in Bharati Mukherjee's fiction and in Bienvenido Santos's short stories, on the other hand, is an endlessly repetitive landscape that simultaneously demands and resists the inscription of ethnicity and race. Even as the writers' styles vary widely, even wildly, America in its perceived impact often assumes a remarkable and terrifying homogeneity, due largely to a mythifying Eurocentric bent. In Mukherjee's short story "Jasmine," the eponymous protagonist, from Port of Spain and new to America, eagerly attempts to reconstruct herself: "She'd managed to cut herself off mentally from anything too islandy. She loved her Daddy and Mummy, but didn't think of them that often anymore" (Mukherjee 1988: 131). At the end of the story, Jasmine is transformed, partly through an affair with the married Bill Moffit, an embodiment of patriarchal privilege, into "a girl rushing wildly into the future" (Mukherjee 1988: 135). We who have lived through that first zeal of re-siting know too well the disappointments and painful revelations that lie in store for the bright-eyed Jasmine, who may have left Trinidad but whom Trinidad will never leave, the Caribbean currents too deep to budge, if not from her own consciousness, at least from the consciousness of those around her. For her every attempt to be prototypically "American" (which she equates partly with material affluence) will be countered by the equally endlessly prototypical "Where are you from?"

How very different are the *manong*, or older brothers, who populate Santos's stories! These lonely, wifeless, and childless men—the grim result of pre–World War II exclusionary, antimiscegenation laws—have no wish, perhaps naively, to aid in their own displacement by exiling their country from their hearts, thereby compounding the original conditions of exile. On the contrary, they keep attempting to re-create the Ilocos region, or Bicol, or Manila—all dear and familiar places, now bathed in the glow of sacred remembrance—in their American lives. By the same token, the intensity of memory makes it all the more difficult to fit into a landscape wiped clean of sentiment but filled with the menace of xenophobia. Hence, memory becomes a double-edged sword, at once revivifying and alienating. Fil, a homely "OT" (old-timer) in "The Day the Dancers Came," wistfully recalls his invitation to dinner, at which he is spurned by a troupe of young visiting Philippine dancers, "they would have something special to remember about us here when they return to our country. They would tell their folks: We met a kind old man who took us to his apartment. It was not much of a place. It was old—like him. When we sat on the sofa in the living room, the bottom sank heavily, the broken springs touching the floor. But what a cook that man was! And how kind! We never thought that rice and *adobo* could be that delicious. And the chicken *relleno*! When someone asked what the stuffing was—we had never tasted anything like it—he smiled, saying, 'From heaven's supermarket,' touching his head and pressing his heart like a clown as if heaven were there" (Santos 1994: 124).

WHOSE AMERICA IS IT?

The traditional concept of America as a Europeanized New World—an oxymoron if ever there was one—has always rested on shaky foundations. When the United States emerged from the 1776 Revolution, the New World was already a de facto postcolonial, multicultural society, a polyglot representation of a nascent global village within its boundaries. Europe was represented by three colonial powers—England, France, and Spain—and by the Dutch. There were the pioneering Native American nations, more than five hundred of them, spread across the continent; Mexicans; African slaves and their descendants; Jews; and even a small community of Filipinos in Louisiana, who had jumped ship to escape their abusive masters on the galleon run between Manila and Acapulco. Tongues and accents varied, as did religious customs, cuisine, clothing—indeed, all the earmarks of what we now term "internationalism" were there from the start. (For all their laudable desire to remake society, the energetic iconoclasts of the 1960s by no means created the joys and pains of multiculturalism. Instead, they were rediscovering what had long been there, but dormant underneath a stifling uniformity.)

While a fledgling United States of America may have defeated a royalist England, gaining political and economic independence, the upstart nation still held culturally to Britannia's umbilical cord. In many ways Merrie Olde England was still home. In the exclusionary history and imagination of white narratives, the Europeanizing of the New World is a constant. This, for instance, is brought home quite clearly by Benedict Anderson, who remarks in an essay on exile and migration on how it was paradoxically possible for Mary Rowlandson, a young seventeenth-century Massachusetts woman, to see English cattle in "deserted English fields" as she was being abducted by a Native American tribe, even though she had never been to England. Thus:

> If one migrated from a village in the delta of the Ganges and went to schools in Calcutta, Delhi, and perhaps Cambridge; if one bore the indelible contamination of English and Bengali; if one was destined to be cremated in Bombay, where was one intelligibly to be home, where could one unitarily be born, live, and die, except in "India"?

> At the same time, for the reasons just detailed, home as it emerged was less experienced than imagined, and imagined through a complex of mediations and representations [Anderson 1994: 319].

In this sense, the tug between Old World and New favored the former, the European narrative assuming a discursive dominance, along with clear-cut notions of nationhood, inevitably relegating to its (negative) margins non-white communities. America as an entity in realpolitik (as opposed to its myth) was undoubtedly "the ambivalent figure" Homi Bhabha refers to, with its problematic "transitional history, its conceptual indeterminacy, its wavering between vocabularies" (Bhabha 1990: 2).

We are too familiar with the classic iconic representation of America: the rugged, fearless, justice-dispensing individual, whether this be John Wayne, Clint Eastwood, or Rambo; the sultry femme of desire, Marilyn Monroe, and her legions of imitators; golden-haired California surfers; endlessly smooth highways, filled with caravans of cars moving toward a bright horizon—toward whiteness. Indeed, in much of Asian Pacific American literature, such "whiteness" is often embodied by the quintessential blonde. (It is no coincidence that in one of her incarnations, Madonna dyed her hair blond.) In *America Is in the Heart* (Bulosan 1991), benevolent, almost saintly, lovely fair-haired white women are representations of the Good America, while gun-toting, roughneck white men represent the Bad America.

In Shawn Wong's *Homebase* (1991: 68, 70), a much later work than Bulosan's, such representations are given a sardonic twist: he talks of his Dream Bride America, a fifteen-year-old "patronizing, slim, long-legged, blonde-haired, full-breasted" cheerleader who persists in telling him that he should "go back home" even when he has made it clear that he is native born and not at all curious about China.

America as both a place and a semi-fictive construct was a trove of subversive contradictions; it was a place whose myths allowed you to be someplace else, to be everywhere else but "here"; it was a place finally that could wind up denying its own place. It was a place where nativity, the state of being "native," lapsed into meaninglessness, came "unmoored," to use Anderson's eloquent term. How then to set roots in such a setting? Biology and culture and art and nurture, certainly, usually. And each community necessarily insists on the primacy of certain patterns, with race almost always assumed to be uniform on the part of its proponents. Away from the land of birth, where the question may not be central to public discussion, race suddenly assumes a pivotal role, along with tradition and ritual.

Race has always figured prominently in the debate on how America should live on in our hearts and minds; the undercurrents of its history/ histories reveal to us how, beneath the wonderful rhetoric and promise of a truly free pluralistic nation—the inherent attraction of infinite accommodation has been the New World's greatest lure—lurks its opposite: the view of an ethnically pure country. Or, at least, a "culturally pure" one. The clichéd image encapsulating that view in a nation of immigrants has been that of the "melting pot." Seemingly benevolent, it gives a respectable face to the idea of purity, for what gets melted are the differences, the "dross"; what remains is a core that is reducible—and reproducible. It is essential to have all the right, predetermined signifiers, from blue jeans to bonds, from hamburgers to suburban homes. An irreparable sense of loss follows, with regret and an abiding sense of melancholy, but the bargain struck, which is often Faustian, is for a new "home." Uniformity becomes the unspoken mantra of this trade-off. And, of course, the question is, Whose standards are we considering? Who built the pot? Who does the "melting"? Who feeds and stokes its fires?

The assimilationist ideology inherent in the melting-pot model stands in contrast with that of the mosaic, whose idea rests on a basic respect accorded to differences, which are viewed as invigorating rather than debilitating, as adding to rather than subtracting from a sense of nation and nationhood. The mosaic as a suggested constitutive signifier of American life points up the wished-for ascendance of pluralism and becomes a de facto recognition and validation of what has always been there: different diasporas existing within the American community. Part of the urgency in investi-

gating the idea of home thus comes directly from the tension between po-
larities—for example, Insider/Outsider, Purity/Hybridity, Stasis/Mobility.

In the aftermath of the 1960s' Civil Rights movement and the
subsequent emphasis on ethnic pride, beginning with the defiantly non-
assimilationist "Black Is Beautiful," what we witness today, the differentiating but not necessarily fragmenting impulse of multiculturalism, reemerged.
And what that implies, as Anderson (1994: 325) puts it, is "that a simple
nineteenth-century version of Americanism is no longer adequate or
acceptable." But far from rendering the discussion simpler, multiculturalism
necessarily complicates investigations of home. For one thing, it seemingly
bestows its imprimatur for adherents to participate in nationalist movements
back in their country of origin, without their American loyalties necessarily
coming into question, which Anderson views as potentially dangerous, for it
could be the "product of capitalism's remorseless, accelerating transformation of all human societies" creating "a serious politics that is at the same time
radically unaccountable" (Anderson 1994: 327).

Beyond that, multiculturalism is neither the New Age panacea—the
key to universal harmony—that its proponents claim it to be nor the
destruction of civilization, the mantra of barbarians at the gate, that the
xenophobic and the zealously Eurocentric would have us believe. But what
makes a discussion of multiculturalism difficult is not so much these two
extremes. It is, rather, the liberal view, which usually winds up engaging in
benevolent appreciation. Under the guise of respecting difference by using
its most visible symbols—dress, song, text, any and all of a culture's pantheon of signs—the liberal model of multiculturalism consigns the Other to,
as the cultural critic Coco Fusco (1995: 103) puts it, "recognizable standards
of difference that rarely question the power relations that define these
distinctions." In that sense, "ethnic" becomes a code word for "peripheral,"
with only those at the center privileged enough to elude its stamp and odor.

Any serious investigation then of multiculturalism must consider the
issue of power, and the necessity of redistributing it, if we are to break away
from the disquieting, ultimately destructive habit of appropriation. And
power therefore has to be seen as an essential component in reconfiguring
home. For one of the blessings of home is to offer its inhabitants the promise
of attainable power. The power of Definition. The power of History. The
power of Language and Representation. The power of Determination, of
helping to shape the meaning of "America" and "American."

Increasingly, being "American" has come to signify for its immi-
grant/exile communities a bifurcation, a tension between return and a
deferral—the emblematic tug concretized by the state of hyphenation. Is that
hyphen a wedge or a bridge between two potentially autonomous states of

being? When Clifford (1994: 308) states that blacks in Britain imagine "ways to stay and be different, to be British *and something else* complexly related to Africa and the Americas," he could very well be talking about Asian Pacific Americans. Whether out of Africa or Asia, the non-Europeanized Old World extends, in ways simultaneously and profoundly dissimilar and similar to England's reach during this country's formative years, to these shores.

That tension and the accompanying debate over homogeneity versus heterogeneity have often yielded rich cultural and social expressions. If conducted without the disabling effects of prejudice and rabble-rousing rhetoric, without the dogma of "P.C.," the debate itself speaks eloquently of a healthy, pluralistic polity and can generate valuable insights into how we can de- and reconstruct ourselves. One can unequivocally say that whenever paradox, of difference unifying, has been viewed as a positive condition, it has been beneficial to America, leading to the liberating formations of a protean society. In 1981, writing on my own experiences as a novice participant in America's burgeoning culture wars, I said, "Should the possibility of paradox disappear, whether apocalyptically or through plain atrophy—should homogeneity become king—then this country's existence will be quite impoverished. Then a fundamental part of the myth will pass away. America will sing, not in a Whitmanesque way of the future, and only mutedly of the present, but mostly and loudly of the past, a child grown stodgy and suddenly very old, content only in its memories of overdevelopment" (Francia 1981: 71).

HOME AND ITS (DIS)CONTENTS

Although substantial Asian immigration to America began with the Chinese coming over because of the California gold rush, the feeling on both sides of the hyphenated divide was that their stay, and that of other Asian immigrants, would be temporary, a trip of sojourners rather than permanent residents. Public debate (if it could be called that) on their status then heavily favored exclusion to inclusion, homogeneity to heterogeneity—a predilection in America's love–hate relationship with immigrants that keeps cropping up like a malignant weed in an otherwise profuse American garden. Over time, over a period of overt racism, accompanied by racist legislation and virulent and violent attacks on Asians of differing nationalities (its dubious height attained by the wholesale incarceration of Japanese Americans during World War II), began the movement toward parity, albeit in fits and starts.

A key moment in that movement came with the 1965 Immigration Act, which increased the flow of so-called Third World immigration, with Asian Pacific Americans benefiting the most. Between 1940 and 1980, that population grew from less than four-tenths of 1 percent to 1.5 percent in 1980 (Daniels 1991: 239, 350). By 1990, the percentage had increased to 3 percent; assuming immigration laws remain the same, by the year 2020, Asian Pacific Americans will number about 23 million, or 7 percent of the total population, with Filipino Americans constituting the largest group (LEAP 1995: 2).

In imaginative ways as varied as their writings, Asian Pacific American writers, whether poets, playwrights, or fictionists, consider the consequences and dimensions of the Asian diaspora. A specific Asian country and culture often foregrounds the work, or at least serves as a background, without preventing the writer from thinking of himself or herself as part of an imagined (though problematic) America. Mukherjee in an interview said that South Asians here "can be Americans in our own way" but not dependent on received notions of what that means: "We don't have to copy any external, outer model of Americanization, and my picture is a very clear-eyed picture of America" (Lavina 1994: 55–57).

The simultaneous embrace of and declaration of autonomy from America inherent in Mukherjee's remarks points to other themes prominent in contemporary Asian Pacific American literature, such as restlessness, rootlessness, exile; "foreignness" and the issue of being bi- or even tricultural; memory and its (dis)abling importance; language; and history.

No longer is home a condition and a place one automatically inherits—a physical and spiritual place beyond question, the background that also foregrounds us. Home becomes a condition to be negotiated, a metaphysical and metaphorical space demanding to be (re)built, with a sense of ownership and prideful autonomy on the part of all its occupants, for, as Salman Rushdie (1991: 149) puts it in *Imaginary Homelands*, "The immigrant must invent the earth beneath his feet." And its inventing, its constructing, in turn demands relentless, passionate questioning, whether of identity, memory, the use of language, or history.

To my mind, the confluence of all these disparate but related elements finds its densest expression in the late Korean American writer and artist Theresa Hak Kyung Cha's *Dictee* (1995), a thoroughly unsettling, intensely personal and feminist, provocative work. Cha works in two opposing directions at once, reconstructing and deconstructing Korean history, both in this country and on the peninsula, and herself, re-viewing the intersections between the personal and the political, between language and silence, between patriarchal traditions and feminist longing and subversion, between an imposed colonial memory and nationalism, in ways antithetical to standard histories and borders. The book is literally a mosaic, combining calligraphy, Greek mythology, photographs, different languages, history, religion—with fragmented but acute language that mirrors and is mirrored by the book's other elements. The work embodies many things (it resists easy categorization), and one of the things it embodies is Cha's militant but also poetic refusal to subscribe to the assimilationist notion of wholeness. For, she asks, where is that fabled wholeness? Certainly not in memory or in history; not in her condition as a Korean American immigrant woman; not in any of those hallmarks conventionally ascribed to the making of a person. For Cha, restlessness is the condition of the fragmented exile: "Our destination is fixed on the perpetual motion of search. Fixed in its perpetual exile . . . we are inside the same struggle seeking the same destination" (Cha 1995: 81).

If Cha's representation of the foreign-born Asian Pacific American's sense of displacement is arguably the densest, John Okada's *No-No Boy* is arguably the starkest in portraying the native-born Asian Pacific American's dilemma in coming to grips with a sense of place and belonging. Ichiro, the novel's young Nisei protagonist, struggles with two questions—"What is Japanese?" and "What is American?"—in his attempts to reconstruct his own personal and social identity following his refusal to serve in the army during World War II. As the editors of *Aiieeee!,* the seminal anthology of Asian Pacific American literature point out, Ichiro instinctively knows to avoid a false duality, as shown in an interior monologue addressed to his mother:

> I am not your son and I am not Japanese and I am not American. I can go someplace and tell people that . . . I am not American, true and blue and Hail Columbia . . . I wish with all my heart that I were Japanese or that I were American. I am neither and I blame you and I blame myself and I blame the world. . . . It is so easy and simple that I cannot understand it at all. And the reason I do not understand it is because I do not understand what it was about the half of me which was American and the half which might have become the whole of me if I had said yes I will go and fight in your army because that is what I believe and want and cherish and love [Okada 1976: 16].

In today's postwar America, in the aftermath of the 1960s, the tension may not be that stark, but it is there nonetheless. In his memoir *Turning Japanese,* David Mura recognizes the tenacious hold Japan has on his unconscious: "Much of my life I had insisted on my Americanness, had shunned most connections with Japan and felt proud I knew no Japanese. . . . But perhaps it's a bit ingenuous to say I had no longing to go to Japan; it was obvious my imagination had been traveling there for years, unconsciously swimming the Pacific against the tide of my family's emigration, my parents' desire after the internment camps, to forget the past" (Mura 1991: 9).

Mura's stay in Japan becomes a way of exoticizing and understanding the past—his as well as his parents'; of dealing with being in the midst of a host American society that, in its treatment of the Japanese as well as of other communities of color, was decidedly racist and colonial. And we find throughout Asian Pacific American literature a tone and attitude that are resolutely postcolonial—that is, considering relationships between the (usually white) holders of power and members of marginalized communities that echo those between colonizers and colonized. Granted, the term "postcolonial" is rarely used to describe Asian Pacific American works, but this is due largely to the deliberate avoidance of America's colonial past, both at home and abroad, in much of critical literature, and to America's glossed-over self-portrayal as a benevolent exception in the ranks of Western colonizers and their heretofore interventionist foreign policy.

Viscerally and intellectually, Asian Pacific American writers shun the homogenizing trend of a Eurocentric society and interrogate the claims of the traditional center to primacy, asserting through the language of imagination and through the imagination of language that such a center no longer holds, but that its own does. Or, more accurately, that several centers hold, with "the peoples of the periphery" returning to "rewrite the history and fiction of the metropolis" (Bhabha 1990: 6). In the more succinct phrasing of Rushdie, "The empire writes back."

Thus, viewed within the larger cultural net cast by its constitutive diasporas, Asian Pacific American literature shifts the locus of privilege from Europe not so much to Asia as to the continent's transformed (and transformative) communities here, questioning traditional allegiances and altering the unquestioned emphasis on a hegemonic mainstream in favor of a decentralized, multiethnic community or communities. To seize on a well-known decentered center, consider the fact that a number of significant Asian Pacific American works situate their universe in Chinatown, letting it occupy a prominent position. De-exoticized but not deracinated, Chinatown in the West encompasses both frontier and tradition, a refuge and preserve of "Chineseness" at the very same time that it represents a centrifugal move from the Middle Kingdom. At polar opposites from Roman Polanski's *Chinatown*—a brilliant film noir that nevertheless marginalizes and casts Chinatown well in the Orientalist mold and is certainly symptomatic of the fortune-cookie world of the asexual Charlie Chan—the view from within enables Chinatown to divest itself of inverted commas, "to breathe, to assume a complexity and a human depth that cannot be measured either by simple geographic boundaries or by simple equations" (Francia 1988).

In Kingston's *The Woman Warrior* and Wong's *Homebase,* the community of Chinese immigrants serves as a signifier not only that Charlie Chan is dead, to borrow Jessica Hagedorn's felicitous title for an anthology of contemporary Asian Pacific American fiction, but that the stereotypes suddenly evaporate like fog in the sunlight. The result is to force the reader to relinquish her or his "outsider" status by coming face to face with flesh-and-blood characters. In both Louis Chu's *Eat a Bowl of Tea* (1989) and Fae Mayenne Ng's *Bone* (1993), Chinatown—in New York and San Francisco, respectively—is as much a character as anyone else. Repository of secrets and of communal ways, site of reconstituted clans and immigrant dreams and nightmares, as well as of the pedestrian business of daily living, Chinatown rests in treasured ambivalence. To Chu's Ben Loy and his wife, Manhattan's Mott Street and its environs, as initially nurturing as they are, turn into a claustrophobic world and must ultimately be abandoned. For Ben Loy's father, the Cantonese sojourner, the very same streets, while devoid of Chinese female presences, allow him face but in the end strip him of it. And for the hip Leila, *Bone*'s narrator, Salmon Alley, the street nestled in the bosom of Chinatown, is a sanctuary; it "felt like the only safe place" (Ng 1993: 120). Salmon Alley becomes a precious site where dear and familiar communal Cantonese feelings find an outlet. Chinatown, however, can be suffocating as well, as it is for Leila's younger sister Ona, around whose suicide the narrative revolves, and for Nina, who migrates to New York.

Just as the view of Chinatown is ambivalent, so too is the view of Asia. Sometimes seen as a kind of paradise lost, the country of origin is often never revisited, in the case of immigrants, or visited, in the case of their descendants. That far-off place becomes a way of dealing with displacement, assuming a curative, revitalizing role, never mind the reasons for leaving in the first place. The larger-than-life role that the country left behind assumes is evident in Bulosan and in the short stories of Santos. Its very representation acts as solid counterweight to the feelings akin to weightlessness in the United States, a country that is seemingly indifferent to the past. Santos's *manong* take to memory as compensation and protection. They are like all other immigrants who "began to sense they had traversed new boundaries, some of them not defined by geography—and they anxiously gathered memory around themselves" (Takaki 1989: 74).

More specifically, the writer's seeming obsession with identity stems from a relentless desire to ground the self, wounded by "dislocation," as Bill Ashcroft, Gareth Griffiths, and Helen Tiffin (1989: 8–9), in their study of postcolonial literature, point out, "resulting from migration, the experience of enslavement, transportation, or 'voluntary' removal for indentured labour. Or it may have been destroyed by *cultural denigration,* the conscious and unconscious oppression of the indigenous personality and culture by a supposedly superior racial or cultural model."

Because of displacement and dispossession, and because siting ideas of home within a specific locale no longer proves satisfactory, the need for alternative sites arises. (It could even be a virtual homeland, a new possibility, thanks to cyberspace.) In Asian Pacific American literature, the springboards can often be language, history (whether collective or personal), or memory, often explored conjunctively, each serving as a key to the others. Words become key, both as catalysts and sanctuaries. The Palestinian poet Mahmoud Darwish, exiled from Galilee for twenty-six years, writes: "We travel like other people, but we/return to nowhere./We have a country of words."

Such re-siting makes home movable (sometimes a feast, but more often an occasion for ambivalent melancholy, for disquieting reflection) but not transient, mutable but not amorphous, complex but rarely confusing. By exploring issues of language, history, and memory—usually in service of (re)constructing an identity—the monolithic "I" acquires a deepening; it learns to adapt, to straddle, and to leap about agilely. Part of the identity dilemma of the Asian Pacific American is the reconciliation, within the "I," of the implacable (American) demands of the individual with those of the (often hegemonic and Asian) collective self. How to fuse the seemingly irresistible with the seemingly immovable? That is what Ichiro wishes to achieve in *No-No Boy*, what the narrator in *The Woman Warrior* meditates on. It is both subject and object in Cha's intense meditation in *Dictee*.

And in *Homebase*, the "I" is transformed from a self-focused ego into a point of entry into, and gathering of, the past for the narrator, Rainsford Chan. Through the deliberate act of remembering, through his imaginative voicing of his great-grandfather's and grandfather's personal histories, Rainsford reclaims and revivifies the lifeblood of his forebears, without whom the railroad in the West would never have been possible. (One can see in the fact of the railroad being linked from the West by the Chinese workers and from the East by their mostly European-descended counterparts not just an obvious irony but a symbolic resistance to any facile interpretation of the immigrants' voyage.) Rainsford's own brave act of self-reclamation is in response to his demand that "America must give me legends with spirit" (S. Wong 1991: 95). In other words, the "I" acts also as a source of reckoning with family, as in the poet Li-Young Lee's intimate portrait of his father in his memoir *The Winged Seed* (1995). It becomes a conflicted but gendered pronoun for Sabah, the young Indian American woman in Ameena Meer's novel *Bombay Talkie* (1994).

If memory, language, and history act as landmarks, or pillars, of home, then they help explain the seemingly oxymoronic idea of a moving home. (The exile, like a turtle, carries his or her home wherever he or she is.) For through such "fixtures," the movable home attempts to achieve the stability, the calmness that obtains at the center of the storm and those near-mythical conventional representations of home embedded in our consciousness.

The genesis of an intellectually, emotionally, spiritually, and culturally nomadic home can be ascribed largely to the hostility, and often violence, experienced by Asian Pacific Americans at the hands of the larger society. It is not surprising, then, that in a significant number of Asian Pacific American works, mobility becomes a hallmark of this condition.

It is not the mobility that the American Dream connotes: the upward lift and greater financial and social freedom. In Asian Pacific American creative texts, mobility often translates into lateral and circular movement, seemingly aimless and repetitive, a cruel variation on upward mobility. Nowhere is this more apparent than in Bulosan's *America Is in the Heart* (1991) and in Cynthia Kadohata's novel *The Floating World* (1989). Sau-ling C. Wong has described Bulosan's work as "arguably Asian America's first major mobility narrative" (S.C. Wong 1993: 1230). His novel takes us through a dizzying succession of places. It doesn't really matter where Allos is: he is everywhere and nowhere at the same time, a fugitive whose only crime is the color of his skin. What exacerbates this rootlessness, of course, is feudal agribusiness's voracious appetite, something he had experienced in the Philippines. If dislocation/displacement is a recurring note sounded by Asian Pacific American writers, then incessant physical motion is one of its quintessential features—the ceaseless movement of a caged spirit longing to be free. Self-fulfillment and attainment of community loom as well-nigh impossible goals. Olivia, Kadohata's narrator, accepts her family's peripatetic (and sometimes pathetic) existence as a normal condition, casually ascribing this to three factors: bad luck, racism, and an unhappy marriage. The automobile gradually comes to represent not so much an instrument of liberation, a happy Hollywood-like symbol of the open road, but a vehicle of containment, of aspirations haunted by oppression. Most of the key periods—and men—in her life are associated with cars. Her stepfather is a garage mechanic, her boyfriend Andy wrecks cars for a living, and the job that she takes on at the end of the novel is servicing vending machines on a particular route, for which she needs a car. Appropriately, she grows aware that her father's ghost is shadowing her when she notices a car tailing her.

What keeps both Allos and Olivia rooted (the former to a greater degree) is memory. In Bulosan's case, it is class solidarity as well; Olivia, already "American," is mostly focused on her individuality. Allos remembers his boyhood village, the miseries of a poverty-stricken life, and his stoic mother in the Philippines, vowing to write for his family as much as for himself. Olivia is guided by Obasan's diaries, journals that reveal a strong spirit and an unorthodoxy that reassures Olivia that her own putative rebellions are a necessary act against corrosive fear. If the tangible environment behaves like a faithless lover, then comfort and a healing touch must be both sought and created—sought in a people's history and language, and created by pioneering acts of imagination.

DESIRE UNDER THE REALM

Four hundred years of colonization, both Spanish and American, has inscribed in the popular Philippine imagination strongly rooted but conflicted feelings about a semimythical homeland that extends far beyond its archipelagic shores. This odd sense of nationalism, ironically enough, was the bastard product of colonialism. Prior to the arrival of the conquistador and the Cross, there was no central government to speak of. (There was no need.) In fact, there was no "Philippines" to speak of: the name is derived from Felipe, the Spanish king in whose name the archipelago was claimed in the sixteenth century. Under Iberian tutelage, the locus of those imaginings was Spain. The nineteenth-century heroic genius and novelist José Rizal, an unwitting inspiration for the 1896 revolution against Spain, advocated reforms and a measure of self-government, but still within the protective embrace of Mother Spain. Even these were considered too audacious by the colonizers, who had him executed.

During World War II, the Japanese Imperial Army, which replaced the American occupiers (albeit temporarily), was surprised and disappointed that Filipinos for the most part refused any collaboration in the creation of a Japanese-led Greater East Asia Co-Prosperity Sphere, showing a tenacious (and to nationalists, a disturbing) loyalty to the gringos. While nationalist feeling has grown in the interim, it hasn't done so unfettered by anachronistic longings. Until recently, a small vocal movement existed that advocated U.S. statehood for the country, its proponents willing to give up the tenuous privileges of independence for the longed-for amelioration to be cheerfully prescribed and dispensed by Uncle Sam. These proponents represented in caricaturist extremist the neocolonial coconut—brown outside, white inside. With the ouster of U.S. military bases in 1992, yet another mooring to a colonized past was cut. But the process of political maturation that this represents is undermined continuously by the stranglehold America has on both the popular imagination and the persistent aspirations for a better life, a better "home," harbored by large impoverished segments of the Filipino masses. When kids, from urban slums to posh residential enclaves, sing *White Christmas*, it isn't only because the song is immensely, globally popular, but also because it represents a long-held dream of claiming America as their own—a dream implanted there by the Americans themselves.

In large part, this is due to the educational system put in place during the American colonial era. Patterned naturally after the system in the States, it was meant ostensibly to "democratize" Filipinos—that is, to provide them with the tools for self-government—and it was their alleged inability to do so that provided the dubious justification for American imperialism. In reality, the educational apparatus was an efficient conduit for the transmittal of Yankee values and tastes. Education resulted in American longings lodged in Filipino bosoms. Thus, an immigrant quoted in Yen Le Espiritu's work on the lives of Filipino immigrants says: "When I first came to the United States, I was surprised I knew more about U.S. history and U.S. literature than most average Americans" (Espiritu 1995: 91). Another immigrant, reflecting on how she and her parents lived in the Philippines, comments: "Because of my American way of life, I didn't have a difficult time adjusting in this country. The United States was not a strange place for me" (Espiritu 1995: 91, 55).

The American colonial educators sent several hundred promising students to the United States to study in different colleges and universities. Known as *pensionados,* they were expected to return to the Philippines, fully acculturated, and take part in the running of the colonial administration. Once independence was attained, they were to help take the reins of government (Chan 1991: 75).

It is worth quoting in full Alfrredo Navarro Salanga's short poem "A Philippine History Lesson" (1987), in which the colonialist influence is precisely configured:

> It's history that
> moves us away
> from what we are
>
> We call it names
> assign it origins
> and blame the might
>
> That made Spain right
> and America—bite.
>
> This is what it amounts to:
> We've been bitten off, excised
> from the rind of things
>
> What once gave us pulp
> has been chewed off
> and pitted—dry.

It is imperative to understand the depth to which the myth of a pluralist, democratic America—propagated intensely during the colonial period—resonates in the collective subconscious and in Filipino American literary texts for the simple reason that many of its practitioners were born on Philippine shores. Thus, in *America Is in the Heart*, it makes perfect sense for Allos to assert repeatedly his right to the American Dream, to believe fully that he too can re-create Lincoln's achievement. At the same time, because of the many rude awakenings that he and his cohorts suffer, he recognizes the tremendous chasm between the imaginary home—one that contained the best of both worlds, though implicitly with Anglo culture perched at the top—and the hateful reality of a white xenophobic society. He conflates a kind of Catholic Marianist imagery (a Spanish colonial legacy) in his embodiment of the Good America as virginally beautiful, inevitably blonde, white women—never to be touched or defiled, only worshiped—with his insurgent, socialist anger at the injustice of the Bad America, embodied in violent, Neanderthal white men. Once, after being beaten by white vigilantes, Allos manages to escape their clutches and shortly after is helped by a young white woman. "I almost cried. What was the matter with this land? Just a moment ago, I was being beaten by white men. But here was another white person, a woman, giving me food and a place to rest. And her warmth" (Bulosan 1991: 210).

Several decades later, Jessica Hagedorn (born in Manila and raised there until she was twelve) recalls a trip back to the Philippines in an early poem, "Song for My Father" (Hagedorn 1993):

> i am trapped
> by antiques and the music
> of the future
>
> and leaving you
> again and again
> for america,
> the loneliest of countries
>
> my words change . . .
> sometimes
> i even forget english.

As is typical of this writer, her cross-cultural adventures are suffused with irony, evident in her "forgetting" English in the country that introduced it to the Philippines as a sure-fire method of inculcating the *via Americana*.

That irony, and the ubiquitousness of the American Dream, renders Hagedorn's first novel, *Dogeaters* (1990), in some ways a quintessential Asian Pacific American novel, though Manila is its main setting. The hybridization so endemic in colonized cultures comes across strongly in her portrayals of Rio and Joey, mixed-blood Manileños who represent, respectively, the upper and lower reaches of society. Their hierarchical status is directly related to their hybridity: in a society that reveres light skin and Caucasian features, it is no accident that Joey, who is part African American, should live in a slum, while Rio, with Spanish, white American, and (to a lesser degree) Chinese antecedents, lives in upper-class comfort. Eventually, Rio climbs even "higher"— that is, migrates to the United States, home of Rock Hudson, Elizabeth Taylor, and Montgomery Clift—the Hollywood stars in the American melodramas she loves. Joey descends even "lower" by going underground in order to survive the depredations of a feudal, elitist society. Joey's transformation is much more radical, while Rio's trip across the Pacific is a logical extension of her upbringing.

Bulosan and Hagedorn, as with other Asian Pacific American writers, live in "the most complex cultural space," as Feroza Jussawalla and Reed Way Dasenbrock (1992: 6) call it, "inheriting the english language and much more from their former rulers, yet in many cases drawing on their own received forms and languages as well." Hagedorn intersperses Tagalog idioms and Spanish phrases throughout her novel, without translating them, refusing in effect to play what Gertrude Stein described as the role of "village explainer."

Issues of language are addressed directly by such poets as the West Coast-based Eugene Gloria, who is concerned about the possible disappearance of his parents' tongue. In "The Whisper," the poet notes the loss of language: "The language of the village withered inside her/when she took up the voice of American movies,/and the spirits of the siblings she was born between/hid away beneath the river" (Carbo 1996: 93). And in "In Language": "After we make love, I teach you/words I'm slowly forgetting: names/for hands, breast, hair and river./And in the telling, I find myself/astonished, recalling the music/in my grandmother's words before she left this world— words you/don't forget, like a mandate/from heaven" (Hongo 1993: 90).

In R. Zamora Linmark's often funny novel, *Rolling the R's* (1996), language becomes a ground of contestation, with the public-school system in Hawaii clearly portrayed as a system of acculturation and therefore a diminisher of difference, a way of severing ties with Filipino and local (this indicated by pidgin English) culture. The use of textbook English by the teenage characters is continually appraised by their teachers, Ms. Takemoto and Ms. Takara (with the teachers' ethnicity implying a hierarchy within the local Asian American community). In their report to the parents of one student, Florante Sanchez, the teachers state that in his writing he "uses English properly... uses correct spelling" but that he associates with "Katherine Cruz and Edgar Ramirez. Will you discourage them from further associations with these two? Their use of pidgin endangers Florante's appreciation and skillful usage of the English language." This is immediately followed by an insidiously hilarious pronunciation lesson:

> ... DO NOT Roll The R's. Free. Three. Three. Free. Bery good. V.V.Very. I am Filipino, not Pilipino. Fil. Pil. Fil. Fil, fil. filfilfilfil. Philippines, not Peelipines. My name is Florante. Flo. Flo-rante. Prrrom. Frrrrom [Linmark 1996: 53–54].

Language as a link to a former home, as a source of joy but also of pain—this is evident in "Upon Overhearing Tagalog," by the Seattle-based poet Fatima Lim-Wilson. That tongue she describes as "sparrow chatter," of this her "home, home/for the lullaby din of traffic, the call/of ripe scents rising from the open markets." But those who speak Tagalog are strangers to her and discourage her approach with a "scorching glare." The poet realizes the irony of her situation: "What you share commands severance./Avoid the lock of a familiar glance./Look down, look past, look through" (Lim-Wilson 1995: 4).

Language languishes without memory—or, more specifically, without the memories of where it was learned and loved. The old-timers in Santos's short stories, as we have seen, attempt to preserve their memories of the Philippines. They remember, but more important, they wish to be remembered. In Santos's "Lonely in the Autumn Evening," Ambo remarks sadly:

> But I keep thinking of home, Ben. How would they know out there of our passing? Would we come to them in a dream, speak to them out of a cloud, and tell them goodbye, we have just passed away? No? Then perhaps suddenly in the midst of a day's work on the farm, or silent in the old wooden house by the sea, our name would mingle with their thoughts. Or perhaps it would seem as though someone passed by and he looked like us, a remembered movement of the head, a manner of walking, or a flash of likeness in a stranger's face [Santos 1994: 83].

Memory, of course, is a tricky process—it too can be imagined, implanted. Fed partly by their parents' or grandparents' quasi-romantic views of the Philippines, partly by the continuing emphasis on "roots," and partly out of a deep and abiding dissatisfaction with finding their place in the American sun, many Filipino Americans tend to look upon those shores with utopian longing, making a complex, colonized, wounded culture bear the weight of their desire. A mythified "Philippines" becomes the counterpoint to a demythified "America." And so we have the rich irony of Filipinos swimming in countervailing currents, waving at one another.

Because of colonial longing on the one hand and a compensatory romanticization on the other, the Filipino abroad will find "homeland" perpetually elusive. As the Marxist critic E. San Juan, Jr., points out astutely: "Of all the Asian American groups, the Filipino community is perhaps the only one obsessed with the impossible desire of returning to the homeland, whether in reality or fantasy. It is impossible because . . . the authentic homeland doesn't exist except as a simulacra of Hollywood or a nascent dream of *jouissance* still to be won by national democratic struggle" (San Juan 1991: 124).

THREATS TO THE SERAGLIO

The Asian Pacific American writer's sense of creative nostalgia, the sometimes sentimental identification with a land across the Pacific, with his or her parents' or grandparents' homeland, arises partly out of the continuing reluctance of the larger society here to see Pacific Asian Americans as they are—citizens of color—and as they would be: full-fledged participants in a pluralistic American enterprise. "Homeland" here becomes a refuge, a state of parity, as much a myth in their own hearts as the longed-for America was in Bulosan's. They are, in a spiritual and cultural sense, orphans in this wide land, a condition aptly taken on by the protagonist in Wong's *Homebase*, with priority given to finding a "home"; their literatures can be seen as "the ancient and only refuge of oppressed peoples," but with an imagination that "also offers possibilities of escape from the politics of dominance and subservience" (Ashcroft, Griffiths, and Tiffin 1989: 35).

While it would be simplistic, not to mention patronizing, to view the creative texts of Asian Pacific America strictly through political and sociological prisms—first and foremost, they are literary works—part of what infuses these texts is a fundamental sense of assertion. Or I should say reassertion. Contrary to mainstream depiction, the voices—intimate, loud, desperate, funny, poetic, scared, articulate—of Asian Pacific American writers have always been there. But in the not-so-distant past, they were treated rather like Chang, the narrator's father in *A Feather on the Breath of God*: "Not as one who would not speak but as one to whom no one would listen" (Nunez 1995: 22).

Persistently, what we see in these texts is the "fictional portrayal of characters experiencing disorientation upon their arrival in an alien country or city, struggling to gain acceptance in an indifferent environment, trying to negotiate the often antagonistic borders of language and race, and using the compass of memory to bring about some reconciliation of the life left behind with the discovery of a new life" (Brown and Ling 1991: xii).

Though immigrant parents traditionally emphasized hardships and sacrifices they had undergone for their American-born children—as well they should—as Chan points out, "They knew they could not expect equal treatment" (Chan 1991: 115). With their children, it was much harder: They expected equal treatment but weren't getting it. Like Ichiro in *No-No Boy* (Okada 1976), they didn't know quite where they belonged.

Home in Asian Pacific American literature (and, I dare say, in literatures written from the "margins") evolves into a complex metaphor of the persistent longing for an imagined community, where hybridity becomes the norm—deemphasizing a past with its emphasis on a certain ancestry and the idea of "purity" symptomatic of a monolithic view—and where citizens of color are regularly engaged in the process of attaining power, whether this be for one's own personal life or for a larger context. For hybridity in a postcolonial world can have its own purity as well, where the encounter of two or more cultures is no longer viewed as a butting of heads but as an occasion, a meeting ground, leading to an acceptance of difference on equal terms, "with cross-culturality as the potential termination point of an apparently endless human history of conquest and annihilation" (Ashcroft, Griffith and Tiffin 1989: 36). The everyday world ends up subverted—itself already an indication of emergent power—so that the "strange" and "exotic" become "normal" and "normal" enlarges its scope.

The ever-present danger, of course, is that the acceptance of difference will water it down, hence muting its agency as a catalyst, as in the paradigmatic example of gloriously multifaceted Chinese cuisine revised to fit the stereotypically bland American tongue (and here again, "American" rests in its accustomed monolithic role). To push the conceit, one could say that appropriation is a way of cooking difference, of defanging it and so rendering it palatable, albeit in a fashionably aestheticized manner. Asian Pacific American literature has its share of works that perform this function, exotic eunuchs at the doors of the literary seraglio—splendid in attire, perhaps, but eunuchs still.

What I have focused on here have been texts that in one way or another pose a threat to the sanctity of the seraglio and the palace, texts that are proud of their difference, that are insistent on an autonomy from Asia as well as from a white America but especially insistent on carving out a space that recognizes both: a space distinct but not separate, different from but not alien to, whole but no longer homogenous. Asian Pacific American literature becomes a moving and often provocative argument for the fulfillment of the vision of America—that we move beyond ideologies based on skin color and ethnicity, beyond exclusivist cultural orientation, to an implicit demand that the American Dream work. It seeks to examine, consciously or not, the question Bhabha poses: "What kind of cultural space is the nation with its transgressive boundaries and its 'interruptive' interiority?" (Bhabha 1990: 5). The desire for a home above all bespeaks a love of that which may have been left behind but remains with us all our lives in the blood. It is a condition that the Sri Lankan American poet Indran Amirthanayagam (1992) alludes to in his lyrical poem "You Must Love":

> Love the tongue
> you'll never again
> speak that wrapped you
> and bled you
> and dried up
> some every day
> on the other side
> of the sea

Here we are indeed "on the other side of the sea," looking back and forward simultaneously, navigating new voyages with maps found only within ourselves, in the resiliency of the human spirit. And Asian Pacific American literature, paradox-filled and paradigm-challenging, stands as a remarkable testament to that resiliency and the restless creativity of the hybrid mind.

■ NOTES

Acknowledgment: I would like to acknowledge the invaluable research assistance of Maria Cecilia Aquino Aguilar.

1. I use the term "Asian Pacific American" advisedly. Along with the earlier "Asian American"—evolving out of the need in the late 1960s of communities of color for political and social empowerment—this umbrella phrase should be considered a way of stressing the common historical experience of different groups of Asians in the United States for the purposes of reclaiming various areas of identity, from memory and language to history. The term is not meant—or, at least, I do not intend for it be taken as meant—to oversimplify the differences, including the histories of animosity that existed and may continue to exist among such groups in Asia.

2. Acknowledging the immigrant origins of much of contemporary American society is in no way meant to gloss over the histories of Native Americans, who were here long before anyone else and who have paid a terrible price in terms of, among

other things, their sense of home. Nor is the acknowledgment meant to gloss over the brutal trafficking of slaves from different African homelands, brought here against their will.

■ REFERENCES

Amirthanayagam, Indran
    1992   "You Must Love." *Kenyon Review* (summer).
Anderson, Benedict
    1994   "Exodus." *Critical Inquiry* 20, no. 2 (winter): 314–27.
Ashcroft, Bill, Gareth Griffiths, and Helen Tiffin
    1989   *The Empire Writes Back: Theory and Practice in Post-colonial Literature.* New York: Routledge.
Bhabha, Homi K., ed.
    1990   *Nation and Narration.* New York: Routledge.
Brown, Wesley, and Amy Ling
    1991   *Imagining America.* New York: Persea Books.
Bulosan, Carlos
    1991   *America Is in the Heart: A Personal History.* Seattle: University of Washington Press.
Cacas, Samuel
    1995   "Marketing the Mainline to Manila." *American Demographics* (July): 15–16.
Carbo, Nick, ed.
    1996   *Returning a Borrowed Tongue.* Minneapolis: Coffee House Press.
Carlson, Lori M.
    1994   *American Eyes.* New York: Henry Holt.
Cha, Theresa Hak Kyung
    1995   *Dictee.* Berkeley, Calif.: Third Woman Press.
Chan, Sucheng
    1991   *Asian Americans: An Interpretive History.* Boston: Twayne Publishers.
Chu, Louis
    1989   *Eat a Bowl of Tea.* New York: Carol Publishing Group.
Clifford, James
    1994   "Diasporas." *Cultural Anthropology* 9, no. 3: 302–38.
Daniels, Roger
    1991   *Coming to America: A History of Immigration and Ethnicity in American Life.* New York: Harper Perennial.
Espiritu, Yen Le
    1995   *Filipino–American Lives.* Philadelphia: Temple University Press.
Francia, Luis H.
    1981   "Memories of Overdevelopment." *The Village Voice,* July 22–28, 1981, 14–15, 71.0

1988   "Scrutable Images: Chinatown Demystified." Whitney Museum of
American Art, *New American Film and Video Series* 44, October 11–
November 13.

Fusco, Coco
1995   *English Is Broken Here.* New York: New Press.

Hagedorn, Jessica
1990   *Dogeaters.* New York: Pantheon.
1993   *Danger and Beauty.* New York: Penguin Books.

Hongo, Garrett, ed.
1993   *The Open Boat: Poems from Asian America.* New York: Anchor Books.

Jussawalla, Feroza, and Reed Way Dasenbrock, ed.
1992   *Interviews with Writers of the Post-colonial World.* Jackson: University Press
of Mississippi.

Kadohata, Cynthia
1989   *The Floating World.* New York: Ballantine Books.

Kingston, Maxine Hong
1989   *The Woman Warrior.* New York: Vintage Books

Lavina, Melvani
1994   "Bridging Time and Space." *Little India* 4, no. 6: 55–57.

Leadership Education for Asian Pacifics (LEAP)
1995   *Connections* 9, no. 1.

Lee, Li-Young
1995   *The Winged Seed.* New York: Simon and Schuster.

Lim-Wilson, Fatima
1995   *Crossing the Snow Bridge.* Columbus: Ohio State University Press.

Linmark, R. Zamora
1996   *Rolling the R's.* New York: Kaya Productions.

Meer, Ameena
1994   *Bombay Talkie.* New York: Serpent's Tail.

Mukherjee, Bharati
1988   *The Middleman and Other Stories.* New York: Grove Press.

Mura, David
1991   *Turning Japanese.* New York: Atlantic Monthly Press.

Ng, Fae Mayenne
1993   *Bone.* New York: Hyperion.

Nunez, Sigrid
1995   *A Feather on the Breath of God.* New York: Harper Perennial.

Okada, John
1976   *No-No Boy.* Seattle: University of Washington Press.

Rushdie, Salman
1991   *Imaginary Homelands.* London: Granta Books (Penguin).

Said, Edward
1990   "On Jean Genet's Late Works." *Grand Street* 9, no. 4.

Salanga, Alfrredo Navarro

    1987   "A Philippine History Lesson." In *Versus: Philippine Protest Poetry,* ed. Alfrredo Navarro Salanga and Esther M. Pacheco. Quezon City: Ateneo de Manila University Press.

San Juan, E., Jr.

    1991   "Mapping the Boundaries: The Filipino Writer in the U.S.A." *Journal of Ethnic Studies* 19, no. 1: 117–31.

Santos, Bienvenido N.

    1994   *Scent of Apples and Other Stories.* Seattle: University of Washington Press.

Takaki, Ronald

    1989   *Strangers from a Different Shore.* New York: Penguin Books.

Wong, Sau-ling C.

    1993   *Reading Asian American Literature.* Princeton, N.J.: Princeton University Press.

Wong, Shawn

    1991   *Homebase.* New York: Plume.

About the Contributors

LUCIE CHENG is Professor of Sociology at the University of California, Los Angeles. She writes in the fields of international migration, gender, ethnic relations, and development. She has served as the director of the Asian American Studies Center at the University of California, Los Angeles; is the founding director of the Center of Pacific Rim Studies; chairs the Asia and Asian American Sociological Association; and serves as an officer in many other professional and civic organizations. Recently appointed as an external examiner of City University of Hong Kong, she is also a frequent visiting professor at Nankai University in China and the National Taiwan University.

VISHAKHA N. DESAI is Vice President for Cultural Programs and Director of the Galleries at the Asia Society in New York City.

ARIF DIRLIK teaches at Duke University, where he specializes in China. His most recent publications include *After the Revolution: Waking to Global Capitalism* (Wesleyan University Press); with Rob Wilson, *Asia Pacific as Space of Cultural Production* (Duke University Press); with Ming K. Chan, *Schools into Fields and Factories: Anarchists, the Guomindang and the Labor University in Shanghai, 1927–1932* (Duke University Press); *The Postcolonial Aura: Third World Criticism in the Age of Global Capitalism* (Westview Press); and *What Is in a Rim? Critical Perspectives on the Pacific Region Idea* (Westview Press).

LUIS H. FRANCIA is a poet, critic, and journalist. His poems have appeared in numerous literary journals and anthologies, including the recently published *Returning a Borrowed Tongue* (Coffee House Press 1996). He has published two books of poetry, the latest being *The Arctic Archipelago and Other Poems* (Ateneo de Manila University Press 1992), and edited a seminal anthology of Philippine literature in English, *Brown River, White Ocean* (Rutgers University Press 1993). He is a writer for New York's *Village Voice*, a contributing editor to *A. Magazine*, and the New York correspondent for the New Delhi-based *Cinemaya* and Hong Kong-based *Asiaweek*. Mr. Francia also teaches a course in Asian American literature at Sarah Lawrence College in Bronxville, New York. Along with Eric Gamalinda, he co-edited *Flippin': Filipinos on America*, an anthology of short fiction and poetry by Filipinos writing in America.

NEIL GOTANDA is Professor of Law at Western State University College of Law in Fullerton, California. He has been active in writing on issues of race and was an organizer of the Workshop on Critical Race Theory. He is co-editor of *Critical Race Theory: Key Writings That Formed the Movement* (New Press, 1995). His Asian American interests and activities date to the 1960s and include community work in

San Francisco's Japantown and teaching one of the earliest classes in Asian American studies at San Francisco State University in 1970.

EVELYN HU-DEHART is Professor of History and Ethnic Studies and Chair of the Department of Ethnic Studies at the University of Colorado at Boulder. She has published three books on the Yaqui Indians of northwestern Mexico and Arizona. Her current research focuses on the Chinese diaspora in Latin America and the Caribbean. To date, she has published articles in English, Spanish, and Chinese, on the Chinese in Mexico, Peru, and Cuba, and has lectured extensively on the topic in the United States, Latin America, Europe, and Asia and the Pacific. She received her B.A. from Stanford University and her Ph.D. from the University of Texas at Austin, where she specialized in Latin American–Caribbean history.

SETSUKO MATSUNAGA NISHI is Professor of Sociology at Brooklyn College and the Graduate School of the City University of New York. She was the founding president of the Asian American Federation of New York (1990–95) and chairs the New York State Advisory Committee to the U.S. Commission of Civil Rights. She is the author of numerous monographs and several books focusing primarily on American race relations, including the adaptation of Japanese Americans following their wartime incarceration and the historical and contemporary attitudes toward Asian immigrants. Dr. Nishi has also contributed to the development of social policies and programs for public agencies and private organizations. She received her Ph.D. in sociology from the University of Chicago and an M.A. in sociology from Washington University (St. Louis).

LE ANH TU PACKARD is a Fellow of the Foundation for Indochina Studies, a nongovernment organization established in affiliation with the University of Amsterdam's Faculty of Economics and Econometrics to promote economics research, education and training in the Indochina region. She is also Managing Associate of the Vietnam Investment Advisory Service, a private consulting service that provides services to firms with business activities in Vietnam. Her recent publications include "Vietnam Country Risk Analysis: Methodology and Country-Specific Issues," *Vietnam Business Journal* (1995) and "Emerging Issues for the Transition Economies in Asia," *Indochina Interchange* (1995). Ms. Packard received her M.A. and M. Phil. degrees from Columbia University in New York.

PAUL Y. WATANABE is Co-director of the Institute of Asian American Studies and Co-director of the Ph.D. Program in Public Policy at the University of Massachusetts, Boston. He specializes in the areas of international relations, the foreign-policy–making process, strategic and defense policy, American political behavior, ethnic-group politics, and public policy and Asian Americans. He is the author of *Ethnic Groups, Congress and American Foreign Policy* (Greenwood Press, 1984), as well as of chapters and articles on a variety of subjects. He serves on the boards of the Massachusetts Immigrant and Refugee Advocacy Coalition and the Asian Pacific American Agenda Coalition, among other organizations. Dr. Watanabe received his Ph.D. in Political Science from Harvard University.